# Lifehacker™

# Lifehacker™

## 88 Tech Tricks to Turbocharge Your Day

Gina Trapani

BICENTENNIAL
1807
WILEY
2007
BICENTENNIAL

Wiley Publishing, Inc.

Lifehacker™: 88 Tech Tricks to Turbocharge Your Day

Published by
**Wiley Publishing, Inc.**
10475 Crosspoint Boulevard
Indianapolis, IN 46256
www.wiley.com

ISBN-13: 978-0-470-05065-1
ISBN-10: 0-470-05065-9

Manufactured in the United States of America
10 9 8 7 6 5 4
1B/SZ/RR/QW/IN

For general information on our other products and services or to obtain technical support, please contact our Customer Care Department within the U.S. at (800) 762-2974, outside the U.S. at (317) 572-3993 or fax (317) 572-4002.

*Library of Congress Cataloging-in-Publication Data*
Trapani, Gina, 1975-
  Lifehacker : 88 tech tricks to turbocharge your day / Gina Trapani.
      p. cm.
  Includes bibliographical references and index.
  ISBN-13: 978-0-470-05065-1 (pbk.)
  ISBN-10: 0-470-05065-9 (pbk.)
  1. Computers. 2. Computer software. 3. Internet. I. Title.
  QA76.5.T6736 2006
  004--dc22                                    2006033473

*For Dad*

# About the Author

**Gina Trapani** (`http://ginatrapani.org`) is an independent web programmer and writer whose work has appeared in *Wired* magazine, *The New York Times*, and *Time* magazine. She is the founding editor of Lifehacker.com, the software and productivity weblog, updated several times daily. A Sun Microsystems–certified Java programmer, Gina builds web sites and Firefox extensions. Born and raised in Brooklyn, New York, she now resides in sunny San Diego, California, with her partner.

# Credits

**Executive Editor**
Carol Long

**Development Editor**
Maryann Steinhart

**Production Editor**
Rachel Meyers

**Copy Editor**
Michael Koch

**Editorial Manager**
Mary Beth Wakefield

**Production Manager**
Tim Tate

**Vice President and Executive Group Publisher**
Richard Swadley

**Vice President and Executive Publisher**
Joseph B. Wikert

**Project Coordinator**
Erin Smith

**Graphics and Production Specialists**
Barbara Moore
Heather Ryan

**Quality Control Technician**
Laura Albert

**Proofreading and Indexing**
Broccoli Information Management
Techbooks

**Anniversary Logo Design**
Richard Pacifico

# Contents

# Acknowledgments

First I'd like to thank Lifehacker.com's publisher, Nick Denton, for taking a chance on me as a writer, for funding my compulsive blogging habit, and for backing me in my quest to get Lifehacker into print. Thanks to my agent, David Fugate of LaunchBooks, for recognizing something before anyone else did and for gently leading this newbie author through the process.

Huge thanks to the original lifehackers, Danny O'Brien and Merlin Mann, for inspiring me, Lifehacker.com, and much of the material in this book—but most of all, for being so generous with their ideas, kind, supportive, and hilariously funny.

Thanks to my associate editors at Lifehacker.com, Adam Pash and Wendy Boswell, for their support and coverage while I worked on this book. Thanks especially to Adam for inspiring Hack 23, "Automatically Reboot and Launch Applications," and for continually raising the bar on Lifehacker.com. Thanks to Lifehacker.com guest writer Jason Thomas for contributing Hack 51, "Encrypt Private Email." Thanks to all Lifehacker.com readers for their email, comments, time, and attention. Thanks to my development editor at Wiley, Maryann Steinhart, for saying the words every author hopes (but never expects) to hear from her editor: "Why don't you give yourself an extra day or two for those chapters?"

Thanks to my brother Andrew, who had enough patience to let his annoying little sister use his computer and figure out that fancy new operating system called Windows 3.1—and then later, for teaching me how to program in Java and generally use my geek powers for good.

Thanks to my good friend and sysadmin Mark Wilkie, for answering my questions, killing my runaway processes, covering my client work while I wrote, and making funny faces with me at a Mac running Photo Booth at Fry's.

Thanks to my whole loud and lovable family, the best cheering section anyone could have: Joe and Cheryl, Joey and baby Andrew, Andrew and Alexis, Jeremy and Jared, Loretta, Margaret Mary, and Mom. (Mom, I love you 24.)

Finally, my deepest gratitude goes to my Terra, who, during the writing of this book, made me snacks, patted my back, advised me, bragged about me, listened to my endless prattle, rescued me from procrastination, said nothing while I scribbled a draft at the Padres game, took me out for beach breaks, and endured my absence during many long nights at the computer. I couldn't have done this without you, and I couldn't be luckier to have you.

# Introduction

*"The highest-performing people I know are those who have installed the best tricks in their lives."—David Allen, productivity guru* [1]

Contrary to the popular misuse of the term to denote a computer criminal, a hacker is someone who solves a problem in a clever or non-obvious way. A lifehacker uses workarounds and shortcuts to overcome everyday difficulties of the modern worker: an interrupt-driven existence of too much to do and too many distractions to keep you from doing it. (*Ding! You have 24 unread messages!*)

On a typical day at work your inbox and RSS reader are overflowing with unread items. You've got so many browser tabs open you can't make out the page titles. You can't remember where you saved the latest version of that presentation you were working on last night at home. The second you log onto IM, your project manager messages you: "Got a minute?"

Information, interruptions, and distractions are aplenty but your attention is scarce, life's short, and you need the right information now. How do you know what to concentrate on next? When you decide, will you be able to focus long enough to get anywhere with it? Life hacks are concrete ways you can filter out the noise and get to the signal.

## History

In 2004, tech journalist Danny O'Brien interviewed several people he called "over-prolific alpha geeks"—skilled and highly productive technologists whose continuous output seemed unaffected by the constant disruptions of modern technology. O'Brien hoped to identify patterns in the way these productive techies managed their work processes. Commonalities did emerge, and the term *life hacks* was born.[2]

The so-called alpha geeks had developed secret systems and tricks for getting through their daily drudgery. They used simple, flexible tools such as text files, email, and Unix command line scripts, and avoided bloated, complex software. They imposed their own structures on their information, and set up mechanisms that filtered and pushed the data they needed in front of their eyes at the right time automatically.

The life hacks concept resonated with geeks across the Internet, including the one typing these words. A movement was born. In January of 2005, I began writing Lifehacker.com, a daily weblog devoted to life hacks. Almost two years later, I have the privilege of sharing the best life hacks that came out of that work with you in these pages.

## Why Lifehacker?

My obsession with time-saving computer tricks developed through years computer programming. A programmer builds software that automates tasks to free up humans. A life hack reprograms your personal workflow to save you time and effort. A life hack uses technology in creative, imaginative, and unexpected ways.

The computers that hum away under our desks at home and at the office are incredibly powerful appliances, whose advanced capabilities go untapped by most. Personal computing is richer and more exciting than ever, but it takes insider knowledge and a willingness to go beyond the default settings to truly use it to your advantage.

This book will show you how.

## Characteristics of a Lifehacker

In a spirit of playful curiosity, lifehackers love to discover and design new ways to get things done. When it comes to tech, lifehackers are the ultimate optimists: where there's a will, there's a way. Lifehackers excel at finding that needle in the haystack that is the web. Lifehackers are addicted to the "Ah-HA!" moments in life. Lifehackers go to great lengths to avoid tedious, mundane work: they'd rather spend 2 hours and 59 minutes automating a 3-hour job than doing it manually.

Lifehackers expect to access their data from any Internet-connected device. Lifehackers keep their hands on the keyboard because mousing is inherently inefficient. Lifehackers get lost in their work and have to be reminded when it's lunchtime. Lifehackers live and work on their computers, so their hard drives are their outboard brain.

Lifehackers use creative problem solving to work smart and get more done with less effort.

## Who This Book Is For

This book is a self-help guide for the over-wired and the overwhelmed. Anyone from the technically savvy to the attention-challenged will find something useful in its pages. Seasoned Web surfers, knowledge workers, freelancers, early adopters, aspiring and accomplished geeks, programmers, tweakers, modders, and do-it-yourselfers will want to read this book. Anyone who has inadvertently burned three hours surfing the Web for no discernable reason, anyone who's been buried under a stack of unread email messages, anyone who's frustrated by disorder and wants to apply systematic structure in his life will find this book useful.

## How to Use This Book

This book is divided into 10 chapters. Each describes a principle of the lifehacker and presents a number of hacks that accomplish that goal one way or another. There's something here for beginners as well as the more tech-savvy reader, but not every solution will work for everyone. Each hack has its difficulty level, platform, and cost listed at the top. As much as possible, I chose to use platform-agnostic software that's free or modestly priced.

Most of the hacks are hands-on software tutorials, so read this book near your computer to try them out as you go. Pick and choose the tricks that fit you best, and work them into your day.

You want to be one of those high performers with the best tricks installed in your life. You can be. You have the tools, you have the desire to find out more, and now you have the handbook.

## Companion Web Site

The author has established a companion web site for this book: `http://lifehackerbook.com`. There she provides updates, links, references, and additional tips and tools regarding the hacks in the book. Additionally, you can append the chapter number to the URL (`http://lifehackerbook.com/ch3`, for example) to go directly to a specific chapter's updates.

# References

1. David Allen, *Getting Things Done* (Penguin Books, 2001), 85.
2. "Interview: father of 'life hacks' Danny O'Brien," Lifehacker.com, March 17, 2005 (`http://lifehacker.com/software/interviews/interview-father-of-life-hacks-danny-obrien-036370.php`).

# Lifehacker™

# Free Up Mental RAM

Your mind is a powerful computer. But sometimes it works *against* you instead of with you. Your brain makes complex decisions and stores years' worth of information, yet there's one thing it doesn't do well: think of what you need when you need it.

When you're walking past the dairy section at the grocery store, you don't realize you've only got a day's worth of milk left in the fridge at home. When do you remember the milk? When you're standing in the kitchen with a box of cereal in your hand.

Short-term memory is a lot like RAM, the temporary memory on a personal computer. It's where you keep all the things you see and experience, and the thoughts that pop into your head throughout the day: "Gotta call the vet when I get home." "Didn't realize that new Italian place is there, should invite her out to dinner this weekend." "Wonder how much a Spanish class would cost." "Darn, I never emailed Jim back about those forms!"

Productivity expert David Allen says these types of thoughts all represent unfulfilled commitments you've made to yourself — what he calls "open loops" — that distract and overwhelm you, creating stress, anxiety, and a constant sense that there's too much to do: "Your conscious mind, like the computer screen, is a focusing tool, not a storage place. You can think about only two or three things at once. But the incomplete items are still being stored in the short-term-memory space. And as with RAM, there's limited capacity; there's only so much 'stuff' you can store in there and still have that part of your brain function at a high level. Most people walk around with their RAM bursting at the seams. They're constantly distracted, their focus disturbed by their own internal mental overload."[1]

Whether it's remembering that you're due to make a dental appointment, or stowing away that tidbit of information you found online for next week's presentation, the only way to deal with all the stuff in your head is to get it off your mind and into a system that can help you recall it at the right time.

This chapter explores various capture systems that offload distractions, pop-up thoughts, and to-do lists to your computer for easy recall, timely reminders, and, ultimately, a clear head.

> **NOTE** For updates, links, references and additional tips and tools regarding the hacks in this book, visit `http://lifehackerbook.com/`. **(Append the chapter number —** `http://lifehackerbook.com/ch1/`**, for example — to go directly to a specific chapter's updates.)**

## Hack 1: Email Your Future Self

Level . . . . . . . **Easy**
Platform . . . . **Web**
Cost . . . . . . . **Free**

Every day you've got a lot on your mind and a lot to do. As a result, it can be nearly impossible to remember mundane recurring tasks — like when it's time to change the oil or go to the dentist — or even important yearly events, like friends' and family birthdays.

Lots of PDAs and calendar software applications have some kind of reminder feature, but who knows what you'll be using next year when Mom's birthday rolls around. What you *do* know is that you'll still be checking your email.

There's a simple way to get email event reminders without being tied down to particular software or device. The free, web-based Yahoo! Calendar (`http://calendar.yahoo.com`) can email or text message you event and task information on the days and times you specify. Create a time-based reminder file that emails your future self the data you'll need to know at just the right moment in time with Yahoo! Calendar.

**NOTE** Like Yahoo! Calendar, Google Calendar (http://calendar.google.com), is also a free, web-based calendar that can send reminders via email or SMS (Short Message Service, also called text messaging).

To get your reminder file started, go to Yahoo! Calendar, sign in with your Y! ID, and then follow these steps:

1. Click the Add Event button at the top of the Calendar. The Add Event page opens.

2. Name your event in the Title text box — Mom's birthday, for example.

3. Use the drop-down lists to select the date of your event.

4. Enter the reminder message you want to receive about your event in the Notes text box. Include all the information you'll need to accomplish the task or manage the event.

5. Scroll down to the Repeating section, and click the [Show] link to expand it. Choose to Repeat Every Year.

6. Scroll down to the Reminders section, and click the [Show] link to expand it. Click the Send a Reminder option and use the drop-down lists to set it to send you a reminder anywhere from 5 minutes to 2 weeks before your event. Choose how to receive the reminder: an IM (Yahoo! Messenger), email, or SMS reminder, as shown in Figure 1-1.

   Be sure to check the time zone in which your reminder will be sent. (See the Note at the bottom of the Reminders section. If the time zone is incorrect, click the Change It link to remedy the situation.)

7. Click the Save button at the bottom of the page to save your event.

That's it: you're guaranteed to always get a message from yourself before your mother's birthday: "Order flowers for Mom! Her birthday's in two days!"

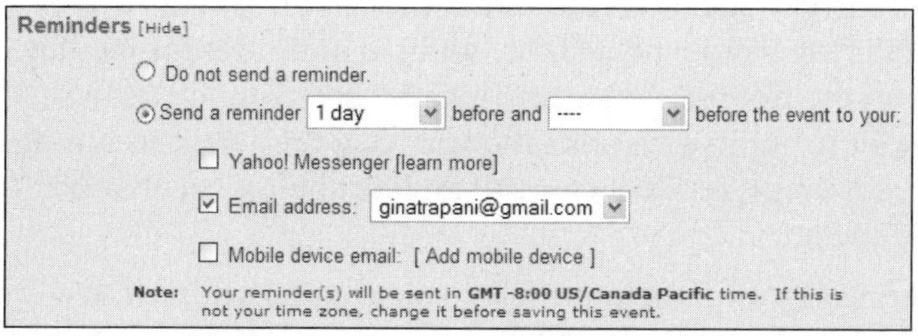

**Figure 1-1** Configure your event reminder on the Add or Edit Event page in Yahoo! Calendar.

Repeat these steps for each event or task you want to remind your future self about. Beyond birthdays, due dates and oil changes, some other ways to use your Yahoo! reminder system include:

- **Remember tasks that need to be done far in advance.** You call the fireplace cleaner guy in February for an appointment and he tells you to try back in July. Add a summer email reminder that says, "Call Joe Fireplace Cleaner at 555-1212 for an appointment." Notice the phone number: make it as easy as possible for your future self to get the task done.

- **Send yourself info on the go.** On Monday, you make plans to go to the roller derby Friday night with friends. So you add an event to your Yahoo! Calendar for 5 p.m. Friday night that sends a text message to your mobile phone: "Gotham Girls roller derby tonight at Skate Key, 4 train to 138th street. Meet outside at 7:15." Directions and specific time are included — the more info, the better.

- **Interrupt yourself.** You're super-involved in a project at work, but you have lunch plans at 1 o'clock across town. So you set up an IM reminder to go off at 12:30 that says, "Lunch at Frank's! Get going or you'll be late!"

- **Don't forget the boring but necessary tasks.** Set up quarterly, monthly, bi-weekly, or weekly reminders for mundane tasks like the following:

  Water the plants

  Get a haircut

  Send the rent check

  Invoice client

  Mail out estimated taxes

  Yahoo! Calendar allows for pretty much any recurring timeframe for events.

- **Get in on events early.** When you find out tickets go on sale in two weeks for your favorite band's next show, set up a reminder for the day before to round up the troops and storm TicketMaster.com. Or send yourself a reminder to get reservations the very day they start accepting them for Restaurant Week, or SMS yourself an hour before an eBay auction is scheduled to end.

- **Create a long-term plan and stick to it.** Say you commit yourself to a year-long savings plan to sock away $200 a month for that vacation to St. Croix. Send yourself an email each quarter that reads, "Hey, self, you should have $xxx in savings right now. Don't forget how great that Caribbean vacation will be!"

■ **Reflect and review.** Each New Year's or birthday, write yourself an email describing your successes and failures of the past year, and your hopes for the next. Schedule it to arrive exactly one year later. Sure, this sounds like a lame high school writing assignment, but it's actually a fun way to surprise yourself with insight into where you are and where you've been.

**NOTE** Backpack (`http://backpackit.com`) is another excellent web application that includes an email or SMS reminder feature.

## Hack 2: Manage a todo.txt File at the Command Line

Level. . . . . . . **Advanced**
Platform. . . . **Windows XP and Vista (Cygwin), Mac OS X, Unix**
Cost . . . . . . . **Free**

A plain text file is a simple and effective way to keep track of your to-do list. But you don't want to fire up a full-fledged text editor like Notepad every time you update or add to your `todo.txt` file. Bypass the time-consuming point-and-click graphical user interface (GUI), and use keyboard commands to search, sort, add, and update `todo.txt` at the command line.

### The Command Line Interface

Before there were windows, icons, and the point and click of the mouse, people performed actions on a computer using text commands at a prompt. Although the command line isn't the most intuitive way to interact with a machine, even in the age of the well-developed GUI, Unix experts, power users, and other people who perform the same actions over and over have turned back to the command line because it saves time. Textual commands keep your hands on the keyboard and enable you to perform repetitive tasks quickly. The command prompt doesn't have check boxes, input fields, tabs, radio buttons, or menus — there's simply one input field.

The disadvantage of the command line is that it's not as easy to intuit the commands you need to get your task done; further, once you learn the commands you need you have to commit them to memory. Still, for something you do daily like manage your to-do list, a command line interface will save you time and effort.

**NOTE** The built-in Windows command line doesn't support the `todo.sh` script described in this hack. Install the free Unix bash emulator Cygwin (`http://cygwin.com`) to run it. See `http://lifehackerbook.com/ch1/` for more information on installing and using Cygwin.

## Why Plain Text?

Plain text is application- and operating-system agnostic. It's searchable, portable, lightweight, and easily manipulated. It's unstructured. It works when someone else's web server is down or your Outlook `.pst` file is corrupted. It's free, and because it's been around since the dawn of computing time, it's safe to say that plain text is completely future-proof. There's no exporting and importing, no databases or tags or flags or stars or prioritizing or Insert-Company-Name-Here–induced rules on what you can and can't do with it.

You want to get information in and out of your `todo.txt` in the least distracting way as possible. You can use a text editor like Notepad to add to the file, search its contents, and update it, but navigating a lengthy text file that way can be cumbersome. That's why I've created a shell script, called `todo.sh`, which edits, searches, and lists items in `todo.txt` without requiring an editor.

## Install todo.sh

Before you use the script, create a `todo.txt` file and save it to your hard drive. Remember its location.

---

**MORE ON PLAIN TEXT**

"Complicated applications crash, or get abandoned by their creators, or just keel over from feature-bloat and become unusable around version 5.0. Power users trust software as far as they have thrown their computers in the past.

One way to think of text files is the grimy residue left over when an application explodes in your face. You put all your data into, say, Palm Desktop, and then one day you lose your Palm or move to a platform that can't read your desktop files. So you export it all into plain text, and try grimly to import it into the next big application. After a while, you just stay with the plain text, because it's easier.

Text files have some concrete advantages, too: you can get stuff into them quickly, and you can search them easily. Getting data in and out fast, and in a non-distracting way, is really the most important thing for a filing system. That is its very point."

— Danny O'Brien, lifehacker researcher[2]

Then, to get started interacting with your todo.txt at the command line, install and configure the todo.sh script. Here's how:

**NOTE** Windows users, all of the following commands should be executed at the Cygwin prompt.

1.  Download the todo.sh package from http://todotxt.com/ download/todo.sh.zip and unzip it. The package contains two files: todo.sh, which is the script itself, and .todo, which contains its configuration settings.

2.  Using the text editor of your choice, edit the section of the .todo file that reads:

    ```
    # Your todo.txt directory
    TODO_DIR="/Users/gina/Documents/todo"
    ```

    Replace /Users/gina/Documents/todo with the path to the directory where your todo.txt is located. For example, it might read:

    ```
    TODO_DIR="C:/Documents and Settings/yourusername/My Documents"
    ```

**NOTE** Some operating systems (like Mac OS X) hide files that begin with a dot like .todo. **For more on how to set Mac's Finder to stop hiding your** .todo **file, see** http://todotxt.com/library/todo.sh.

3.  Make the todo.sh script executable by using the following command:

    ```
    chmod +x todo.sh
    ```

4.  Move the .todo configuration file to your home directory like so:

    ```
    mv .todo ~/.
    ```

5.  Type ./todo.sh to see the usage message:

    ```
    ./todo.sh
    Usage: todo.sh  [-fhpqvV] [-d todo_config] action [task_number]
    [task_description]
    Try 'todo.sh -h' for more information.
    ```

Now you can execute commands on todo.txt. However, you don't want to type todo.sh every time — that would get tiresome quickly. Instead, alias the todo.sh command to a single key, such as T. To do so, add the following line to your command prompt configuration file. (In Windows/Cygwin, that file is ~/.profile; for Mac OS X users, it's ~/.bash_profile; and for Linux users, it's ~/.bashrc.)

```
alias t='/path/to/todo.sh'
```

Replace `/path/to/todo.sh` to the full qualified path of your script.

For updated instructions, notes, and more information about setting up `todo.sh`, go to `http://todotxt.com`.

## Using todo.sh

The `todo.sh` script provides several commands for interacting with your `todo.txt` file. It assumes the file contains exactly one task per line.

For example, to add a task using `todo.sh`, type:

```
t add "ask Tom if he wants that old bike in the garage"
```

When you press Enter, that text is appended to the end of `todo.txt`. Notice that quotes are required around the text of the task. Alternatively, simply type `t add` and enter your task at the prompt — no quotes required.

To list all the items in `todo.txt`, type:

```
t list
```

Here's an example result of using the `t list` command:

```
01 ask Tom if he wants that old bike in the garage
02 pick up the dry cleaning
03 RSVP to the co-op board meeting
```

You'll notice that every task has a number (which is actually the line number it appears on in `todo.txt`). Use those numbers to reference lines and perform other actions. For example, you can delete line 3 using `t del 3`, or replace the contents of line 2 with `t replace 2`. Get a complete description of all the commands available in `todo.sh` by running `t -h`.

Although being able to edit a text file without a GUI editor is convenient, the real power in `todo.sh` comes from its capability to search and sort your `todo.txt`. First, however, be sure your list can be filtered.

## Create a Sortable, Searchable todo.txt

An effective to-do list has all the information you need to answer the question: "What should I work on next?" Sort and search your to-do list using three important filters:

- **Context.** *Getting Things Done* author David Allen suggests[3] splitting up your task lists by context — that is, the place and situation where you'll work on the job (indicated by the shorthand character for "at," @). Messages that you need to send go in the @email context; calls to be made, @phone; and household projects, @home. That way, when you've got a few minutes at the laundromat with your cell phone, you can easily check your @phone tasks and make a call or two while you have the opportunity.

■ **Project.** The only way to get through a project is to split it up into small, doable chunks. Those small tasks move a large undertaking forward, so you need to access all the tasks associated with a large project. To move along a project like "Cleaning out the garage," for example, you want to choose the next logical action for that project on your task list. "Clean out the garage" isn't a good to-do item because it's actually a collection of many smaller tasks, but "Call Goodwill to schedule pickup" in the Clean Out Garage project is.

■ **Priority.** Your to-do list should be able to tell you what the next most important thing for you to get done is — either by project or by context or overall. For example, a call back to a potential client on the verge of closing the deal might be higher priority than a call to an existing client just to check in and see how things are going. Or getting back to a co-worker who's waiting on you to complete a project will have a higher priority than scheduling a lunch with friends. In general, to-do items with deadlines within the next few days are always higher priority than tasks with a flexible deadline (that is, within the next few weeks). Your to-do list should let you see which tasks are higher priority than others, so you don't leave your co-worker hanging while you make restaurant reservations with friends.

This is possible even in a simple, unstructured `todo.txt` file.

**NOTE** See Hack 60, "Make Your To-Do's Doable," for more on writing a manageable to-do list that doesn't paralyze you with overwhelming tasks.

### Building Your todo.txt

Taking the context and project into consideration, a single line in your `todo.txt` file might read:

```
+garage @email ask Tom if he wants that old bike
```

The plus sign indicates a project or a job that involves several tasks to complete. Here `+garage` is shorthand for the Clean Out Garage project. The @ sign indicates the context — or time, place, situation, or toolset — where you can complete the task. In this example, `@email` is the context where you can complete the task. Finally, "Ask Tom if he wants that old bike" is a brief but specific description of the task.

## List Tasks with todo.sh

The todo.sh script can extract sub-lists from your to-do list based on context, project, priority, or keyword.

Suppose the contents of your todo.txt are:

```
do the laundry
+book @computer Edit todo.txt hack
+garage @phone Schedule Goodwill pickup 555-1212
@phone Thank Mom for the package
+taxreturn @homeoffice Gather documents
+website @online Update FAQ
+garage @shopping Bike rack at Lowe's
+taxreturn @email ask Don at Acme about the 1099
+garage @email Neighbors re: joint garage sale Sat, June 10
```

What do you do with that? It depends on the situation.

Let's say it's April 1 and you've got to get moving on the income tax return front. The following command says, "Show me only the tasks associated with the tax return project":

```
t list taxreturn
```

The result is:

```
+taxreturn @homeoffice Gather documents
+taxreturn @email ask Don at Acme about the 1099
```

Or you can list all the tasks you can do to move along your tax return project when you have email access like this:

```
t list taxreturn @email
```

Which returns:

```
+taxreturn @email ask Don at Acme about the 1099
```

List all the phone calls you have to make, or all the items you have to pick up at the store using t list @phone or t list @shopping, respectively.

## Prioritize Tasks

When you're comfortable with this system, a problem arises: long task lists in no particular order except the one you entered them in. For one more layer of prioritization in todo.txt, optionally add precedence to a task in the form of a letter enclosed in parentheses to the beginning of its line.

For example, in the following list, there's an (A) in front of high-priority actions, a (B) next to less important actions, and no priority rating for the other items:

```
(A) do the laundry
(B) +book @computer Edit todo.txt hack
+garage @phone Schedule Goodwill pickup 555-1212
(A) @phone Thank Mom for the package
+taxreturn @homeoffice Gather documents
+website @online Update FAQ
+garage @shopping Bike rack at Lowe's
+taxreturn @email ask Don at Acme about the 1099
(B) +garage @email Neighbors re: joint garage sale Sat, June 10
```

Prioritize tasks using todo.sh with the pri command. For example, to prioritize the task on line 4, use the command t pri 4 A. The todo.sh script will prepend an (A) to the beginning of line 4.

Because todo.sh automatically orders task lists alphabetically, all tasks are listed in order of priority (see Figure 1-2). Also, priority items are color-coded for easy visual identification (although you can't see that in a black-and-white picture).

You can view a short movie on using todo.sh commands at http://todotxt.com/library/todo.sh.

## More Uses for todo.txt

The beauty of the text file format is its flexibility and portability. Stow your todo.txt file on your USB drive for use on any computer; automatically text message your grocery list or phone calls to make to your cell phone or PDA for reference on the go; incorporate your todo.txt into your computer desktop wallpaper; manipulate the file with any application or shortcut that can process text files. Truly, the uses for text files are limited only by your imagination.

```
$ t list
03 (A) @phone Thank Mom for the package
09 (A) do the laundry
01 (B) +book @computer Edit todo.txt hack
08 (C) +garage @email Neighbors re: joint garage sale June 10
02 (C) +garage @phone Schedule Goodwill pickup 555-1212
06 +garage @shopping Bike rack at Lowe's
07 +taxreturn @email ask Don at Acme about the 1099
04 +taxreturn @homeoffice Gather documents
05 +website @online Update FAQ
--
TODO: 9 tasks in d:/data/gina/docs/todo/tests/todo.txt.

gina@scully ~/docs/todo/tests
$
```

**Figure 1-2** The todo.sh script sorts and color-codes prioritized items.

A community of users and developers have come together to discuss and devise creative uses for `todo.txt` and shortcuts in doing so. Visit `http://todotxt.com` and join the mailing list to ask questions, make suggestions and explore other ways you can put `todo.txt` to work for you.

# Hack 3: Develop Your (Digital) Photographic Memory

Level....... **Easy**
Platform.... **Web and email-enabled camera phone**
Cost ....... **Free for Flickr limited account, $29.95/year pro subscription**

The miniscule size and large memory capacity of modern digital cameras and camera phones can turn anyone into a constant, impromptu photographer. Documenting your world and the information in it has never been easier and faster than it is now. A ubiquitous capture device can change the way you remember (and forget) things for good. With a photo-sharing service like Flickr (`http://flickr.com`), you can capture and file away your digital photographic memory in the Internet cloud from wherever you are.

> **NOTE** Several photo-sharing services such as Kodak Easy Share and Snapfish can publish your digital photos and serve the purpose detailed here. This hack uses Flickr as an example because of its useful tagging and upload-by-email feature.

## Tag Your Photos on Flickr

When you add photos to your account on Flickr, you can assign keywords or tags to those photos, indicating what's in them or any other meta information you want to include. You can use the tags later to slice and dice your photos by keyword.

For example, you can view your own (or another user's, or all users') `sunset` tag to see all the photos of the sun going down (see Figure 1-3).

You can configure the privacy setting on any given photo to: viewable only by you (private), by all (public), or only by contacts that you list as friends, family, or both.

**Figure 1-3** All of ginatrapani's photos tagged sunset on Flickr.

## Upload Photos to Flickr from Your Camera Phone

You can upload photos to Flickr through the web application or various uploading programs. But to publish photos from your camera phone, use Flickr's upload by email capability. To enable upload by email, visit `http://flickr.com/account/uploadbyemail` while you're logged into Flickr. You'll be assigned a secret email address that will publish photos sent to it in your Flickr account.

Using a special message format, you can set the privacy and tag photos you email from your phone. Tag photos in a message using the **tags: x "y z"** syntax in the subject or on a new line in the body of a message. Also, using suffixes like **+private** or **+ff** added to the secret upload email address Flickr supplies, you will mark the photo as private or viewable by your friends and family.

For example, say you're at Fry's Electronics and spot a hard drive you're interested in, but you want to research it more online when you get home. You could create a new message with the photo on your phone, and use the email address Flickr supplied you for upload. That message might look like this:

```
To: foo10bar+private@photos.flickr.com
Subject: Seagate 300GB tags: "to research" "frys" "to-do"
Body: [Photo attachment]
300GB, 7200RPM, USB 2.0, too spendy?
```

Adding +private to the address means you won't subject your friends to your blatant consumerism (it marks the photo as viewable by you only). Tagging the photo "to-do", "to research", and "frys" will help you remember to find out more about the drive and where you saw it when you get home.

**WARNING** Before you start uploading photos to Flickr from your camera phone, be sure that your mobile phone plan supports emailing photos and that it won't cost you an arm and a leg. When it comes to emailing photos, even 1 cent per kilobyte in data transfer adds up fast!

## Your Photo Reference

Having mastered on-the-fly tagging and privacy settings, you'll want to check out some more creative uses for a personal photo database made with your camera phone on the go:

- **Business cards.** Instead of letting that stack of business cards you collected at the conference collect dust in your desk drawer, snap a picture of each and upload them all to Flickr with tags (people's names, conference name) and descriptions of who they were, where and when you met, and whether you want to follow up about something. Be sure to mark these as private!

- **Photo recipe box.** Eat something at a restaurant or a friend's house you'd like to try to make at home? Take a picture, add some details about the ingredients, and tag it `"cooking"` as shown in Figure 1-4. Keep track of all your favorite meals with snapshots that make answering "What should we have for dinner tonight?" as simple as browsing your `"meals"` Flickr tag. You can even tag by ingredients like `"chicken"`, `"vegan"`, or `"spicy"` so you've got some ideas when your vegetarian brother-in-law comes over for dinner.

**Figure 1-4** A Flickr photo of a recipe tagged `"cooking"`.

- **Wishlist.** When you're out and about shopping, take a photo of the items you want to get or to price compare. Possible tags include `"wishlist"` and `"to research"`.

- **Wine labels.** When your sweetheart remarks how much she loves the bottle of wine you got out at dinner, snap a photo of the label so you can surprise her with a bottle at home. Start your personal wine database with label photos to keep track of what you liked and didn't.

- **Text or URLs.** Maybe a sign at that landmark describes the history of the place. Or you'll never remember that Web site address you saw on a billboard up the street. Take a pic and send to Flickr tagged `reference` or `to visit`.

- **Store hours of places you frequent.** Next time you're at the local post office or bank, snap a photo of the business hours so you've got a quick reference for what's open when.

- **Home inventory.** A fantastic way to keep track of your home inventory is to snap pictures of serial numbers and include prices of your valuables. They'll come in very handy in case your laptop gets swiped or there's a fire or flood in your home.

- **Where you parked.** Was it level E or F? Snap a quick photo of the sign closest to where you put your car and save yourself a whole bunch of wandering through the parking lot or garage later on.[4] (Flickr isn't required for this one.)

## Hack 4: Install Your Personal Wikipedia

Level. . . . . . . **Advanced**
Platform. . . . **Windows XP and Vista**
Cost . . . . . . . **Free**

The collaboratively edited Wikipedia (`http://en.wikipedia.org`) is a vast, searchable repository of information, constantly written and re-written by its readers. Don't you wish you or your group could have your own editable encyclopedia of brain dumps and documentation like Wikipedia? You can. MediaWiki (`http://mediawiki.org/wiki/MediaWiki`), the software that runs Wikipedia, is freely available for anyone to install. In this hack, you set up MediaWiki on your Windows PC and add and edit pages to your new, local *personalpedia*.

**NOTE** MediaWiki is advanced wiki software that requires Apache web server, the PHP scripting language, and the MySQL database server installed to run. If this makes your head spin, a simpler (and less featured) alternative to MediaWiki is the excellent Instiki, which is covered in Hack 5.

## What You Need

- **A Windows computer**, not already running Apache web server.
- **WAMP server software**, the all-in-one PHP/MySQL/Apache installation for Windows XP, available as a free download at http://en.wampserver.com.
- **MediaWiki**, available as a free download at http://mediawiki.org/wiki/MediaWiki.

## What to Do

Setting up MediaWiki involves configuring the WAMP web and database servers as well as the MediaWiki source files. Here's how to get all the components installed and working together.

**WARNING** Running a server on your personal computer can be a security risk. Make sure you are behind a firewall that prevents unauthorized access to your server. See Hack 85, "Firewall Your Computer," for more information.

1. Download WAMP and install it in the C:\wamp\ directory. (If you must install it elsewhere, make sure the folder you choose has no spaces or special characters in its name.) Check the Autostart option. When the installation completes, visit http://localhost/ in your web browser to see the front page of your new web server (see Figure 1-5).

2. You're already behind or running a firewall (right?) but just to be on the safe side, you're going to assign a password to your new database server. (It's good to be healthily paranoid where security's concerned.) From the homepage of your WAMP installation (http://localhost), go to the Tools section and click the PHPmyadmin 2.7.0-pl2 link (your version may be more recent).

3. Then, click the Privileges link. Check all users except root, and click Delete.

**Figure 1-5** The WAMP server front page.

4. Click the Edit button next to the root user, and change the password to something you'll remember and save. Now PHPmyadmin no longer has to access your database, because it doesn't have your new password. You can remedy that easily.

5. Open the `C:\wamp\phpmyadmin\config.inc.php` file in a text editor. Change the line that reads:

   ```
   $cfg['Servers'][$i]['password'] = '';
   ```

   to

   ```
   $cfg['Servers'][$i]['password'] = 'yournewpassword';
   ```

   Where `yournewpassword` is the password you just set up in PHP-myadmin. Refresh the PHPmyadmin interface in your web browser, and you should be able to view your database information.

6. Unzip and untar the MediaWiki package you downloaded. Rename the resulting folder (probably called media-wiki-1.6.3, although your version may differ) to mywikipedia and move the entire directory to `C:\wamp\www\mywikipedia`.

7. Access your new MediaWiki installation at `http://localhost/mywikipedia`. Click the Set the Wiki Up! link. The screen that opens requires all of MediaWiki's configuration options.

8. This will seem like a long, complicated questionnaire but it really isn't. Accept all the default values *except* you must set a site name (mine is Ginapedia), WikiSysOp password, and your database password. The Database User can be root and the password whatever you chose in

step 2. (Alternately, create a non-root database user with fewer rights in phpMyAdmin and use that instead.)

9. When you've finished configuring your wiki, click the Install! button and let MediaWiki work its magic. If all goes well, you get a message at the bottom of the screen that reads, "Move the config/LocalSettings.php file into the parent directory, then follow this link to your wiki." To do that, cut and paste the `C:\wamp\www\mywikipedia\config\ LocalSettings.php` file to `C:\wamp\www\mywikipedia\ LocalSettings.php`

   Then click the link to visit your new wiki installation, located at `http://localhost/mywikipedia`.

10. You might notice that the image in the upper-left corner isn't very personal. To set it to something you like, crop and resize an image of your choice to 135×135 pixels, and save it as `C:\wamp\www\mywikipedia\ skins\common\images\mywikilogo.jpg`. Then, open the `c:\wamp\ www\mywikipedia\LocalSettings.php` file and change the line that reads:

    ```
    $wgLogo = "$wgStylePath/common/images/wiki.png";
    ```

    to:

    ```
    $wgLogo = "$wgStylePath/common/images/mywikilogo.jpg";
    ```

    Refresh the wiki front page to see your new logo.

## You're Ready to Go

Now you've got a clean, new, customized local installation of MediaWiki all ready to use however you please. As evidenced by Wikipedia, the best application of a wiki is group collaboration. However, wikis come in handy for individual use as well, to track lists, notes, links, images, or anything else you want to search or reference over time.

Wikis are especially good for writing projects because they keep every page revision history and allow for easy adding and editing of pages. My co-editors and I at Lifehacker.com use a MediaWiki installation to collaborate on site ideas and drafts. I use a wiki to keep personal notes on programming techniques, to track software serial numbers, and to save quotes I like as well as other relevant links and articles.

**NOTE** View a video demonstration of using MediaWiki to write a novel at `http://lifehackerbook.com/links/mediawiki`.

To begin editing a page in your new wiki, simply click the Edit link at the top of a page, as shown in Figure 1-6.

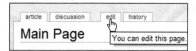

**Figure 1-6** Click the link to edit your MediaWiki wiki.

The text of the page is displayed inside an editable text area. You'll see some square brackets and other markup revealed. This is the special formatting markup called Wikitext that lays out MediaWiki pages.

## Brief Wikitext Primer

- Denote a page's section header with two equal signs prefixed and suffixed around the section name, like so:

  ```
  == Section Header Name ==
  ```

- A subsection uses three equal signs:

  ```
  === Subsection Name ===
  ```

- Create a link to an external web page with square brackets containing first the URL followed by the text of the link, like this:

  ```
  [http://lifehacker.com Lifehacker]
  ```

- External links off of the MediaWiki site are followed by a little arrow, as show in Figure 1-7.

- Links to a page inside your wiki — a page called Favorite quotes, for example — would be achieved like this:

  ```
  [[Favorite Quotes]]
  ```

MediaWiki's User Guide offers a full reference for MediaWiki markup at http://meta.wikimedia.org/wiki/MediaWiki_User%27s_Guide:_ Editing_overview.

**NOTE** Later in the book you'll find hacks that explain how to assign a domain name to your home web server and how to access a home server behind a router/firewall.

**Figure 1-7** Link to another web site in MediaWiki.

# Hack 5: Keep an Instiki Wiki Hyperlinked Notebook

Level....... **Medium**
Platform.... **Windows XP and Vista, Mac OS X**
Cost ....... **Free**

A wiki is an editable web site, where you can add any number of pages and update the text of those pages right inside your web browser. Wikis are perfect for a team of people collaboratively editing information — Wikipedia (http://en.wikipedia.org) is the quintessential example of this — but a wiki is also useful to an individual as a searchable, versioned, digital notebook.

Imagine storing and editing your to-do lists, bookmarks, snippets of text, project notes, reference material, or anything you wanted on your home computer from anywhere just using a web browser — no disks, thumb drives, text editors, or file transfers required. This is possible with a personal wiki.

In this hack, you install a server and wiki software on your home computer using Instiki (http://instiki.org/show/HomePage), a package that's perfect for beginners. Instiki is easy to install and to use.

**NOTE** If you're interested in trying out a wiki without installing it, visit PB Wiki (http://pbwiki.com) for a free hosted wiki solution.

## Installing Instiki

Instiki is server and wiki software all rolled into one package, and it's written in a language called Ruby.

**WARNING** Running a server and opening a port on your home computer is a risky undertaking. Make sure your computer is either behind a firewall or running firewall software, has all the latest security updates, and has been thoroughly scanned for viruses and spyware before you begin.

### Windows Installation

1. Download Ruby (http://rubyforge.org/frs/?group_id=167). Click the latest stable release .exe file, which at the time of writing is ruby182-15.exe. Run the installer, and accept the license agreement

and all the default settings, including `C:\ruby\` as the installation folder.

2. Download the Instiki zip package from `http://instiki.org/show/HomePage` and unzip to a folder on your hard drive. Move and rename the folder to `C:\instiki`.

3. From the Start menu, choose Run. Type **cmd** in the Open text box and click OK to open a Windows XP command line. Change to the Instiki directory like so:

```
cd \instiki\
```

4. To start the Instiki server, enter:

```
ruby instiki
```

The output will look like this:

```
C:\instiki>ruby instiki
=> Starting Instiki on http://0.0.0.0:2500
=> Data files are stored in C:/instiki/storage/2500
[2005-09-16 12:45:20] INFO WEBrick 1.3.1
[2005-09-16 12:45:20] INFO ruby 1.8.2 (2004-12-25) [i386-mswin32]
[2005-09-16 12:45:20] INFO WEBrick::HTTPServer#start: pid=4008
port=2500
```

### Mac Installation

Setting up Instiki is a lot less complicated for Mac users. On the Instiki download page (`http://rubyforge.org/frs/?group_id=186`), use the MacOS binary link to get the Instiki disk image (`.dmg`) file. Mount the disk image and simply double-click the Instiki icon to start the wiki (no Ruby or text commands required). When Instiki has started, use the Wiki option in your menu bar to quit Instiki.

### Configure Instiki

When the Instiki installation is complete, switch to your web browser. Go to `http://localhost:2500` to begin Instiki setup. Give your new wiki a name and a password. I'm calling mine Gina's Notebook, as shown in Figure 1-8.

Click Setup to save your settings.

## Instiki Setup

Congratulations on succesfully installing and starting Instiki. Since this is the first time Instiki has been run on this port, you'll need to do a brief one-time setup.

1. **Name and address for your first web**
   The name of the web is included in the title on all pages. The address is the base path that all pages within the web live beneath. Ex: the address "rails" gives URLs like /rails/show/HomePage. The address can only consist of letters and digits.

   Name: Gina's Notebook        Address: mynotebook

2. **Password for creating and changing webs**
   Administrative access allows you to make new webs and change existing ones. Everyone with this password will be able to do this, so pick it carefully.

   Password: ******        Verify: ******

   [ Setup ]

**Figure 1-8** Setup screen for an Instiki web.

## You're Ready to Go

When you click the Setup button, a page opens, prompting you to enter text; this is your home page. Here's where things get interesting.

On the right is a quick guide to Instiki's wiki syntax — that is, the ways you can bold and italicize your text, add external links, and reference new pages. Instiki uses CamelCase to identify page names, so if you type MyToDoList, Instiki automatically creates a reference to a new page because it's several words squashed together mixed case (each word begins with a capital letter, but there are no spaces between them).

Figure 1-9 shows the following example text using Instiki's syntax typed into the page:

```
I _need_ a place to *write things down.*
Hello, "Lifehacker":http://lifehacker.com readers.
This here will be MyToDoList.
```

You'll notice that you can set the username of the text author, which defaults to AnonymousCoward. To track who wrote what, replace AnonymousCoward with your name.

Then, click Submit to save your text, and the bold and italic formatting is applied as indicated. Figure 1-10 shows the result of saving the preceding example text, with *need* in italics, **write things down** in bold, and the word Lifehacker set as a link to http://lifehacker.com.

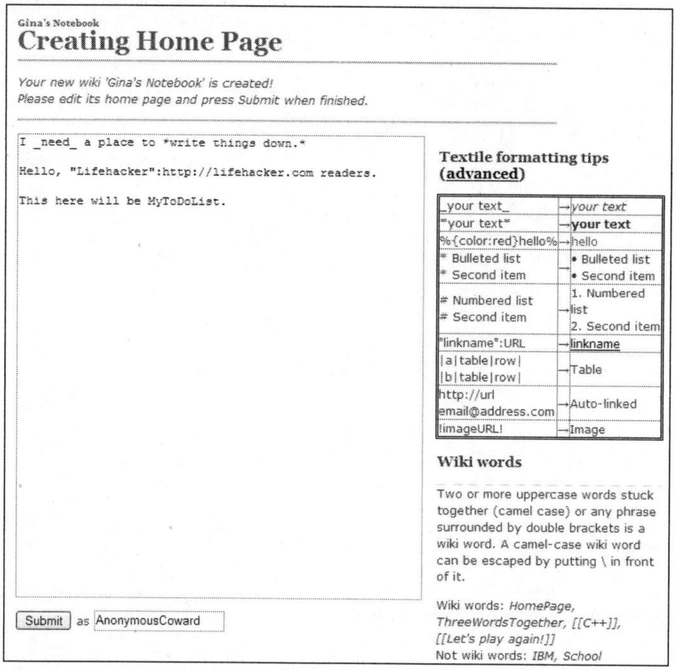

**Figure 1-9** Page creation using Instiki's default formatting.

Notice the question mark next to MyToDoList? That means that it's a new page, which hasn't yet been officially created. (Remember that Instiki uses CamelCase to identify page names.) Create it by clicking the question mark and, in the new page that opens, fill in text for your new MyToDoList page in the notebook. Figure 1-11 shows an example.

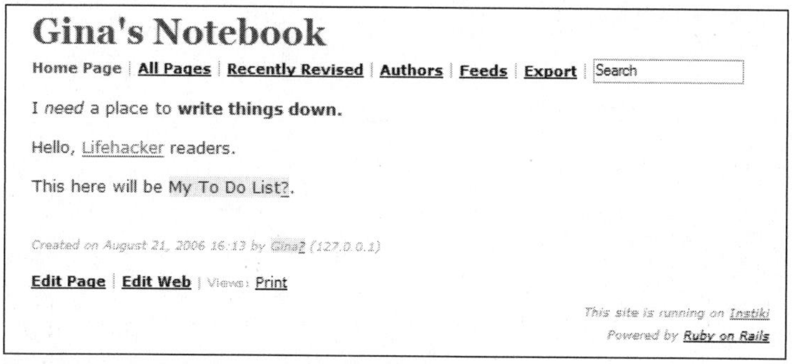

**Figure 1-10** Saved home page in Instiki.

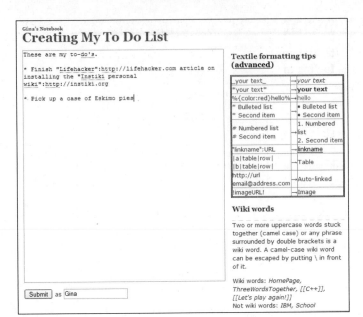

**Figure 1-11** Creating a bulleted list on a new page in Instiki.

Save the text and the MyToDoList page appears as shown in Figure 1-12. Return to your home page using the Home Page link. You can see that MyToDoList now links to your newly created page, as shown in Figure 1-13.

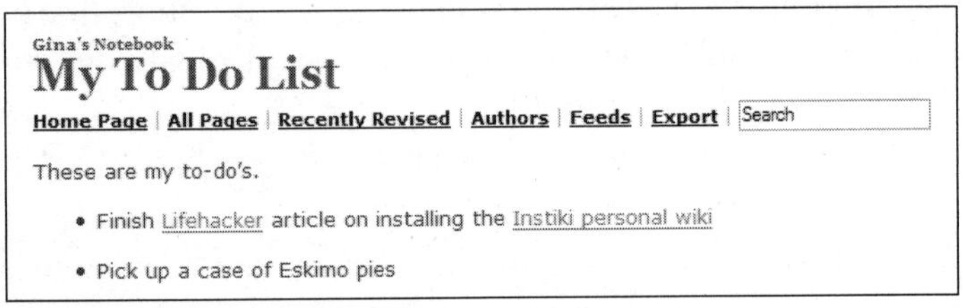

Gina's Notebook

## My To Do List

**Home Page** | **All Pages** | **Recently Revised** | **Authors** | **Feeds** | **Export**   Search

These are my to-do's.

- Finish Lifehacker article on installing the Instiki personal wiki
- Pick up a case of Eskimo pies

**Figure 1-12** Saved MyToDoList page in Instiki.

## Gina's Notebook

Home Page | **All Pages** | **Recently Revised** | **Authors**

I *need* a place to **write things down.**

Hello, Lifehacker readers.

This here will be My To Do List.

**Figure 1-13** Saved home page with working internal link to the MyToDoList page.

> ### AUTOMATICALLY START UP INSTIKI WITH WINDOWS XP
>
> **Get your Instiki wiki to start whenever your computer boots up with a simple batch script. Save the following into a file named** `startwiki.bat`**:**
>
> ```
> cd \instiki\
>
> ruby instiki
> ```
>
> **Create a Windows XP shortcut to** `startwiki.bat` **and place it in your** `C:\Documents and Settings\All Users\Start Menu\Programs\Startup` **folder. That will run Instiki automatically when your computer starts up. See Hack 82, "Clean Up Your Startup," for more on starting programs automatically in Windows.**

## Securing and Accessing Your Wiki

If you're going to be accessing your personal wiki from anywhere, that means anyone else will be able to edit it, too — and you may not want that. Set a password on your Instiki wiki to make it editable and readable by no one but you. Click the Edit Web link inside Instiki (bottom of page), and establish a password for your web.

If your computer is not behind a router or firewall, you can now read and write to your personal wiki from any Internet-connected computer by typing your home computer's IP address or domain name plus `:2500` into a web browser's address field. Determine your computer's IP address at `http://whatismyip.com`.

Here are examples:

```
http://123.456.789.0:2500
http://mycomputer.homeip.net:2500
```

If you're on a corporate or university network, most likely your computer's IP will not be accessible from any other Internet-connected computer.

The extra 2500 addresses Instiki, which runs on port 2500, Ruby's default port. This works well because if you use Hack 35, "Run a Home Web Server," you may have Apache web server listening on port 80. Ports 80 and 2500 do not conflict so both can run simultaneously, but to reach your Instiki wiki, you must add the `:2500` to the end of your computer's address.

## Hack 6: Take Great Notes

Level . . . . . . . **Easy**
Platform . . . . **Pen and Paper**
Cost . . . . . . . **Free**

Like it or not, your work life involves meetings — status meetings, planning conference calls, brainstorming sessions, meetings for the sake of meetings. But a meeting is only as valuable as the action taken after everyone's left the conference room.

Whether you're headed to a business meeting, a university lecture, or a conference session, taking effective notes is a critical skill that moves your projects, your career, and your education forward. This hack covers three practical note-taking methods, as well as how to make your own custom notepaper.

## Method 1: Symbolize Next Actions

Using notepaper or a simple text file on your laptop, indent each line of your notes in from the left margin. Then, use a simple system of symbols to mark off four different information types in the column space left in the margin. The following table describes the most useful symbols:

| SYMBOL | DESCRIPTION |
| --- | --- |
| [ ] or ☐ | A square check box denotes a to-do item. |
| ( ) or o | A circle indicates a task to be assigned to someone else. |
| * | An asterisk is an important fact. |
| ? | A question mark goes next to items to research or ask about. |

After the meeting, a quick vertical scan of the margin area makes it easy to add tasks to your to-do list and calendar, send out requests to others, and further research questions.[5]

## Method 2: Split Your Page into Quadrants

Another way to visually separate information types is to split your note-taking page into quadrants and record different kinds of information — like questions, references, to-do lists, and tasks to delegate — into separate areas on the page. Rumor has it this is how Bill Gates — someone known for taking amazingly detailed meeting notes — gets it done.[6]

## Method 3: Record and Summarize

The Cornell note-taking method works best for students or researchers digesting large amounts of information on a daily basis. The purpose of this system is to avoid re-copying your notes after the fact; to simply get it right the first time. To use this method, separate the page into different areas, as shown in Figure 1-14.[7]

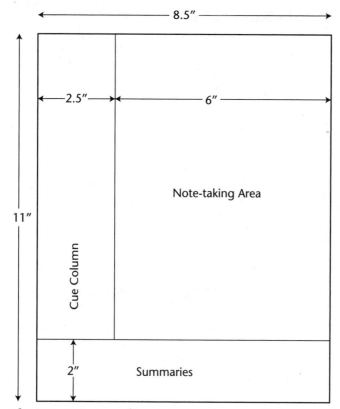

**Figure 1-14** A page split up into areas for use with the Cornell note-taking method.

Use the page sections as follows:

**Note-taking area:** Record the lecture, discussion, or meeting as completely as possible using brief sentences in paragraphs. This area will contain the meat of the information to which you will refer later. Capture general ideas and when the meeting leader or instructor moves on to a new point, skip a few lines and begin a new paragraph.

**Cue column:** Jot questions and one-liners that connect main ideas in your notes in the cue column. Later, during a study or review session, cover up the right side of the page and use the left column's cues to help yourself recall facts.

**Summary:** After the class or meeting, write a sentence or two summarizing the content of your page of notes at the bottom of the page. Use the summary section to scan your note pages and quickly find topics of discussion.

## Create Your Own Custom Note Paper

There are a few free web applications out there that produce custom PDF's of formatted, lined note paper. Print out several copies before your next meeting or class and put them in your notes binder.

- **The Notepaper Generator** (`http://simson.net/notepaper/index.cgi`) at Simson.net creates a PDF file of a lined page with a small monthly calendar in the header and an optional summary box in the upper-right corner. Choose your font face and optionally include punch holes as well.

- **The Cornell Method PDF Generator** (`http://eleven21.com/notetaker`) prints pages split into the Cornell note paper style with unlined, ruled, or graphed sections. Optionally include your name, the date, and the name of your class, and up to four punch holes for use in a binder. Also, choose the line darkness on a scale from gray to black.

- **Michael Botsko's Notepad Generator** (`http://botsko.net/Demos/notepad_generator`) makes a PDF notes template that includes your name, the page number, date, and project name, and splits the page into two sections: one for notes (with lines) and the other for action items with due dates. It also has optional punch holes.

# References

1. David Allen, *Getting Things Done* (Penguin Books, 2001), 22.
2. "Interview: Father of 'Life Hacks' Danny O'Brien," Lifehacker.com. (`http://lifehacker.com/software/interviews/interview-father-of-life-hacks-danny-obrien-036370.php`).
3. *Getting Things Done*, 143.
4. Merlin Mann, "How Do You Get Creative with Your Phonecam?" 43 Folders. (`http://43folders.com/2005/09/21/how-do-you-get-creative-with-your-phonecam`).
5. Michael Hyatt, "Recovering the Lost Art of Note-taking," Working Smart. (`http://michaelhyatt.blogs.com/workingsmart/2005/04/recovering_the_.html`).
6. Ron Howard, "Post BillG Review." (`http://weblogs.asp.net/rhoward/archive/2003/04/28/6128.aspx`).
7. "The Cornell Note-Taking System," Brigham Young University. (`http://ccc.byu.edu/learning/note-tak.php`).

# Firewall Your Attention

Your attention is your most endangered resource. The technical props of modern work life — email, instant messaging, mobile devices, and constant Internet connectivity — make limitless amounts of information always available at the press of a button. Every minute of every day advertisements, software notifications, ringing phones, blinking voice mail signals, and buzzing pagers vie for your attention. But there are a finite number of minutes, hours, and days in your life.

Modern gadgets and software are designed to help you multi-task. The evolution from the textual command line to a graphical user interface on personal computers made it possible to have a dozen windows open on one screen simultaneously, each doing a different job. The problem is that modern computing devices have outpaced humans' capabilities to multi-task.

Further, email software and cell phones and instant messenger make you reachable and interruptible at any moment in time. We live in a culture of constant connectivity, so we respond to those interruptions in kind. But this type of interruption-driven existence can have a devastating effect on your mental focus and your ability to perform. It makes for workers who are distracted, irritated, overwhelmed, and run ragged.

Psychiatrist Edward Hallowell calls the condition ADT (Attention Deficit Trait), a workplace-induced attention deficit caused by the constant distraction of high-tech devices. He says, "It's sort of like the normal version of attention deficit disorder. But it's a condition induced by modern life, in which you've become so busy attending to so many inputs and outputs that you become increasingly distracted, irritable, impulsive, restless and, over the long term, underachieving. In other words, it costs you efficiency because you're doing so much or trying to do so much, it's as if you're juggling one more ball than you possibly can."[1]

A University of California at Irvine study showed that businesspeople are interrupted once every 11 minutes on average during the work day.[2] A recent *Time Magazine* article, which cited that study, points out that many well-known successful people make a point to shut out these types of interruptions:

> Some of the world's most creative and productive individuals simply refuse to subject their brains to excess data streams. When a New York Times reporter interviewed several recent winners of MacArthur "genius" grants, a striking number said they kept cell phones and iPods off or away when in transit so that they could use the downtime for thinking. Personal-finance guru Suze Orman, despite an exhausting array of media and entrepreneurial commitments, utterly refuses to check messages, answer her phone, or allow anything else to come between her and whatever she's working on. "I do one thing at a time," she says. "I do it well, and then I move on."[3]

Orman knows that the key to overcoming ADT is to fully focus on one task at a time. Give yourself the time and space to dig into a problem and reach that state of mind called *flow*, when you're fully immersed in your task, effortlessly successful, and oblivious to time and external factors.

To get into this zone, block out irrelevant distractions and only let in the information you need to get the job done. Like a computer system firewall that blocks potential intruders, the techniques presented in this chapter will help you firewall your most precious resource.

## Hack 7: Limit Access to Time-Wasting Web Sites

Level. . . . . . . **Advanced**
Platform. . . . . **All (Firefox)**
Cost . . . . . . . **Free**

Picture this: you sit down at your computer to write a report that's due the next day. You fire up a web browser to check the company intranet for a document. For a split second you glance at your home page. "Wow!" you say. "The Red Sox won in the 17th inning! Let me see what happened..."

Three hours later, no report's been written, and you want to throw yourself out the window.

Sound familiar?

It's too easy to scamper down the rabbit hole of the Web when you've got pressing tasks to work on. At one point or another, you've probably burned a few hours clicking around Wikipedia, Amazon.com, eBay, Flickr, or Google

News and afterward hated yourself for it. Surfing efficiently is an exercise in discipline and sometimes outright abstinence. This hack uses JavaScript to blank out certain web sites during times you're supposed to be working.

First, identify the biggest offenders — the sites you can spend hours clicking around for no particular reason except boredom, procrastination, or lack of more creative ways to spend your time. For me, two of these sites are Flickr (`http://flickr.com`) and Metafilter (`http://metafilter.com`), so this example uses them.

The morning's a good time to buckle down and slog through the bulk of the day's work, so that's the worst period to waste hours looking at your buddies' kitten photos on Flickr. Things tend to slow down around 3 o'clock in the afternoon, so treating yourself to a little recreational surfing then may be OK.

To help yourself limit unproductive surfing, use this Invisibility Cloak user script that turns time-wasting web sites blank before 3 p.m. (or whatever time you configure). Here's how to enable the Invisibility Cloak.

## Install the Invisibility Cloak

The Invisibility Cloak JavaScript requires the Firefox web browser with the Greasemonkey extension to run. Here's how to get it set up.

1. Download and install the Greasemonkey Firefox extension from `http://greasemonkey.mozdev.org`. (For detailed instructions on how to install a Firefox extension, see Hack 71, "Extend Your Web Browser.")

2. Using Firefox with Greasemonkey installed, go to the Invisibility Cloak user script page at `http://lifehackerbook.com/ch2/cloak.user.js`.

3. Click the Install button at the top right of the page (see Figure 2-1).

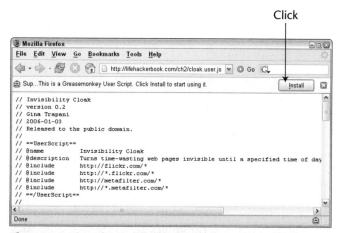

**Figure 2-1** View the Invisibility Cloak user script in Firefox.

## Set Which Sites Should Wear the Cloak

The Invisibility Cloak script is auto-configured to work on Metafilter (`http://metafilter.com`) and Flickr (`http://flickr.com`), but you want to it to work on the sites you choose.

1. In Firefox, select Tools → Manage User Scripts to edit, add, and remove sites that should wear the cloak for you, as shown in Figure 2-2.

2. Use a wild card operator — the asterisk (`*`) — to indicate all pages on a site. For example, `http://flickr.com/*` will apply the Invisibility Cloak to all the pages on the Flickr.com domain.

3. When the Invisibility Cloak is enabled (the Enabled check box is selected), visit one of the specified web sites before 3 p.m. and you get the message shown in Figure 2-3.

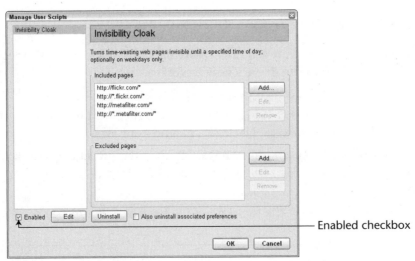

Enabled checkbox

**Figure 2-2** Add and edit web sites that should wear the Invisibility Cloak in the Manage User Scripts dialog box.

**Figure 2-3** Cloaked web site before 3 p.m.

## Customize the Script

You can customize the Invisibility Cloak script further by hand-editing the code. Following is the JavaScript body of the script. You'll edit the bold lines in a minute.

**NOTE** The ⊃ symbol is not part of the code. It merely indicates that the code line was too long to fit on one line in the book, and the code on the following line is actually a continuation of the first line.

```
// Invisibility Cloak
// version 0.2
// Gina Trapani
// 2006-01-03
// Released to the public domain.
//
// ==UserScript==
// @name          Invisibility Cloak
// @description   Turns time-wasting web pages invisible until ⊃
a specified time of day; optionally on weekdays only.
// @include       http://flickr.com/*
// @include       http://*.flickr.com/*
// @include       http://metafilter.com/*
// @include       http://*.metafilter.com/*
// ==/UserScript==
//
```

```
// ==RevisionHistory==
// Version 0.1:
// Released: 2006-01-03.
// Initial release.
//
// Version 0.2:
// Released: 2006-01-18.
// Includes option to not apply cloak on the weekends.
// ==/RevisionHistory==



(function () {
  // EDIT THE NEXT LINES TO SET THE HOUR AFTER WHICH SITES SHOULD APPEAR
  // HOURS IN MILITARY TIME, SO 15 = 3PM
  var surf_time_after = 15;
  // TAKE OFF CLOAK ON WEEKENDS?
  var cloak_off_weekends = true;
  // END EDIT

  var tstamp = new Date();
  var its_the_weekend = false;
  if (tstamp.getDay() == 6 || tstamp.getDay() == 0)
  {
      its_the_weekend = true;
  }

  var readable_time = '';
  if (surf_time_after > 12 )
  {
     readable_time = surf_time_after - 12;
     readable_time = readable_time + 'PM';
  } else {
     readable_time = surf_time_after + 'AM';
  }

  if (tstamp.getHours() < surf_time_after )
  {
     if (cloak_off_weekends == true)
     {
        if (its_the_weekend == false)
        {
           var b = (document.getElementsByTagName("body")[0]);
           b.setAttribute('style', 'display:none!important');
           alert("You can surf after "+ readable_time + "; right ↩
now, get back to work!");
        }
     } else {
           var b = (document.getElementsByTagName("body")[0]);
           b.setAttribute('style', 'display:none!important');
           alert("You can surf after "+ readable_time + ";  right ↩
```

```
now, get back to work!");
      }

   }

})();
```

To change the time your Invisibility Cloak comes off, follow these steps:

1. Go to the script at `http://lifehackerbook.com/ch2/cloak
   .user.js`. In Firefox, choose File → Save Page As. Save the script
   to your computer, and then open the `cloak.user.js` file in a text
   editor. Change the number 15 (which represents 3 p.m. on the
   24-hour clock) in the line that reads `var surf_time_after = 15;`
   to your desired time.

2. By default, the cloak is not applied on weekends. To change that setting, edit the line that reads:

   ```
   var cloak_off_weekends = true;
   ```

   to

   ```
   var cloak_off_weekends = false;
   ```

3. You can also change the message the cloak displays when you visit a
   restricted site. Edit the line:

   ```
   alert("You can surf after "+ readable_time + ;⤵

   "; right now, get back to work!");
   ```

   to include your custom message inside the quotation marks. (The
   `readable_time` variable represents the time you set on the 12-hour
   clock with AM or PM specified.)

4. Save your changes. In the Manage User Scripts dialog box, uninstall the
   Invisibility Cloak. Then, open your edited `cloak.user.js` file in Firefox and choose Install to use that version.

# Hack 8: Permanently Block Time-Wasting Web Sites

Level........ **Advanced**
Platform.... **Windows XP and Vista, Mac OS X**
Cost ....... **Free**

Is there a web site that's utterly toxic to your mental state or ability to work?
Maybe you grind your teeth over your ex's weblog, which details every
moment of her happy new life without you. Maybe you've lost hours of your

life trolling eBay auctions and you simply can't impulse-buy another auto-graphed Neil Diamond record. Perhaps online backgammon can snatch away hours of your day at the office.

The preceding hack describes how to block time-wasting web sites during certain times of the day and week. Alternatively, you can block sites at *all* times, until you explicitly release the restriction. This hack fakes your computer into thinking that those problem sites live on your hard drive — which obviously they don't — and forces a `Server Not Found` error when your fingers impulsively type out that tempting, time-sucking URL.

Here's how.

## Windows

1. Using Notepad or some other text editor, open the file named `hosts`, which is located in the following directory:

    **Windows XP and Vista**: C:\WINDOWS\SYSTEM32\DRIVERS\ETC

    **Windows 2000**: C:\WINNT\SYSTEM32\DRIVERS\ETC

    **Windows 98\ME**: C:\WINDOWS\

2. Add the following on its own line in the `hosts` file:

    ```
    127.0.0.1 ebay.com games.yahoo.com evilex.com
    ```

    Replacing the sites listed with the domains that you want to block.

## Mac OS X

1. In Finder, from the Go menu, choose Go To Folder.

2. In the Go To Folder dialog, type `/etc/`.

3. From the `/etc/` folder window, open the `hosts` file in a text editor.

4. Add the following on its own line in the `hosts` file:

    ```
    127.0.0.1 ebay.com games.yahoo.com evilex.com
    ```

    Replace the sites listed with the domains that you want to block.

## The Result

After you've completed the steps for your operating system, save the `hosts` file and quit your editor.

Now when you visit one of your blocked sites, you get a `Server Not Found` error. (If you're running a web server, at home as detailed in Hack 35, your own server's files appear.)

The advantage of this method over Hack 7 is that the sites are blocked from every browser on that computer, not just Firefox. The downside is that when you decide it's an OK time to browse eBay, you've got to manually comment out the following line in the `hosts` file by adding a # to the beginning of the line:

```
#127.0.0.1 metafilter.com flickr.com
```

And that's a deliberately huge pain that can help keep your wandering clicker in line when you're under deadline.

# Hack 9: Reduce Email Interruptions

Level....... **Easy**
Platform.... **All**
Cost ....... **Free**

Unlike phone calls and instant messenger, email was never intended for real-time communication. However, most people treat it as if it were. You most likely work with your email program open all day long, while it checks for new messages every 5 minutes, and notifies you of unread incoming email on the spot.

It's so difficult to ignore that little unopened envelope, isn't it? Maybe those new messages contain juicy gossip, or photos of the baby, or heaping praise from the boss. Maybe they contain details of an emergency that has to be dealt with right this second. Most likely they contain misspelled details of how to buy "cheap V1@gr@" but nevertheless, the impulse to look at them is powerful. Unread email is just another shot of the information drug your hungry mind craves. It cries out to you, "Open me! Open me!"

However, when you need to focus, do yourself a favor: actively control when you check your email. Two strategies can help.

## Shut Down Your Email Program

The simplest (but perhaps least practical) way to stop letting your inbox run your day is to quit your email software. Make your default work mode email-free. Open your inbox only at designated processing times. Commit to just two or three times during a workday — say, first thing in the morning, just after lunch, and an hour before you leave — to check for and process unread messages. This means responding, filing, and taking any action those messages warrant on the spot.

**NOTE** Hack 46, "Decrease Your Email Response Time," provides strategies for processing email right off the bat to avoid a pileup of read-but-not-processed messages.

## Set Your Client to Check for Messages Once an Hour

Your work situation may demand that your email program be open all the time — say, if you work in Outlook using its calendar and tasks lists. You can still reduce the constant interruption of the new mail notification: set your mail client to check for new messages once an hour.

By default, Microsoft Outlook checks for unread email every 5 minutes. That means — what with spam, cc-happy co-workers, mailing lists, and bored friends at work — you potentially can be interrupted 12 times an hour, or 108 times during a 9-hour workday by a new email message. Change this setting to every 60 minutes to reduce the number of interruptions from 108 to 9 times a day.

The method for changing that setting varies, depending on your email program. If you use Microsoft Outlook, choose Tools → Options. In the Mail Setup tab, hit the Send and Receive button to change the frequency setting, as shown in Figure 2-4.

The amount of time you choose to check for new messages is up to you, but even once an hour can be excessive. If you're truly ready to toss the email monkey off your back, try processing email two or three times a day, at times you determine.

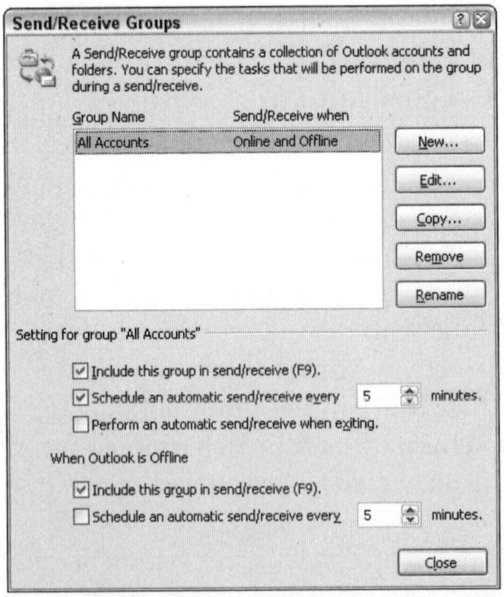

**Figure 2-4** Microsoft Outlook Send/Receive options.

# Hack 10: Split Your Work Among Multiple Desktops

Level. . . . . . . **Easy**
Platform. . . . **Windows XP, Mac OS X**
Cost . . . . . . . **Free**

The more space you have to lay out your materials, the easier it is to get a job done. Imagine a cook in a kitchen with restricted counter space. She has to remove the first ingredient from the refrigerator, put it on the counter, chop, measure, and add it to the recipe. To use more ingredients she has to return the first to the refrigerator to make room for the second, and so on. But what if she had a larger countertop that could accommodate all the ingredients at once? The chef could spend less time switching between ingredients and more time cooking.

The same concept applies to the amount of screen real estate you have on your computer monitor. Modern operating systems make multi-tasking with overlapping windows on one screen possible, but that requires some amount of task switching and window resizing to get to what you need. A recent survey by Jon Peddie Research[4] showed that multi-monitor computer setups can increase a computer worker's productivity by 20 to 30 percent.

In fact, Microsoft Corporation founder Bill Gates splits his work up onto three screens that make up one desktop: "The screen on the left has my list of emails. On the center screen is usually the specific email I'm reading and responding to. And my browser is on the right-hand screen. This setup gives me the ability to glance and see what new has come in while I'm working on something, and to bring up a link that's related to an email and look at it while the email is still in front of me."[5]

To use physical multiple monitors, your computer has to have multiple video cards or one video card capable of multiple monitors. If you don't have that capability, use virtual desktops instead to separate your work into four distinct workspaces and focus on one at a time.

For example, use one desktop for the task at hand; the second for your task resource documents, calendar, or to-do list; the third for web access; and the last for email. Here's how to get it set up.

## Windows XP

Download the free Microsoft Windows Virtual Desktop Manager (MSVDM) from http://microsoft.com/windowsxp/downloads/powertoys/ xppowertoys.mspx. After installing MSVDM, right-click your Windows taskbar and select Toolbars → Desktop Manager. The MSVDM toolbar displays buttons labeled 1 through 4. Switch to another desktop by pressing a button, or use the Quick Preview button to see all four desktops in quadrants on your screen, as shown in Figure 2-5.

Assign a different desktop background to each desktop to distinguish them visually. To do so, right-click the MSVDM toolbar and choose Configure Desktop Images, as shown in Figure 2-6.

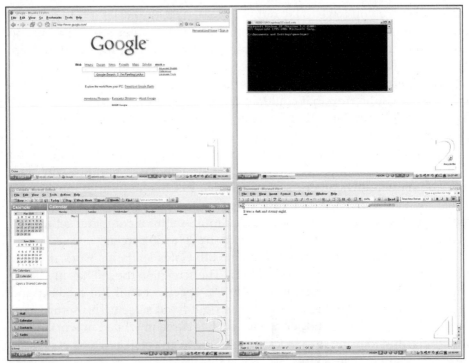

**Figure 2-5** View all four virtual desktops using Microsoft Windows Virtual Desktop Manager.

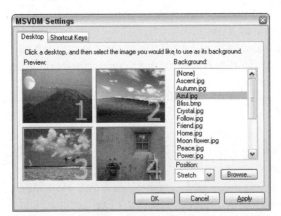

**Figure 2-6** Choose a wallpaper image for each desktop in Microsoft Windows Virtual Desktop Manager.

## Mac OS X

If you're running Mac OS X 10.4 (Tiger), VirtueDesktops (`http://virtuedesktops.info`) is a free virtual desktop manager. Download the latest version, unzip it, and drag and drop it into your Applications folder. Start up VirtueDesktops, and a virtual desktop menu appears in the status bar. Choose Preferences from that menu, and within the Triggers area, configure your preferred keyboard shortcuts for switching between desktops. By default, the Option+Tab key combination displays all four desktops which you can navigate using the arrow keys, as shown in Figure 2-7.

> **NOTE** The latest version of Mac OS X 10.5, Leopard, will have virtual desktops (called Spaces) built right in. More information on using Spaces is available at `http://apple.com/macosx/leopard/spaces.html`.

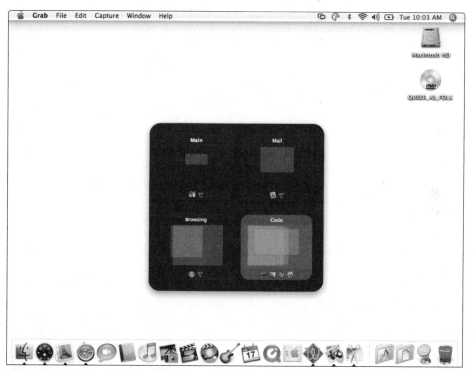

**Figure 2-7** Create and manage four virtual desktops on Mac OS X 10.4 with VirtueDesktops.

# Hack 11: Build a No-fly Zone

Level . . . . . . . **Easy**
Platform . . . . **All**
Cost . . . . . . . **Free**

Many modern office spaces have open layouts to "promote interaction between departments" — which means they're set up to distract you all day long. Low-wall cubes, side-by-side desks, required use of an instant messenger (IM) — all make for a workday that's interruption-driven instead of task-driven. Then there's the management strategy to encourage personnel intermingling that seats employees who do involved mental work such as programming or number-crunching next to loud sales people yammering away on the phone.

For anyone who doesn't have her own office with a door that can be closed, getting actual work done at the office can be a serious challenge. Co-workers stopping by, IM windows popping up, getting dragged off to meetings or hijacked to deal with the latest department crisis are all time-suckers that can leave you worn out at 6 p.m., wondering where the day went.

When you're just a cog in the machine, changing your office's culture might not be possible. But for your own sanity and productivity, do what you can to protect yourself from extraneous interruptions at the office.

## Set Yourself up to Get into the Zone

It takes 15 minutes of uninterrupted time to get into "the zone," that wonderfully productive place where you lose all sense of time and space and get a job done. Protect yourself from interruptions before you start on an involved mental task to give yourself that 15-minute runway.

Forward your office phone to voice mail and silence your cell phone. Shut down instant messenger. If it must be on, set your status to Busy or Here but working, chat later. Shut down your email client. If you're waiting for a crucial message, set your email program to receive messages quietly (no sound) and forward any must get-through email to your phone.

Shut down every application running on your computer that doesn't have to do with the task at hand. If you don't need the Web to complete your task, disconnect your machine from the network. I know — it's extreme, but I'm serious. If you're a programmer, download language documentation locally before you start to avoid the temptation of the web browser.

## Make Yourself Inaccessible

If your office uses Outlook or a shared calendar, schedule an appointment with yourself that shows you as busy during the time you're working on your task to avoid meeting requests during that time. (This is especially useful for recurring tasks such as to write weekly status reports.)

Signal to your co-workers in whatever ways are possible that you shouldn't be interrupted unless absolutely necessary. If it's acceptable at your workplace, put on headphones — noise-canceling headphones are best — and listen to music to block out sound. (A former co-worker of mine once confessed that he put on headphones without anything playing on them just so people wouldn't randomly address him.)

**NOTE** See Hack 16, "Drown Out Sound with Pink Noise," for more on masking office noise.

If interruption by your manager or co-workers is a big problem, work out a way you can signal that you're available to chat or that you're super-involved at the moment at your desk. Make an agreement with others that when the sock's on the door, they won't stop by asking if you want to get coffee or what you thought of last night's episode of *Lost*.

## Work at Quieter Times and in Zoned-Off Spaces

If all else fails, find times and space at your office where it's easier to get work done. Come in a little earlier or stay later or move your lunch break to the opposite time of your co-workers. A couple of programmers I know who worked at a frenetic office used to schedule a two-hour meeting together in a conference room a couple of times a week, where they'd go with their laptops to code in peace and quiet. A complete change of scenery can help boost your productivity as well as keep you from the ringing phone and chatty cube mate.

## Hack 12: Filter Low-Priority Email Messages

Level. . . . . . . **Easy**
Platform. . . . **All**
Cost . . . . . . . **Free**

You're head-down at work on that important presentation that's due in two hours. BING! An unopened envelope appears in your system tray.

"You have 1 unread message."

Maybe it's your co-worker with game-changing information about the presentation. Maybe it's your boss asking to see you right away. You switch and take a look at your inbox. Oh. Aunt Eunice forwarded you a picture of a kitten in a tutu. Again.

Millions of email messages course over the internet wire per second, and some days it feels like a big chunk of them land in your inbox. Your spam filter helps shuttle junk mail out of sight, but what about messages from cc-happy co-workers, Aunt Eunice's forwarded emails, and mailing list messages that clutter your inbox with low-priority noise?

## Filter Low-Priority Messages

Set up rules — also called email filters — to make low-priority messages skip your inbox and file themselves away someplace less urgent. A mail filter is a list of conditions that trigger an action you define on an incoming email message. Filters can be as simple as "Delete any message from annoying.person@ example.com," or can get more complex, like "Any message that doesn't contain any one of my five email addresses in the To: field and does not have the word URGENT in the subject line should be moved to the Not Important folder."

The exact steps for doing this vary depending on your email software. The following examples use the excellent, free, cross-platform email program Thunderbird, available at `http://mozilla.org/products/thunderbird`.

To configure your email filters in Thunderbird, select Tools → Message Filters, and click the New button. Figure 2-8 displays a rule that files Aunt Eunice's forwarded messages and any messages from a mailing list to a folder called Later.

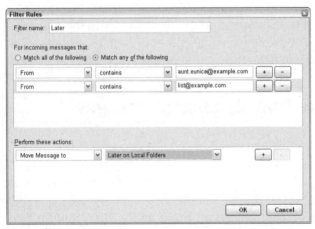

**Figure 2-8** Mail filter that moves low-priority incoming messages to a folder called Later in Mozilla Thunderbird.

## Filter CC'ed Messages

One of the most common misuses of email — especially in an office situation — is carbon copying anyone and everyone even tangentially related to the topic on a message. It's safe to assume that messages not directed to you (that is, your email address is not in the To line) are less urgent and more informative: CC'ed messages most likely don't require a response or action on your part. On a day when you're firewalling your attention to only the most important disruptors, set up a rule that shuttles email you've been CC'ed on out of your inbox and into a separate folder for searching and browsing later.

To do so, first create a CC folder in your email program. Then, set up a rule (filter) to say, "If my email address does not appear in the To field, file this message," as shown in Figure 2-9.

**NOTE** Hack 48, "Master Message Search," provides tips for digging up messages based on specific criteria.

When the filter is enabled, all new messages that arrive without your email address in the To field are automatically filed in the CC folder.

**Figure 2-9** An email rule that moves messages not directed to either of two email addresses to a folder called CC.

# Hack 13: Clear Your Desktop

Level....... **Easy**
Platform.... **Windows XP and Vista, Mac OS X**
Cost ....... **Free**

It's amazing how fast your computer's desktop can fill up with shortcuts and files and turn into a virtual candy store of colorful icons beckoning your mouse pointer: "Click me! Click me!" Most modern software puts a shortcut to itself on your computer desktop by default when you install it. Your web browser and email program might save files they download directly to your desktop. It's tempting to leave documents on your desktop because you'll know they'll be in sight at all times. But at what cost?

A cluttered virtual desktop is as bad as a cluttered physical desktop. It's visually distracting and makes it easy to get derailed from the task at hand. ("Hey, lemme watch that funny .avi movie just one more time!")

Clear your virtual desktop by removing all the icons you don't need. To maintain a completely clear desktop with absolutely nothing taking up space, you can disable Desktop icons entirely. Here's how.

## Windows

1. Drag and drop all the files you've saved on your desktop into the My Documents folder. (See Hack 52, "Organize My Documents," for ways to get your My Documents folder under control.)

2. Delete all the shortcuts to software applications on your desktop that already exist in Windows' Start menu.

3. To disable Desktop items entirely, in Windows XP, right-click the Desktop, and from the Arrange Icons By submenu, deselect Show Desktop Icons. In Windows Vista, right-click the Desktop, and from the View submenu, clear Show Desktop Icons.

4. Enable the Quick Launch toolbar to start up programs without having to navigate the Start Menu. Add shortcuts to programs or documents you open often to this toolbar for easy access. The limited real estate is a good thing: choose only the items you *launch* often. (For example, if you open the status.xls spreadsheet every other day, use a shortcut to that document, instead of a shortcut to Excel.) As for all your other programs? Fear not: they're still accessible, safely tucked away in the Programs folder.

## Mac OS X

Mac applications are a lot less likely to add shortcuts to your Desktop; but it is still easy to save downloaded files to your Mac's desktop. Here's how to clear up things and still make all your favorite applications and documents accessible.

1. Drag and drop all the files on your Desktop to your Documents folder in Finder.

2. Delete any shortcuts left on your Desktop.

3. Drag and drop your frequently launched programs to the Dock (to the left of the Trash Bin).

4. For easy access to your Documents and Applications folders, drag and drop them to the Dock as well. When clicked, the Applications folder will reveal a vertical menu of items, as show in Figure 2-10.

Make it a habit to file away programs and documents in folders rather than on your desktop to maintain a clutter-free virtual work environment.

**Figure 2-10** Place the Applications folder on the Dock as a menu to access all your software.

# Hack 14: Make Your House a Usable Home

Level....... **Easy**
Platform.... **All**
Cost ....... **Free**

Ever been on the way out the door and you can't find your keys? Dashing around the house tearing through every nook and cranny in a stressed-out frenzy isn't the best way to start the day. But we've all been there.

It's so easy to sabotage yourself every day without even realizing it. The moment you put your keys in the pocket of the jacket you tossed over the kitchen chair you didn't think, "I'm going to make it really difficult for myself tomorrow morning when I have to leave for the big interview." Yet there are so many small ways in which you can unconsciously make life harder on yourself. Personal sabotage — whether it's in the form of convincing yourself you'll magically remember to pick up milk at the store or thoughtlessly surfing the Web when you've got a looming deadline — is a reversible habit with a little thought and planning.

Just the way a basketball teammate tips the ball when the slam dunker leaps to make the basket, you can be your own teammate and set yourself up for success in life and work.

Take a look at your living space with a focus on usability. Your home should be a tool that helps you get things done, a space that's a pleasure to be in and a launch pad for daily tasks as well as your life goals. Whether you want to relax after work, phone a family member, or keep track of a dry cleaning receipt, there are lots of simple ways to create a living space that makes getting things done a breeze.

## Create a Place for Incoming Stuff

Every day you walk into the house with your hands full of mail, pockets full of change, and a cell phone that needs recharging. Instead of dumping that pile of bills onto the coffee table, scattering a mess of pennies and dimes on your dresser, and tossing the phone onto a table, create useful places to drop off stuff without having to think: say, a change jar that goes to Coinstar every few months, an indoor mailbox for you and your housemates, and a phone-charging center with an easily-accessible plug. Fact is, after a long day at work, you don't want to have to think about where to put stuff when you walk in the door. So make it a no-brainer.

## Put Items You Need to Remember in Your Path

Make it hard to forget where you put your keys, your cell phone, that check you're supposed to mail, or the dry cleaning receipt. Section off a space near the door where you can easily pick up items on your way out. Hang a key rack. Place a snail mail outbox nearby for letters and bills that need to get dropped at the post office. The door of my old apartment was metal, so I kept a few magnets stuck to it to hold receipts, mail, and notes I'd be sure to see on my way out the door.

## Stow Away Stuff You Don't Use; Put Stuff You Do Within Easy Reach

Surround yourself with the things you use and either get rid of the things you don't, or stow them away. For example, if you've ripped all your audio CDs to MP3 and only listen to them in that format, then why line your living room walls with CDs that never get touched? Box up your CDs and store them up on a high shelf in the closet to make room for the things in the living room that you do use. In the kitchen, if you rarely make waffles but you're on a grilled cheese kick, put the waffle-maker on the top shelf and leave the Foreman grill at eye level.

## Strategically Place Items to Make Tasks Easy

Having all the things you need to complete a task on hand is half the battle. One of my favorite household life hacks is the sheet-folding trick: fold the flat and fitted sheets into a set and place them *inside* one pillowcase, along with any other pillowcases for those sheets. The convenient packaging precludes the need to rummage through the linen closet matching up sheet sets when the time comes to make the bed.

There are lots of ways to make tasks easier with strategic placement. If your telephone directory is digital, print out a copy and leave it by the phone at home so you don't have to consult your cell phone or boot up the computer to find a number. Make recycling easy by placing the bin in the area where the most paper or glass is generated — say, the home office or kitchen. If you're bleary-eyed and fumbling for the TV remote each day to check the weather, give yourself a break. Invest in a cheap thermometer and place it in the bedroom window just by your closet, so you know what kind of outfit to choose without any hassle.

Alternatively, keep your laptop in the bedroom and use it as your alarm clock and weather notifier, in case of rain or snow. Use an Alarm Clock widget (available at `http://widgetgallery.com/view.php?widget=39123`) to start playing music at a time you determine. Then schedule a task that launches a weather report web page as well. (See Hack 23, "Automatically Reboot and Launch Applications," for more on launching a web page at a specific time.)

## Make Task-Based Centers

Place all the items you need to complete a task in an area sectioned off for that activity — like a computer repair center, a bill-paying center, or a gift-wrapping center. Keep ink and paper next to the printer; folders and tabs on the filing cabinet, and stamps, envelopes, and address stickers in a mail center. Incorporate the defragging process — placing related items next to one another — into your regular cleaning routine.

## Leave Writing Material Everywhere

Keep pens and pads all over the house: by the phone, on the kitchen counter, on the night table, in the bathroom. You never know when a thought that needs to be recorded will strike. An idea, a forgotten to-do, the solution to a problem you're having at work, a dream you want to remember, an image or drawing, a phone number — all should all be jotted down without effort. Easily available capture tools keep nagging thoughts from cluttering your mind.

## Set up an Inbox

Make a place to put real-life items that come streaming into your day, so you can process them at times *you* determine instead of letting them interrupt you. Snail mail, receipts, business cards, random paperwork, notes you've scribbled to yourself should all be shuttled directly into your inbox for later sorting and processing. A plastic or metal office inbox does just fine; any kind of box or even designated desk space would work. You get bonus points if you can get your housemate or partner to get an inbox, too; that way you can leave things for him or her to see without piles of stuff gathering around the house.

## Collaborate with Housemates

Simple tools can make sharing household tasks easy. Place a magnetic dirty/clean flippy sign on the dishwasher so everyone knows when it has to be emptied and when it can be loaded. Stick a magnetic whiteboard to the fridge with an ongoing shopping list. Use it to leave notes or to-do lists, too, such as "Call plumber about the toilet! 555-3456." A magnetic whiteboard calendar is also a handy way to keep track of household schedules, especially for busy families.

**TIP** The Grocery Shopping Helper (available at `http://lifehackerbook`
`.com/ch2/groceryhelper`) creates a list of shopping items with the aisle
they're located in at your local store. Print out a copy to keep on your fridge,
and list the quantity next to items you need. Then, sort needed items by aisle to
make grocery shopping a breeze.

## Hack 15: Sentence Stuff to Death Row

Level . . . . . . . **Easy**
Platform . . . . **All**
Cost . . . . . . . **Free**

Endless streams of information compete for your attention. RSS feeds, mailing
lists, and news sites are all great ways to keep up with what's going on in the
world and within your industry. However, because putting your ear to yet
another new information channel is so easy, it's equally easy to find yourself
swimming in a sea of unread items that pile up while you're focusing on other
things. Prune your information channels down to the ones most worth your
time to keep up a solid attention firewall. One technique for doing so is sen-
tencing certain information streams to a virtual death row.

Maybe it's the mailing list you once enjoyed and participated in with relish,
but that has become more boring than informative. Maybe it's that weblog that
seemed so fun and original six months ago that's slowly lost your interest.
Whether you're de-cluttering your home or your digital space, sometimes it's
hard to know what you can safely toss and what to hang onto. A simple
method for choosing what goes and what stays is to make a folder called
`Death Row` on your hard drive, in your email program, or RSS reader — or in
all three. Place any feeds, lists, or files you're not sure are useful to you anymore in there.

Give yourself six weeks. If within that time, you never looked up something
in that feed, or list, or used one of those files, out it goes. If you did use an item,
reinstate it into your regular rotation.

## Hack 16: Drown out Sound with Pink Noise

Level . . . . . . . **Easy**
Platform . . . . **Mac OS X, Windows**
Cost . . . . . . . **Free**

If your co-worker's conversation down the hall is distracting you, or your downstairs neighbor's television is blaring up through your floor, block out the sound with a soft static noise. Pink noise masks ambient sounds like passing car subwoofers or neighborhood industrial noise.

## Mac OS X

A free software application for Mac OS X, called Noise (see Figure 2-11), plays distraction-drowning pink noise continuously. You can download it from `http://blackholemedia.com/noise`.

## Windows

Pink noise and white noise CDs and MP3s are available for purchase online and offline. Set them to play on repeat using any digital music player or CD player on your computer to replace Noise's functionality.

## Hack 17: Keep Software from Stealing Focus

Level....... **Easy**
Platform.... **Windows XP**
Cost ....... **Free**

Ever been typing in a document or a password prompt and have a pop-up take over as the active window? It's not hard to instant message a password to a stranger or unknowingly reboot your computer because a Windows Update prompt asked while you weren't looking. An application focus thief breaks into your workflow without warning or permission. Not only can it steal the window focus, it can take over your *mental* focus. Why should Windows interrupt you on your time? The short answer is, it shouldn't.

A free Windows enhancement called Tweak UI can disable focus-stealing applications. Download the free Tweak UI from the Microsoft web site at `http://microsoft.com/windowsxp/downloads/powertoys/xppower toys.mspx`. Click the TweakUI.exe link in the column on the right side.

Once Tweak UI is running, under the General options, in the Focus panel, select Prevent applications from stealing focus, as shown in Figure 2-12.

**Figure 2-11** Mac OS X Noise in action.

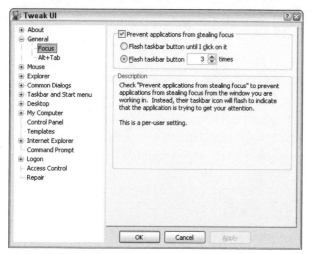

**Figure 2-12** Configure Windows application focus settings in Tweak UI.

Tweak UI unlocks lots of other Windows settings as well. It's worth a look around the software for other options to configure Windows just to your liking.

# References

1.  Alorie Gilbert, "Why Can't You Pay Attention Anymore?" CNET News.com (`http://news.com.com/Why+cant+you+pay+attention+anymore/ 2008-1022_3-5637632.html`).
2.  Jerry Useem, "Making Your Work Work For You," *CNN Money*, March 2006 (`http://money.cnn.com/magazines/fortune/fortune_archive/ 2006/03/20/8371789/index.htm`).
3.  Claudia Wallis and Sonja Steptoe, "Help! I've Lost My Focus," *TIME Magazine*, Jan 16, 2006 (`http://time.com/time/archive/preview/ 0,10987,1147199,00.html`).
4.  Ivan Berger, "The Virtues of a Second Screen," *The New York Times*, April 20, 2006 (`http://nytimes.com/2006/04/20/technology/20basics .html`).
5.  Bill Gates, "How I Work: Bill Gates," *Fortune Magazine*, Mar 30, 2006 (`http://money.cnn.com/2006/03/30/news/newsmakers/gates_ howiwork_fortune`).

# Automate Repetitive Tasks

You want to spend your time doing interesting work, not slogging through tedium. Faced with a dull, tiresome task, a lifehacker opts to spend three hours and 55 minutes automating it rather than four hours actually doing it.

Computers are built to take the burden of menial tasks out of human hands. Refrigerators switch on and off to maintain a certain temperature. Your paycheck is directly deposited into your account without anyone having to visit the bank. Streetlights snap on at dusk so humans don't have to canvass the neighborhood flipping switches. And you can automate personal computing tasks to run in the background automatically.

If you examine your work processes over time, you'll notice that certain activities come up over and over again, whether it's filing email messages into the same folders, cleaning up your hard drive, or downloading new songs from your favorite bands' web sites. Program your computer to perform these tasks once, and you'll never have to do them by hand again.

Every computer operating system can execute automated tasks on a recurring schedule, but few personal computer users take advantage of this capability. It's a shame. Granted, the initial time investment of automating a job can seem high, but in the long run, the payback more than makes up for it.

A computer isn't like a car: you don't have to be at the wheel to drive. Set up your computer to run itself while you're asleep or at lunch or in a meeting. It can do routine maintenance, fetch files from the Web, and back itself up. Save yourself from the doldrums of tedious work with the following hacks that automate important — but boring — tasks so you can concentrate on more appealing work.

## Hack 18: Automatically Back up Your Files

Level....... **Medium**
Platform.... **Windows XP and Vista**
Cost ....... **$75 and up**

More and more, the fragments of your life exist as particles on a magnetic disk mounted inside your computer. The photos from your one-year-old niece's birthday, the interview you did with great-grandpa Gus, your working manuscript of the Great American Novel, the first email messages you exchanged with your spouse — not to mention crucial professional data — all reside on that spinning magnetic platter susceptible to temperature changes, power surges, fire, theft, static, and just plain wear and tear.

Hard drives fail. It's a fact of computing life. It's not a matter of whether your computer's disk will stop working; it's a matter of when. The question is how much it will disrupt your life — and it won't if you have a backup copy.

Backing up your data could possibly be the dullest — yet most indispensable — thing you do on your computer. But who remembers to do it? You don't have to.

In this hack you'll automate nightly, weekly, and monthly local and off-site backups for your PC using free software. This system will even email you if something goes wrong, so it's the ultimate "set it and forget it" situation. Once you get this up and running, you'll never have to worry about losing data again.

### What You'll Need

- A Windows XP or Vista PC.
- **SyncBack Freeware version 3.2.** Available as a free download from `http://2brightsparks.com/downloads.html`.
- **An external hard drive.** Purchase an external hard drive that connects via USB or FireWire, depending on your computer model. (Consult your PC's user guide for the ports are available on your machine.) When deciding capacity, go for 10 times the amount of data you want to back up. For example, if the size of your My Documents folder is 10 GB, then look to purchase a 100 GB hard drive. (If a drive the size you need isn't available, calculate the size of your home directory without space-hogging subdirectories, like My Music, My Videos, and My Pictures. You have the option to reduce the number of copies you keep of those large files to save space.)

■ **An off-site, FTP server (optional).** If you want off-site backup — in case of fire, flood or theft — purchase an ongoing backup hosting plan on a server that provides FTP access. For less than $10 a month, you can get several gigabytes of storage at a web (or purely backup) hosting provider.

## Configure the Backup System

You can create multiple schedules and notifications and back up over the internet to remote servers with the SyncBack backup software. While both Windows XP and Vista come with a built-in backup utility, neither offers the options and flexibility of SyncBack.

**NOTE** Vista's backup utility has one advantage over SyncBack — it displays a file's past versions inside its Properties dialog box, which is a nice perk.

To get your automated, worry-free backups up and running, follow these steps:

1. Get the SyncBack software — SyncBack Freeware v3.2 — available for download at `http://2brightsparks.com/downloads.html`. Install the application.

**NOTE** SyncBackSE version 4.0 is also available to buy at $25. This hack uses the free SyncBack version 3, which does not offer the advanced features of version 4, such as backing up open files, unlimited zip file size, and encryption.

2. Connect your external hard drive to your computer. Turn it on. Name it Backup and browse to it in Explorer. (On my computer, for example, it's the `G:\` drive.)

3. Create four folders: `nightly`, `weekly`, `monthly-even`, and `monthly-odd`, as shown in Figure 3-1. You'll store your backups in these folders.

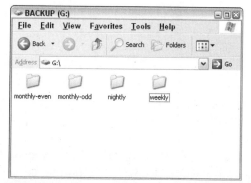

**Figure 3-1** Backup folders on the external drive.

4. Fire up SyncBack. Create a new profile called `Local Nightly backup`. Set the Source to your My Documents folder (or wherever you store your important data), and the destination to your backup drive's `nightly` folder, as shown in Figure 3-2.

5. Select the directory to backup. Choose to back up your entire Source directory or select specific subdirectories to get backed up. This option comes in handy, if say, you have a few space-hogging directories (like My Videos and My Music) and you don't have the space to keep four copies (one in each of the `nightly`, `weekly`, and two monthly folders) of those big files on your backup drive.

   To do so, select Let Me Choose Which Sub-Directories to Include from the Sub-dirs drop-down list (just below the Destination field) and, on the Simple tab, choose Backup the Source Directories Files Including Selected Sub-Directories.

6. Click the Sub-Directories tab. If you have hundreds of subdirectories, it'll take SyncBack some time to traverse the tree and display them. Go grab a cup of coffee and come back to check off the directories you want backed up each night. That's when you tell SyncBack to ignore the My Music, My Pictures, and My Videos folders each night when it runs.

7. Really effective automation runs without intervention or interruption, but lets you know if something goes wrong. Enable the advanced options in SyncBack by clicking the Expert button at the bottom.

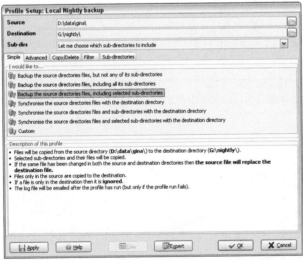

**Figure 3-2** Nightly Local backup profile window in SyncBack.

8. To monitor whether your nightly backup runs without a hitch, in the E-mail tab, check the Email the Log File When the Profile Has Run option. You don't want an email every day; you just want one if things go awry, so also check the Only Email the Log File if an Error Occurs option. See Figure 3-3.

9. Set your SMTP server options as well and then click the Test Email Settings button to make sure you can receive messages, as shown in Figure 3-3.

**NOTE** Your SMTP options specify what server you use to send mail. Check with your email service provider for your hostname and port information. The To and From fields should contain your email address.

10. Select the Misc tab, and click the Schedule button. Here you tell Windows XP to run this nightly backup every evening (or early morning) at, say, 2:00 a.m. Be sure to set the Windows password you use to log into your computer for this scheduled task by clicking the Set Password button.

11. Wash, rinse, and repeat to create a profile called Local Weekly Backup. Set the Destination to your backup drive's Weekly folder and set the profile to run once a week (say, at 3:00 a.m. Saturday morning). The subdirectory and email settings should remain the same for this profile.

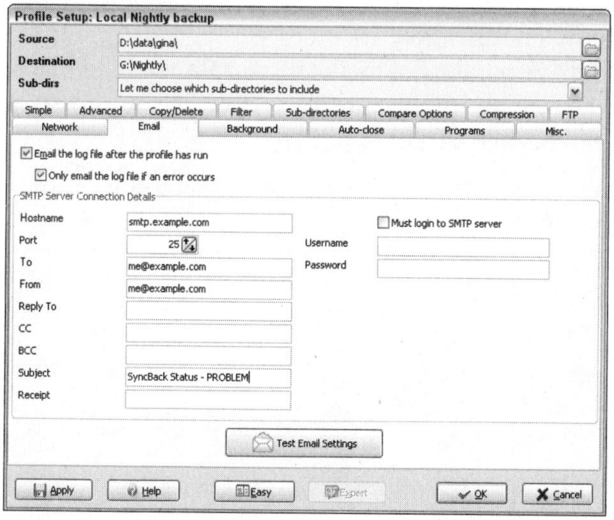

**Figure 3-3** Email settings for the Local Nightly Backup profile in SyncBack.

12. Configure your bi-monthly local backup. You could set up a single monthly backup profile that runs once a month, but using that scheme, you run the risk of losing data. Here's how. Say you do a massive file deletion or update on the last day of the week and month. Those changes would replicate to all three backup copies (Nightly, Weekly, and Monthly), and you'd have no backup of anything before your deletion or update.

   To avoid this, set up two local bi-monthly backup profiles, one of which runs on even months, and the other runs on odd months: Local Bi-Monthly (even) Backup and Local Bi-Monthly (odd) Backup, respectively. When you set up the schedule for the Local Bi-Monthly (even) profile, from the Schedule tab, choose Monthly from the Schedule Task drop-down, and then click the Select Months button. Check off the even months of the year, as shown in Figure 3-4.

13. Set up the bi-monthly (odd) profile the same way, with odd months checked off.

You can test your new backup profiles by doing a Simulated Run to see what files would get copied where without actually copying them. To do so, select a profile to test in SyncBack and select Task → Simulated Run. Depending on how much data you have, a test run can take a long time.

After all four profiles have run (in at most two months from setup), you'll have four copies of your most important data on your external drive getting updated every night, week, and month. If something goes wrong and the backups fail, you receive an email notification.

This means that when hard drive breaks down, the most data you'll lose is a day's worth. And if you overwrote an important file — even if you did so a month ago — you can recover a backed up copy.

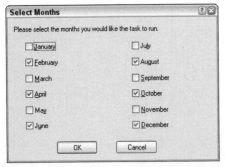

**Figure 3-4** Run the Local Bi-Monthly (even) Backup on even months.

## Off-Site Backup

Your backup plan doesn't stop there. If your computer's hard drive buys the farm, you're covered, but what if your house burns down or gets burglarized? You want your most important data somewhere off-site as well. That's where your FTP server comes in.

Create a last SyncBack profile called Remote Nightly Backup that sends all your important data over the wire from, say, your hard drive in New York to your FTP server in Atlanta. In the FTP tab, enter your server's information as shown in Figure 3-5.

> **TIP** If you don't like the idea of your data on someone else's server, check out the Compression tab, where you can configure a profile that zips up your files and applies password to them. Run that profile before your remote backup FTP for a little extra security.

That's it! When your multi-profile, automated backup system is up and running you can rest easy knowing that when catastrophe strikes — or if you simply upgrade to a new computer — your data is safe and sound, with five different copies stored on- and off-site. Figure 3-6 shows the list of backup profiles set up in SyncBack in this hack.

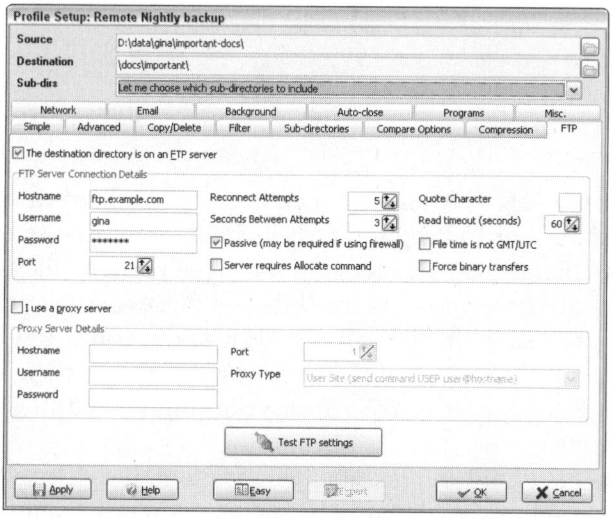

**Figure 3-5** Remote nightly backup to an off-site FTP server.

**Figure 3-6** SyncBack Local and Remote backup profiles.

Backup geeks and the curious should be sure to explore all of SyncBack's tabs and options. For example, in the Autoclose tab, you can set SyncBack to shut down any programs with a word you specify in the title bar before it runs a backup job. The Programs tab sets commands to run before and after backup happens, handy for database or source repository dumps, grabbing files you want to back up from the Web, or anything else you want to move or copy when a profile runs.

# Hack 19: Automatically Defragment Your Hard Drive

Level....... **Medium**
Platform.... **Windows XP**
Cost ....... **Free**

The digital footprint of your life gets ever bigger on your computer hard drives, so it's more important than ever to keep those disks healthy to preserve your critical data. As files change, get deleted, or are over-written, they become fragmented on your hard drive, split up into bits and pieces located at different physical points on the disk. In the same way it takes you a few moments to turn to page 8 to finish reading that front page newspaper article, drive heads have to work a little harder to read and write fragmented files scattered across your hard drive.

Luckily Windows comes with a built-in disk maintenance tool that defragments your hard drive — rearranges the file bits and pieces in an order optimized for your computer. Running a *defrag* is a long, tedious process (especially as hard drives get larger and larger), so it's a perfect candidate for automation.

In this hack, you set up a regular disk defragmentation that will automatically run at night while you sleep, and keep your computer's hard drive in tip-top shape.

**NOTE** Windows Vista defragments your hard drive on a weekly basis by default. Apple says[1] that there is little benefit to defragmenting your Mac's hard drive because technology built into the Mac OS prevents excessive disk fragmentation.

Here's how to set up regular drive defragmentation using Windows Scheduled Tasks.

1. From the Control Panel, choose Scheduled Tasks. (In some Windows configurations, Scheduled Tasks is listed in the Control Panel's Performance and Maintenance section.) Select Add Scheduled Task.

2. The Scheduled Task Wizard opens. Click Next to add a task. The Defrag .exe utility isn't listed in the program options. Click the Browse button to find it (usually located at `C:\Windows\system32\defrag.exe`).

3. Give the task a name and a frequency, as shown in Figure 3-7.

**NOTE** The frequency with which you defragment your drive depends on how often large files change on your hard drive. For a home computer that's not reading and writing large files most of the day, monthly will do. For a work computer constantly in use, weekly should be sufficient.

4. Choose a time to defrag. Your computer cannot be in use (that is, writing files) while defrag is running, so schedule the job to start at a time when you won't be using it, like 1 a.m. on Saturday morning.

5. Enter your Windows password. Windows will ask you to enter an administrative username and password, which it needs to run this job on its own. When finished, click Next. At the last screen of the wizard, check Open Advanced Properties For This Task When I Click Finish. Then click Finish.

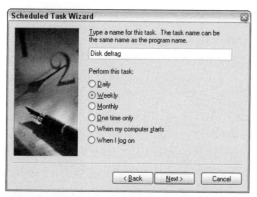

**Figure 3-7** Name and choose a frequency for the defrag task.

6. In the Advanced Properties dialog boxs Run text box, enter the letter of the hard drive you want to defragment, like `C:`, as shown in Figure 3-8, after the `defrag.exe` command.

7. As previously mentioned, defrag only if your computer is idle. No other processes can be writing to disk while defrag is running, so set the task to only run if your computer's not doing anything else. For example, if you set defrag to run at 1 a.m. and you have a late work night, or another scheduled job is downloading a huge video file, you want to put off the defrag task until the other work is complete. To do so, on the Advanced Properties dialog box's Settings tab, select Only Start the Task if the Computer Has Been Idle for at Least and enter a desired number of minutes, like 10, as shown in Figure 3-9.

8. Click OK to save the settings on your automated defragment task.

If you have more than one hard drive in your computer, use these steps to create a separate task for each drive, using the appropriate drive letter.

**Figure 3-8** Add the drive letter to the defrag.exe command.

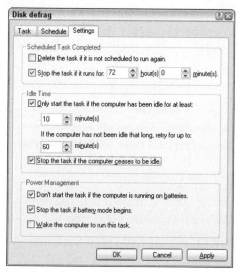

**Figure 3-9** Begin defragmenting only if the computer isn't doing anything else.

# Hack 20: Automatically Empty Your Digital Junk Drawer

Level. . . . . . . **Advanced**
Platform. . . . **Windows XP and Vista**
Cost . . . . . . . **Free**

During the course of a work day, you save all sorts of disposable files on your computer: video, images, and songs meant for a single viewing or listen, PDF files you have to print, software installers and zip files you extract and do whatever you need with the contents. The end result is a lot of digital detritus clogging your hard drive for no good reason. But you don't want to clean up after yourself every time you work with a set of files you don't need to keep.

In this hack, you schedule a virtual janitor script that sweeps through your hard drive every night and deletes any files in your digital junk drawer that have been sitting around for more than $x$ days, like old garbage starting to stink. This program constantly recovers space on your hard drive so you don't have to worry about getting the dreaded Low Disk Space message while you're in the middle of something important.

> **WARNING** This script and the instructions for use require comfort with executable script editing and automated file deletion, which are not to be taken lightly. Pointed at the wrong directory, this script could damage your PC.

To put your janitor to work, first create your virtual junk drawer folder. Then you'll configure the janitor to clean out the files older than a number of days you determine from that folder. Finally, you'll schedule the janitor to clean up at a regular, convenient time.

Here's what to do:

1. Create a directory in your main documents directory that is going to serve as a holding pen for temporary, disposable files. Mine is in `D:\data\gina\junkdrawer`, so that's how I'll refer to it for the rest of this hack.

2. Download the `janitor.vbs` script, available at `http://life hackerbook.com/ch3/janitor.vbs`. Save it in your documents. (Mine is located in `D:\data\gina\scripts\janitor.vbs`.)

3. Set your web browser and email client to save downloaded files and message attachments to your junk drawer.

   Firefox users, select Tools → Options → Downloads. Set the directory to which Firefox should download automatically in the Download Folder section, as shown in Figure 3-10.

4. Using a plain text editor such as Notepad, open the `janitor.vbs` file and edit the following sections to set the path to your `junkdrawer` directory, and how many days old files should be when they get deleted.

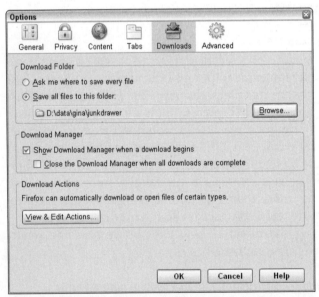

**Figure 3-10** The Firefox Downloads dialog box set to save to the junkdrawer directory.

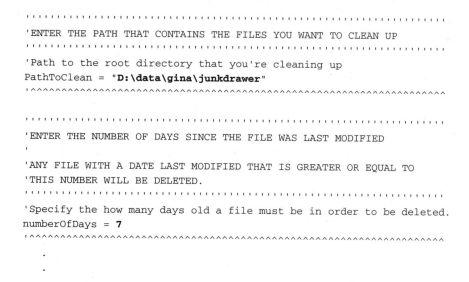

```
'''''''''''''''''''''''''''''''''''''''''''''''''''''''''''''''''
'ENTER THE PATH THAT CONTAINS THE FILES YOU WANT TO CLEAN UP
'''''''''''''''''''''''''''''''''''''''''''''''''''''''''''''''''
'Path to the root directory that you're cleaning up
PathToClean = "D:\data\gina\junkdrawer"
'^^^^^^^^^^^^^^^^^^^^^^^^^^^^^^^^^^^^^^^^^^^^^^^^^^^^^^^^^^^^^^^^^


'''''''''''''''''''''''''''''''''''''''''''''''''''''''''''''''''
'ENTER THE NUMBER OF DAYS SINCE THE FILE WAS LAST MODIFIED
'
'ANY FILE WITH A DATE LAST MODIFIED THAT IS GREATER OR EQUAL TO
'THIS NUMBER WILL BE DELETED.
'''''''''''''''''''''''''''''''''''''''''''''''''''''''''''''''''
'Specify the how many days old a file must be in order to be deleted.
numberOfDays = 7
'^^^^^^^^^^^^^^^^^^^^^^^^^^^^^^^^^^^^^^^^^^^^^^^^^^^^^^^^^^^^^^^^^
        .
        .
        .
```

In the line that begins PathToClean, replace D:\data\gina\junkdrawer with the path to your junk drawer folder. Also, change the line numberOfDays to your preferred time frame. I'm happy deleting stuff 7 days old, but you might want to start with a month (30) or two weeks (14).

**WARNING** This script deletes files from your hard drive, from any directory that you specify. If you enter C:\Windows\system32, for example, you could do irreparable damage to your computer. So make absolutely sure the PathToClean is set to a directory with files Windows does not need to function and files you don't care about losing.

Also, this script deletes files *x* days older than the files's Last Modified date. It is possible that a file's Last Modified date is already older than the number of days you specify, even if you've just downloaded the file. Keep this in mind when you're saving files to your junk drawer. Only save stuff in your junk drawer that are OK to lose.

When your junk drawer is set up and the script is configured, double-click janitor.vbs to run it. It will check your junk drawer and all its subdirectories for old files and delete any it finds. Empty subdirectories will be deleted as well. If all goes well, you see a pop-up box that reads, "The directory has been cleaned up!" as shown in Figure 3-11.

**Figure 3-11** Janitor completion pop-up.

**NOTE** **If you get a message along the lines of "no script engine for file extension .vbs," download the Windows XP Scripting Host from** `http://microsoft.com/downloads/details.aspx?FamilyID=C717D943-7E4B-4622-86EB-95A22B832CAA&displayLang=en`**. This installation requires a restart.**

When your script is pointed to the right place and you've run it and are happy with the results, you want to schedule your virtual janitor to sweep through every day.

Select Control Panel → Scheduled Tasks and then File → New. Name your new task **Clean out junk drawer**. Double-click the task, and set the Run: line to where your script lives, as shown in Figure 3-12.

Click the Set Password button and enter your Windows password. This authorizes Windows to run the script on its own.

On the Schedule tab, set the job to run each day at a convenient time. On a computer that stays on all night, you can run the script in the wee hours of the morning. To test the new job, right-click Clean Out Junk Drawer in Scheduled Tasks and choose Run. You should get the "The directory has been cleaned up!" message again.

**Figure 3-12** Make the Janitor script a scheduled task.

---

**ABOUT VISUAL BASIC**

Many viruses and spyware use Visual Basic, the language this script is written in, to do bad things like spam your friends and steal your credit card number. This doesn't mean Visual Basic is inherently bad, it means it's oft been used for evil. As a result, many spyware scanners and virus protection programs will sound off all sorts of alarms and even disable Visual Basic scripts entirely in the name of protecting you. This script is benign. It does nothing harmful except delete files from a directory you specify. Whitelist and allow it to execute no matter what your virus protection and spyware cleaner says; it's kosher.

---

Now your virtual janitor is set to clean up after you. Remember, the key to this system is to *move files out of your junk drawer if you'll need them long term.* Otherwise, they will be irrecoverably lost.

**NOTE** Danny O'Brien developed the concept of the janitor script, and programming help was generously provided by Brian Plexico. Variations on this script with extra features are available at `http://lifehackerbook .com/ch3/.`

# Hack 21: Automatically Download Music, Movies, and More

Level....... **Advanced**
Platform.... **All**
Cost ....... **Free**

Your web browser does a good job of fetching web documents and displaying them, but there are times when you need an extra-strength program to get those tougher download jobs done.

A versatile, old school Unix program called wget is handy tool that makes downloading tasks very configurable. Whether you want to mirror an entire web site, automatically download music or movies from a set of favorite weblogs, or transfer huge files painlessly on a slow or intermittent network connection, the wget program — the non-interactive network retriever — is for you.

## Install and Run Wget

Download the Mac or Windows version of wget from `http:// lifehackerbook.com/links/wget`. After downloading, extract the files to `C:\wget` on Windows or `/Applications/wget` on the Mac.

To run wget, launch a command line (the Mac Terminal, or Windows Command Prompt). At the command line prompt, switch to the directory where wget is installed by typing

```
cd c:\wget\
```

on Windows, or

```
cd /Applications/wget/
```

on the Mac. Then type the wget command you want from the following examples and press Enter.

The format of wget commands is:

```
wget [option]... [URL]...
```

URL is the address of the file(s) you want wget to download. The magic in this little tool is the long menu of options available that make some highly customized and scriptable downloading tasks possible. This hack covers some examples of what you can do with wget and a few dashes and letters in the [option] part of the command.

> **NOTE** For the full take on all of the wget program's secret options sauce, type
> **wget --help at the command line or check out the complete wget manual**
> **online, available at** http://gnu.org/software/wget/manual.

## Mirror an Entire Web Site

Say you want to back up your blog or create a local copy of an entire directory of a web site for archiving or reading later. The following command saves all the pages that exist at the example.com web site in a folder named example.com on your computer:

```
wget -m http://example.com
```

The –m switch in the command stands for *mirror this site*.

Say you want to retrieve all the pages in a site *and* the pages to which that site links, you'd go with the following command:

```
wget -H -r --level=1 -k -p http://example.com
```

In plain English, this translates into: Download all the pages (-r, recursive) on http://example.com plus one level (--level=1) into any other sites it links to (-H, span hosts), and convert the links in the downloaded version to point to the other sites' downloaded version (-k). Also, get all the components like images that make up each page (-p).

**WARNING** Those with small hard drives, beware! This command downloads a *lot* of data from large sites that link a lot more (like blogs). Don't try to back up the internet, because you'll run out of disk space!

## Resume Partial Downloads on an Intermittent Connection

Say you're using the wireless connection at the airport, and it's time to board the plane — with just a minute left on that download you started half an hour ago. When you make it back home and reconnect to the network, you can use the -c (continue) option to direct wget to resume a partial download where it left off.

Say you want to download the 89 MB installer file for free office suite software, OpenOffice.org (http://openoffice.org). Use the following wget command:

```
wget http://ftp.ussg.iu.edu/openoffice/stable/2.0.2/OOo_2.0.2_Win32Intel_
install.exe
```

Mid-download, you get the boarding call and have to close your laptop and get on the plane. When you reopen it back home, you can add a -c to your wget command, and resume fetching the partially downloaded file, like this:

```
wget -c http://ftp.ussg.iu.edu/openoffice/stable/2.0.2/OOo_2.0.2_
Win32Intel_install.exe
```

This feature comes in handy when you're sharing bandwidth with others or need to pause a download while you work on another bandwidth-intensive task. For example, if that movie download is affecting the quality of your internet phone call, stop it and resume after you've hung up the phone using the wget -c switch.

**NOTE** Most — but not all — servers on the Internet support resuming partial downloads.

Also, if the URL of the file you're downloading contains ampersand (&) characters, be sure to enclose it in quotes in the command, like this:

```
wget -c "http://example.com/?p1=y&p2=n"
```

## Automatically Download New Music from the Web

These days there are tons of directories, aggregators, filters, and weblogs that point off to interesting types of media. You can use wget to create a text file list of your favorite sites that, say, link to MP3 music files, and schedule it to automatically download any newly added MP3s from those sites each day to your computer.[2]

Here's how:

1. Create a text file called `mp3_sites.txt`, and list URLs of your favorite sources of music online (like `http://del.icio.us/tag/ system:filetype:mp3` or `http://stereogum.com`), one per line.

2. Use the following wget command to go out and fetch those MP3s:

```
wget -r -l1 -H -t1 -nd -N -np -A.mp3 -erobots=off -i mp3_sites.txt
```

   That `wget` recipe recursively (`-r`) downloads only MP3 files (`-A.mp3`) linked from the sites (`-H`) 1 level out (`-l1`) listed in `mp3_sites.txt` (`-i mp3_sites.txt`) that are newer (`-N`) than any you've already downloaded. There are a few other specifications in there — like to not create a new directory for every music (`-nd`) file, to ignore `robots.txt` (`-erobots=off`), and to not crawl up to the parent directory of a link (`-np`).

When this command is scheduled with the list of sites you specify, you get an ever-refreshed folder of new music files wget fetches for you. With a good set of trusted sources, you'll never have to go looking for new music again — wget will do all the work for you.

> **TIP** Use this technique to download all your favorite bookmarks for offline usage as well. If you keep your bookmarks online in del.icio.us, use wget to download the contents of your favorite pages to your hard drive. Then, using Google Desktop Search, you can search the contents of your bookmarks even when you're offline.

## Automate wget Downloads on Windows

To schedule a wget download task to run at a certain time, open a new document in a plain text editor like Notepad. Type the wget command you want to schedule, and save the file with a `.bat` extension, such as `getnewmusic.bat`.

In Windows Task Scheduler, browse to `getnewmusic.bat` in the Programs section and set the schedule as usual.

> **NOTE** See Hack 19, "Automatically Defragment Your Hard Drive," for more details on setting up a recurring job in Windows Task Scheduler.

# Hack 22: Automatically Email Yourself File Backups

Level........ **Advanced**
Platform.... **Windows XP and Vista**
Cost ........ **Free**

When my sister-in-law asked me how she could back up her master's thesis without any special equipment or software, I had to think for a minute.

"Email it to yourself," I finally told her.

Emailing yourself important documents that change often is a quick and dirty — yet very effective — form of backup, especially if you're using a web-based email solution such as Gmail (`http://gmail.google.com`) or Yahoo! Mail (`http://mail.yahoo.com`).

By regularly emailing yourself a copy of a file you've been slaving over for months — or hours — you're storing it off-site on your mail server, where it'll be safe in case of drive failure, theft, fire, or flood. Plus, you build up a directory of document versions over time, all in your inbox. Even using the more complex and thorough backup system detailed earlier in Hack 18, a few copies of that key document in your email inbox can give you an extra sense of security *and* accessibility.

Of course, you don't want to go through the work of attaching a document to a new email and sending it manually four times a day. In this hack you'll use a scriptable Windows program to do it for you. Schedule this program to run daily or hourly, or however often you need for quick and easy, versioned, off-site backup of your most important working documents.

## Set up the Email Script

The main act in this emailing show is a small, free utility called Blat, available for download at `http://blat.net`. Blat sends email with attachments from the command line. Unzip Blat into the `C:\Blat250\` directory.

Using Notepad or another text editor, make a list of all the files you want to email yourself, separated by commas. Save that file as `C:\Blat250\full\files-to-backup.txt`. A sample `files-to-backup.txt` might look like this:

```
d:\data\Important Document01.doc, d:\data\Career-changing-Presentation.ppt
```

List as many files as you like — just make sure there are commas between them.

Now you have to set your email SMTP server and From: address. To do so, from the Windows command line (in Windows XP, Start → Run, cmd), switch to the Blat directory (`cd c:\blat250\full\`). Then run the following command, substituting your SMTP server and your address for smtp .example.com and yourname@example.com:

```
Blat -install smtp.example.com you@example.com
```

That tells Blat how to send the message and from whom.

**NOTE** Check with your Internet service provider for your SMTP server settings.

Now, create your auto-email backup script by entering the following into a new text document:

```
c:
cd \
cd Blat250\full\

Blat -body "Just in case." -s "[backup] Important files" -to ↵
you@example.com -af files-to-backup.txt
```

Replace you@example.com with the email address where you will store your backups.

(Remember, ↵ indicates that the code line continues on the next line. It should all be on one line in your editor.)

Finally, save this new file as C:\Blat250\full\email-file-backups.bat. (Make sure this file has the .bat extension and that it's not a .txt file.)

You're ready to test the email script. In Windows Explorer, browse to the C:\Blat250\full\ directory. Double-click your new script, email-file-backups.bat (see Figure 3-13).

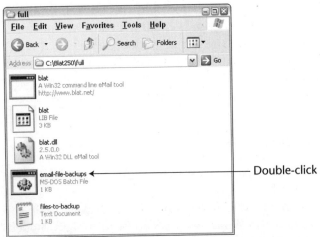

**Figure 3-13** The contents of the C:\Blat250\full\ directory.

A command window pop ups, with Blat doing its thing. Within a few seconds, all the files you listed in `files-to-backup.txt` should appear in your email inbox.

### Why Not Just Save Files to Flash Drives or a CD?

The key here is that the files become available from anywhere you can get your mail. In the case of web-based mail like Gmail or Hotmail, that's any Internet-connected computer with a web browser. If your laptop is stolen, thumb drive is lost, CD goes bad — you have your files up in the cloud. This works especially well for work files you've edited at home.

## More on Emailing Yourself Backups

Here are some more tips and notes that will help you make the most of this hack.

### Email Backup Filtering

You'll notice that the subject line of your email is "[backup] Important files" (that's set by the `-s` switch in the `blat` command in your `.bat` file). Use message filters and the word [backup] in the subject line to dispatch these messages from your Inbox to a Backups folder automatically, so they don't get in your way.

> **NOTE** See Hack 12, "Filter Low-Priority E-mail Messages" for more on using email filters.

### Scheduling

Finally, you can use Windows Task Scheduler to set your script to run at certain times. If you're rapidly changing a set of documents throughout the day, once an hour might be an appropriate recurring schedule; otherwise, once a day could work. Other considerations include your email provider's storage capacity and how many versions of your documents you want to store.

### File Size and Type Limitations

Keep in mind that this method is not meant for use with very large files. Your email host only provides so much disk space, and some SMTP servers limit the size and number of attachments you can send at a time. Limitations depend on your provider. (For example, if you're a Gmail user, `.exe` file attachments don't make it through the Gmail spam filters.)

The bottom line is that this hack is not for backing up more than just a handful of smallish files, like Office documents.

### Troubleshooting

If your script doesn't work, from the command line, change directories with this command: `cd c:\Blat250\full`. Then run the script from there (just type `email-file-backups.bat`) and watch the output. If there's a problem connecting to your SMTP server, it'll be listed there. There are tons of switches and options for Blat — if you need to specify a non-default mail port, or username and password to log onto your SMTP server, for instance. Run `Blat -h` to see the full rundown.

Also, the Blat Yahoo! Group (`http://groups.yahoo.com/group/blat`) is active and the archives contain a lot of helpful troubleshooting information and tips.

## Hack 23: Automatically Reboot and Launch Applications

Level . . . . . . . **Easy**
Platform . . . . **Windows XP and Vista**
Cost . . . . . . . **Free**

Windows PC users know that every once in awhile, your computer can slow down or run into problems that are magically resolved when you restart. A PC that's on continuously 24 hours a day — especially when it's hard at work at night, running automated tasks outlined in this chapter — can benefit from a regular reboot to clear out memory and end any hanging software processes. Furthermore, chances are you start your work day with a set number of software applications, like Microsoft Outlook and your morning paper web sites.

In this hack, you'll schedule an early morning reboot and launch the software you need to get to work before you even sit down at your desk.

### Automatically Reboot Your Computer

It's the middle of the night. Your computer has backed itself up, degfragged the hard drives, and fetched you new music from all over the Web. Now it's time to begin the new day with a fresh start.

Select Start → Control Panel → Scheduled Tasks. In the Scheduled Tasks window, choose File → New → Scheduled Task. Name the new job Reboot. Right-click the task and choose Properties. In the Run text box, enter the following, as shown in Figure 3-14.

```
C:\WINDOWS\system32\shutdown.exe -r -t 01.
```

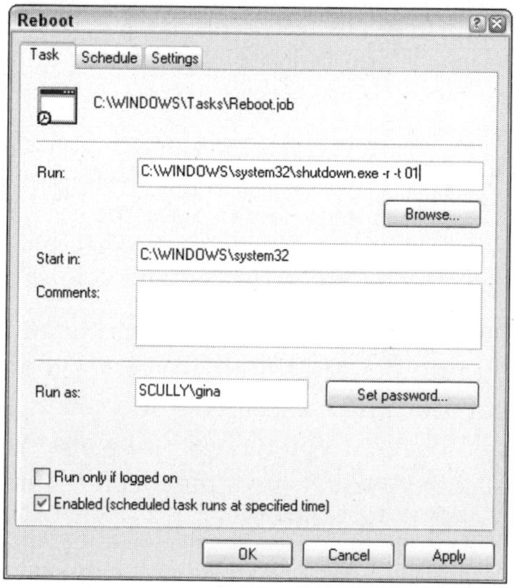

**Figure 3-14** The Reboot scheduled task.

You don't want your PC to reboot if it's in the middle of something else, so on the Settings tab, select the Only Start This Task If The Computer Has Been Idle For At Least option, and enter a time frame, like 10 minutes. If your Windows login has a password, you'll have to enter it to authorize Windows to run the task as you.

Set the task schedule to Daily, one hour before you usually sit down at your computer. If the Reboot job doesn't run because the computer is busy at that time, it shouldn't try again after you start working, so on the Settings Tab, make sure the Retry Up To option is set to 60 minutes.

## Automatically Launch Software or Documents

Schedule the applications you normally launch by hand to start up on their own before you sit down at your computer in the morning as well. Enter the path to any software program in a new scheduled task's Run text box. For example, provided it's been installed in the default location, Microsoft Outlook 2003 launches with the following command:

```
"C:\Program Files\Microsoft Office\OFFICE11\OUTLOOK.EXE"
```

Additionally, you can launch specific documents instead of just programs. For example, if you absolutely must start the day editing Chapter 3 of your book, create a task that is simply the path of the document:

```
"d:/data/gina/docs/lifehacker-book/chapter3.doc"
```

That will open the `chapter3.doc` file in Microsoft Word automatically. Or schedule a WinAmp or iTunes playlist to launch and begin playing first thing in the morning for a custom alarm clock.

> **NOTE** Set the most important thing you have to work on the next morning automatically. Hack 61, "Set up a Morning Dash," explains how to make the first hour of the day the most productive.

If you schedule your Reboot task an hour before you arrive at work, have the auto software launch job run about 15 minutes after that. That way your computer will restart, and then launch your morning programs so you can just walk in, coffee in hand, and get started. (However, if you have a password set up on your PC — always a good idea security-wise — programs can't start automatically after reboot until you've logged in by hand.)

## Automatically Start a Web Browsing Session

If you spend time browsing the Web at work, chances are you have a set of pages that you visit to start the day, like your morning paper. Your computer can easily fetch your favorite web pages before you reach your desk so that your morning reads are waiting for you.

Set up a task to open the Firefox web browser the same way you did with Outlook. Then add all the pages you'd like to load automatically, separated by a space to the Run line. The resulting command could look something like this:

```
"C:\Program Files\Mozilla Firefox\firefox.exe" lifehacker.com
nytimes.com gmail.google.com
```

> **NOTE** The free Firefox web browser is available for download at `http://mozilla.org/products/firefox`. Firefox is a superior web browser for many reasons; in this case its tabbed browsing feature makes opening several web pages in one window possible.

In this case, when you arrive at your computer, a Firefox window will be open with all your morning sites pre-loaded.

> **NOTE** Special thanks to Lifehacker.com associate editor Adam Pash for his contributions to this hack.

# Hack 24: Automatically Log Your Progress in a Spreadsheet

Level....... **Medium**
Platform.... **Windows XP or Vista with Microsoft Excel**
Cost ....... **Free**

A spreadsheet is a great way to track progress on any type of undertaking that involves numbers — like how much weight you've lost, how many widgets you made, how many miles you ran, or how many cigarettes you smoked. But who remembers to update his spreadsheet by hand?

Instead, use a simple scheduled script that prompts you to add data to your spreadsheet log. For example, if you're trying to lose weight, you could use this script to automatically remind yourself to record your current weight with the dialog box shown in Figure 3-15.

Simply enter your current weight into the text box, click OK, and the script automatically appends the current date and your weight to a two-column Excel spreadsheet — without ever having to open Excel.

Schedule this script to run when you log on every morning or once a week. With it you'll never forget to log your current weight again, and you can make shiny line charts graphing your diet progress in Excel once you've added enough data.

Here's how to set it up:

1. Download the `weightlogger.vbs` script from `http://life-hackerbook.com/ch3/weightlogger.vbs` and save it to your computer. Here's the complete code listing (you'll edit the bold lines):

```
''''''''''''''''''''''''''''''''''''''''''''''''''''''''''''''''''''''
'TITLE:      Weight Logger
'DESCRIPTION:    Appends your current weight to an Excel spreadsheet
                 with today's date
'CREATED BY:    Gina Trapani - lifehacker.com
'CREATE DATE:   07/28/2005
'
'INSTRUCTIONS:    1. Enter the filename you'd like to append your
                     weight to make sure to only change the text that
                     currently reads:
'  "C:\Gina\logs\weight.xls". The path must be surrounded by quotes.
''''''''''''''''''''''''''''''''''''''''''''''''''''''''''''''''''''''
```

```
Dim xlApp, xlBook, xlSht
Dim w, filename, currentRow, lastVal


filename = "C:\Gina\logs\weight.xls"


w = InputBox("Today's weight?", "Weight tracker")

Set xlApp = CreateObject("Excel.Application")
set xlBook = xlApp.WorkBooks.Open(filename)
set xlSht = xlApp.activesheet

xlApp.DisplayAlerts = False

'write data
currentRow = 2
lastVal = xlSht.Cells(2, 2)
while lastVal <> ""
    currentRow = currentRow + 1
    lastVal = xlSht.Cells(currentRow, 2 )
wend

xlSht.Cells(currentRow, 1) = Now
xlSht.Cells(currentRow, 2) = w

xlBook.Save
xlBook.Close SaveChanges = True
xlApp.Quit

'deallocate
set xlSht = Nothing
Set xlBook = Nothing
Set xlApp = Nothing
```

2. Create a new spreadsheet called weight.xls. The Column A header is Date and the Column B header is Weight.

3. Using your favorite text editor, open the weightlogger.vbs file you just downloaded. Change the line that reads:

   ```
   filename = "C:\Gina\logs\weight.xls"
   ```

   to contain the path to where your weight.xls spreadsheet resides on your hard drive. Save your changes. Be sure to enclose the file path in quotes.

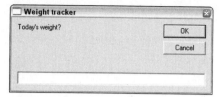

**Figure 3-15** Spreadsheet log update dialog box.

**TIP** If you're using the `weightlogger.vbs` to track progress on something other than weight loss, you can modify the script to reflect that. For example, the line that reads

```
w = InputBox("Today's weight?", "Weight tracker")
```

**could be changed to**

```
w = InputBox("Miles run today?", "Running log").
```

4. Double-click the `weightlogger.vbs` script. A dialog box prompts you for your weight. Enter a number and click OK. Your current weight is entered into `weight.xls`.

**NOTE** The free Windows XP Script Engine is required to run VBS scripts. If you get a message along the lines of "no script engine for file extension .vbs," download the engine from `http://microsoft.com/downloads/details.aspx?FamilyID=C717D943-7E4B-4622-86EB-95A22B832CAA&displayLang=en`. The installation does require you to restart your computer.

5. Schedule regular weigh-in prompts using Windows Scheduled Tasks. Set the `weightlogger.vbs` script task to run every day or every week, at your discretion.

## References

1. "About Disk Optimization with Mac OS X," Apple documentation (`http://docs.info.apple.com/article.html?artnum=25668`).
2. Jeffrey Veen, "MP3 Blogs and wget" (`http://veen.com/jeff/archives/000573.html`).

# Streamline Common Tasks

Shortcuts get you where you want to go faster, but they take some time to learn. The difference between taking the main roads across town and taking the back roads may be that the main roads are easier but take longer. If you drive across town every day, however, it's worth your time learning the back road shortcuts.

The same principle applies to your work processes. No doubt you perform dozens of repetitive actions every day, like typing www.google.com into your browser's address bar, or clicking the Start button and navigating to the Programs menu, or typing "Let me know if you have any questions" at the end of an email. These are opportunities for shortcuts that can add up to large savings over time. Every movement, every task, every action is a candidate for optimization and streamlining.

Imagine that in working a few new shortcuts into your day, you save 2 seconds on each of four tasks you perform 20 times a day. That amounts to about 2 and a half minutes of saved time a day, which adds up to 667 minutes or more than 11 hours a year (taking into account weekends and two weeks of vacation). All told, you can save more than an entire workday every year just by learning how to search Google or sign an email taking the back roads.

The key is teaching yourself the shortcuts that will benefit you most. Identify the activities you perform most often, learn the shortcut, and then train yourself to use it every time. At first a shortcut may be hard to remember, but with practice it becomes second nature.

The hacks in this chapter streamline common computer processes so you can spend less time moving the mouse and tapping the keyboard and more time getting things done.

## Hack 25: Search the Web in Three Keystrokes

Level........ **Easy**
Platform..... **All (Firefox)**
Cost ........ **Free**

If you're online at work, chances are you search for information on the Web several times a day. There are dozens of ways to do a web search from your desktop, but the most common method takes the longest:

1. With your web browser open, select the entire URL of the current page in the address bar.

2. Replace it by typing **www.google.com**.

3. Press Enter.

4. Type your search term — say, **lifehacker** — into the search box.

5. Click the Google Search button or press Enter.

You'd probably follow these same steps for lots of other web searches, too, like at Yahoo!, Amazon.com, or Wikipedia.

There is a much faster way.

The free, open-source web browser Firefox (`http://mozilla.org/ products/firefox`) comes equipped with a Google web search box built into its chrome, in the upper-right corner, as shown in Figure 4-1.

You can execute a web search from this box without ever taking your hands off the keyboard; you only need to use the key combination Ctrl+K. Here's how to google lifehacker using this shortcut:

1. With the Firefox web browser open, press Ctrl+K.

2. Type **lifehacker**.

3. Press Enter.

The Search Bar doesn't just work for Google. It comes preloaded with Yahoo!, Amazon.com, eBay, Answers.com, and Creative Commons searches as well. Visit Firefox Add-ons at `https://addons.mozilla.org/ search-engines.php` to get other useful engines such as the Wikipedia, IMDB (Internet Movie Database), the Merriam-Webster dictionary, Weather.com, and Ask.com.

Google search bar

**Figure 4-1** The Mozilla Firefox web browser comes with a search box built in the right of the Go button.

Firefox magically transports you to the search results page for lifehacker without your ever visiting the Google homepage. This method cuts your search down to three keystrokes plus your typed search terms — and no mouse movement.

To page to another search engine, use Ctrl+↓ or Ctrl+↑. For example, to search for lifehacker on Amazon.com:

1. Press Ctrl+K to move the cursor to the Search box.

2. Press Ctrl+↓ twice to switch to Amazon.

3. Type **lifehacker** and press Enter.

**TIP** To open your search results in a new tab from the Firefox Search Bar, press Alt+Enter (instead of just Enter) after entering your search term.

There are several alternatives to the Firefox/Google search bar, including the Google Toolbar for Internet Explorer (available at `http://toolbar .google.com/T4/`) and Google Desktop Search (see Hack 53, "Instantly Retrieve Files from Your Hard Drive," for more info).

Most application launcher programs like Quicksilver for Mac (`http:// quicksilver.blacktree.com`) and Launchy for Windows (`http://www .launchy.net`) also support quick web search queries, as do widget engines such as Yahoo! Widgets (`http://widgets.yahoo.com`) and Mac OS X Dashboard.

Lastly, you can embed a series of search engine input boxes right on your Windows desktop; see `http://lifehackerbook.com/ch4/desktopsearch` for more on that.

# Hack 26: Quick-Launch Software Applications

Level....... **Medium**
Platform.... **Windows XP and Vista, Mac OS X**
Cost ....... **Free**

The graphical user interface revolutionized personal computing because it made using a computer so much easier and visual. However, using the mouse is one of the most inefficient ways to drive a computer. Think about it: you must move your hand from the keyboard to the mouse pad, drag the pointer across the screen and center it over a button or icon, then double-click the area to open a document or launch an application.

You can save an enormous amount of time by using keyboard shortcuts to navigate your computer's operating system and programs. This hack describes how to bypass the mouse and launch programs and documents without ever taking your hands off the keyboard.

## Windows: Essential, Built-In Keyboard Shortcuts

Microsoft Windows has several keyboard shortcuts built into it that, when memorized, can significantly reduce the number of times you reach for the mouse during your workday. Here are some of the essential shortcuts for navigating Windows:

| SHORTCUT | TO |
| --- | --- |
| Alt+Tab | Cycle through open programs (release keys when you see the screen you want). |
| Windows+D | Show the desktop. |
| Windows+L | Lock your workstation. |
| Windows+R | Show the Run box. |
| Ctrl+Esc | Open the Start menu. |

**TIP** Alt+Tab, which displays a mini-menu of your running programs, is my most frequently used Windows key combination. The free Alt+Tab Power Toy Windows add-on — available for download at `http://microsoft.com/windowsxp/downloads/powertoys/xppowertoys.mspx` — presents a much more informative visual choice by displaying previews of the open windows as you cycle through them.

The following are indispensable editing shortcuts:

| SHORTCUT | TO |
| --- | --- |
| Ctrl+S | Save the current document. |
| Ctrl+C | Copy selected text to clipboard. |
| Ctrl+X | Cut selected text or object and place on the clipboard. |
| Ctrl+V | Paste the contents of the clipboard into the current document. |
| Ctrl+Z | Undo the last action you performed. |

| SHORTCUT | TO |
|---|---|
| Ctrl+Y | Redo the last action you undid. |
| Ctrl+B | Bold the selected text. |
| Ctrl+I | Italicize the selected text. |
| Ctrl+U | Underline the selected text. |

You might use some of these shortcuts all of the time, and some none of the time. To find the key combinations most useful for your workflow, look over the complete list of Windows keyboard shortcuts at `http://support` `.microsoft.com/default.aspx?scid=kb;en-us;301583`.

## Windows: Define Your Own Keyword Shortcuts

With Microsoft Windows you can create shortcuts to documents, folders, and applications and place them on your desktop for easy access. But lifehackers who want to avoid the mouse whenever possible can also launch these shortcuts using a keyword you define. Here's how:

1. Create a folder where your keyword shortcuts will live. In this example, the shortcuts folder is located at `C:\Documents and Settings\` `penelope\shortcuts\`.

2. Navigate to any program in the Start Menu (like Microsoft Word.) Right-click its icon and choose Send to Desktop (Create Shortcut).

3. Drag the new Microsoft Wordshortcut from your desktop to the shortcuts folder you set up.

4. Rename the shortcut by selecting it, pressing F2, and typing **wrd**.

5. Repeat steps 2–4 for any documents or folders you'd like to open with a few keystrokes, as shown in Figure 4-2.

**Figure 4-2** Shortcuts to the Firefox web browser, Thunderbird email client, iTunes music player, Chapter 4.doc Word document, and My Documents folder, all renamed short, memorable keywords: ff, email, music, ch04, and docs.

6.  Add the shortcuts folder to the Windows path to make them runnable. To do so, select Settings → Control Panel → System (listed under Performance and Maintenance on some systems), and click the Advanced tab. Click the Environment Variables button, and append the shortcuts folder you created to the Path variable, as shown in Figure 4-3. Make sure the existing Path value ends in a semicolon (;) and that you add a semicolon to the end of the shortcuts directory.

Click OK and then click OK again to save the new Path value.

Now you're ready to use the shortcuts. Press the Windows+R key combination to bring up the Windows Run dialog box. Type the keyword you set up — for example, **wrd** to launch Microsoft Word — and press Enter. Word will start.

> **NOTE** Windows will launch the first thing that matches a word typed into the Run dialog box. For example, if you name your browser's shortcut web, entering web in the Run dialog box won't open Firefox or Internet Explorer as you'd expect — it launches the C:\Windows\Web folder, which comes first in the Path variable.

There are several application launchers available for Windows, including SlickRun (http://bayden.com/SlickRun, free), Launchy (http://launchy.net, free), AppRocket (http://candylabs.com/approcket, $18) and Colibri (http://colibri.leetspeak.org, free). The advantage of the method described here is that it requires no additional software or cost.

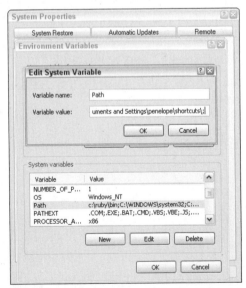

**Figure 4-3** Add the shortcuts folder to the end of the Path variable.

## Mac OS X: Quicksilver Keyboard Commander

Free software Quicksilver (`http://quicksilver.blacktree.com`) for Mac OS X puts a keyboard-based interface to your Mac at your fingertips. At its most basic level of functionality, Quicksilver launches applications and opens documents. Quicksilver's greatest advantage is that it indexes your Mac's hard drive, so no keywords have to be pre-configured; every document and application can be accessed with Quicksilver immediately. Here's how to use Quicksilver as a keyboard launcher.

1. Download and install the latest version of Quicksilver from `http://quicksilver.blacktree.com`. As of writing, OS X 10.4 (Tiger) users want beta 48; 10.3 (Panther) users should get beta 36.

2. To invoke the Quicksilver commander, press Ctrl+Spacebar (Quicksilver's default invocation key combination). Begin to type the name of the application or document you'd like to open, like **Wor**. Quicksilver suggests Microsoft Word as a match and displays a drop-down list of other possible matches on the right, as shown in Figure 4-4.

3. Press Enter to open Microsoft Word, or press the down arrow key to choose another option. Quicksilver adapts its suggestions to your most-used applications and documents, so next time you invoke Quicksilver with Ctrl+Spacebar, and type **Wor**, it will suggest the item you've launched before at the top of the list.

Quicksilver is not just a keyboard launcher; in fact, it would take an entire book just to describe the various actions you can perform on a Mac using it. To find out more, browse the Quicksilver manual at `http://docs.blacktree.com/quicksilver/overview`, or Mac expert Merlin Mann's excellent introduction to Quicksilver at `http://43folders.com/2006/07/26/macbreak-quicksilver/`.

**Figure 4-4** Quicksilver launcher matches programs that contain WOR in the title.

# Hack 27: Save Time with Text Substitution

Level. . . . . . . **Advanced**
Platform. . . . **Windows XP and Vista**
Cost . . . . . . . **Free**

If you spend your day at a keyboard, chances are you type particular phrases several times throughout the day, like "Thanks for contacting us." Maybe you've acquired a maddening habit of typing *teh* instead of *the* when your fingers are really flying over the keys. Perhaps you enter the current date into documents all the time, or you tend to use Internet acronyms like IMO for "in my opinion."

These are all situations in which text substitution can save you time. Define short abbreviations for phrases you use often, or misspellings you're prone to, and automatically expand those abbreviations to their full, intended form. This hack explains how.

## AutoHotkey Hotstring

The free, open-source AutoHotkey software automates tasks on Microsoft Windows. AutoHotkey has many features and possibilities for scripting actions on your PC, but this hack concentrates on its Hotstring feature, which expands abbreviations to pre-defined, reusable text snippets.

**NOTE** AutoHotkey requires advanced scripting with special formatting for its text substitution feature. Readers looking for a simpler (but less robust) solution should consider a commercial product called ActiveWords (http:// activewords.com, $49.95), which is easier to configure.

For example, a running AutoHotkey script can expand the letters btw to by the way, or output the current time and date when you type ldate. Here's how to set up your first AutoHotkey script:

1. Download and install AutoHotkey from http://autohotkey.com/ download.

2. Create or choose a directory for your AutoHotkey scripts. Using any text editor, create a new file and enter one line that reads:

   ```
   :*:teh::the{Space}
   ```

   This tells AutoHotkey that any time you type *teh*, to replace it with *the* immediately. (The * part of the command says *immediately*, and the {Space} after the instructs AutoHotkey to insert a space after the correction.)

3. Save the file as `first.ahk`.

**CAUTION** Make sure the `.txt` extension is not added onto the file. If you're using Notepad, in the Save As dialog, enclose the filename in quotes — `"first.ahk"` — or select All Files from the Save As Type drop-down to avoid the `.txt` extension being added automatically.

4. Using the AutoHotkey Compiler (installed in the AutoHotkey folder in your Start menu under Programs as `Convert .ahk to .exe`), choose the `first.ahk` script for compilation, as shown in Figure 4-5, and click the Convert button.

    AutoHotkey generates a file called `first.exe` in your scripts folder.

5. To run your script, double-click the `first.exe` file. An AutoHotkey icon appears in your system tray. With `first.exe` running, try typing *teh* in any context or program. It will be replaced by *the*.

**NOTE** There are some instances where you don't want *teh* replaced with *the* — in words like statehood and Tehran, for example. This script leaps into action only when you've typed *teh* with a space before it *and* after it.

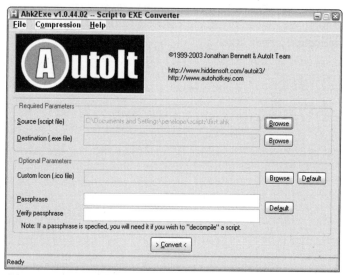

**Figure 4-5** Compiling the first.ahk script to first.exe.

## Personalize the Script

Now, there are many more uses for AutoHotkey Hotstrings than just common misspellings. If you answer customer email, you can program long snippets of formatted text to magically appear with a few keystrokes. Common Internet abbreviations such as btw and afaik can auto-expand to their full English phrases (by the way; as far as I know). Fill in web forms that ask for your address and phone number with auto-expanding Hotstrings. Personalize the text substitution by sending a string into it. For example, *John tx* becomes *Thanks for writing us, John*.

The anatomy of an AutoHotkey Hotstring is as follows:

```
:*c:Btw::By the way
```

The `*c` represents the options set for this substitution. In this case, `*` means the replacement should happen immediately (not after a pre-defined activation key like Enter or Spacebar is pressed); `c` means the abbreviation is case-sensitive. `Btw` is the abbreviation, and `By the way` is the phrase that will replace it.

The following code is a fully functioning AutoHotkey script with some common usage examples. Download your copy from `http://lifehackerbook.com/ch4/sample.ahk` and modify it for your own purposes.

> **NOTE** The script defines an activation key: a special key that triggers replacements specified to go only when the key is pressed. In this sample script, you define the activation key as Enter.

```
; Sample AutoHotkey Script with common usage examples
; Lines that start with a semicolon are comments and may be deleted
; Define the Hotstring activation key as Enter (`n)
#Hotstring EndChars `n

; COMMON MISSPELLINGS
; automatically replace without the activation key (*)
:*:teh ::the{Space}
:*:Gian ::Gina{Space}
; automatically replace without the activation key, case-sensitive (*c)
:*c:Gian ::Gina{Space}
:*c:gina ::Gina{Space}

; ABBREVIATIONS
; automatically replace without activation key, case-sensitive (*c)
:*c:btw::by the way
:*c:Btw::By the way
:*c:afaik::as far as I know
```

```
:*c:Afaik::As far as I know
; not case-sensitive
:*:omg::Oh my God

; PERSONAL INFORMATION
; replace only after the activation key is hit
; immediately after the case-sensitive abbreviation (oc)

; for example, trigger the name replacement by typing
; nam{Enter}

:oc:nam::Gina Trapani
:oc:ast::1 Commercial Street
; so, typing "asterisk" nothing gets replaced
:oc:acty::Provincetown, MA 02657
:oc:ph::508-555-1212

; QUICK EMAIL RESPONSE
; replace these when the activation key is hit
; after the case-sensitive abbreviation (oc)
:oc:bg::Best,{Return}Gina
:oc:faq::Read more in our FAQ, located at
http://www.lifehacker.com/software//lifehacker-faq-028869.php. {Return}
:oc:tc::Take care{!}
; Bracketed characters {!} and {Return}
; represent special characters and keys typed literally
; ie, an exclamation point and the Enter key

; the text inside the parentheses is outputted exactly how it appears
; with the exact formatting preserved
:oc:ccontact::
(
    +-------------------------------+
    | Gina Trapani                  |
    | 1 Commercial Street           |
    | Provincetown, MA 02657        |
    | Phone: 508-555-1212           |
    | Email: gt@example.com         |
    +-------------------------------+
)
; paste anything on the left of the abbreviation into the ^v area
; in the replacement
; ie "John tfyn" becomes "Thanks for your note, John."

:oc:tfyn::^+{Left}^xThanks for your note, ^v.
; "Jill dr" becomes "Dear Jill, "

:oc:dr::^+{Left}^xDear ^v,{return}
```

```
; replace when typed automatically, no activation key required (*)
:*:gt@::gtrapani@example.com

; DATES
; replace these as soon as they are typed, no activation key needed (*)

:*:ttoday:: ; Will look like September 19, 2006
FormatTime, CurrentDateTime,, MMMM dd, yyy
SendInput %CurrentDateTime%
return

:*:ldate:: ; Will look like 9/19/2006 3:53 PM
FormatTime, CurrentDateTime,, M/d/yyyy h:mm tt
SendInput %CurrentDateTime%
return

:*:ddate:: ; Will look like 2006-09-19_15-53
FormatTime, CurrentDateTime,, yyy-MM-dd_H-mm
SendInput %CurrentDateTime%
return
```

For more information about AutoHotkey scripts and Hotstring options, consult the documentation at `http://autohotkey.com/docs/Hot strings.htm`.

> **NOTE** You can't recompile an AutoHotkey script while it's running. First, stop the `.exe` file. To do so, right-click the AutoHotkey icon in your task bar and choose Exit. Then, recompile the modified script and launch the updated `.exe` **file.**

You can also use the compiled AutoHotkey scripts on other computers even if AutoHotkey is not installed, so the `.exe` files are perfect for toting around on a thumb or flash drive or emailing to yourself for use anywhere. (Hack 34, "Carry Your Life on a Flash Drive," has more on taking your most useful apps with you on a USB drive.)

One AutoHotkey enthusiast used the Wikipedia's huge list of common misspellings (`http://en.wikipedia.org/wiki/Wikipedia:Lists_of _common_misspellings`) and created an enormous AutoHotkey script that auto-corrects them. The resulting compiled Universal AutoCorrect program is available at `http://lifehackerbook.com/ch4/autocorrect.exe`. The AHK source file is also available for you to inspect, modify, and add your own common misspellings, at `http://biancolo.com/content_show .cfm?content_id=25569`.

# Hack 28: Text Message Efficiently

Level . . . . . . . **Easy**
Platform . . . . **Mobile phone with SMS capabilities**
Cost . . . . . . . **Dependent on your plan**

More and more modern cell phones and plans feature Short Message Service (SMS), the capability to send a text message to another phone or email address.

To the uninitiated, texting can seem inconvenient, but text messages have numerous advantages over voice calls. Human beings read text faster than listening to speech. Text messages are archived, searchable, and can never be misheard or cut off by bad reception. Texting someone gets info into his hands when he's away from his desk without requiring that he stop everything to pick up the phone to talk. Text messages get right to the point, cutting out time-wasting small talk, throat-clearing, and the energy it takes to get back into the flow of what you were doing before the phone rang. Text messages can be heard in a noisy situation like a party or concert. Texting various web services can retrieve helpful information you need on the go such as directions, addresses, and phone numbers.

For those of you with an SMS-capable mobile phone, this hack presents a few power-texting tips that can help you get the most out of SMS.

## What You Can Do with SMS

Texting can help you get things done. For example:

- **Send reminders** — Text your spouse on her way home from work to *pick up milk at the store*. Remind your teenager to *call when you get there*. Text your future self-reminders about to-do's or appointments.

- **Search the Web** — Several mobile search services like Google SMS (`http://www.google.com/sms`) and 4INFO (`http://4info.net`) will text you information by SMS request. For example, you can text GOOGL (or 46645) the message *star wars 11215* to find show times for the latest Star Wars film in the 11215 ZIP Code. Get flight arrival times, weather, sports scores, dictionary definitions, stock prices, and more via SMS. (See Hack 38, "Search the Web from Your Phone," for more.)

- **Find a friend in a loud place** — You're at a concert trying to meet up with a friend and you can't hear a thing. This is the time to text. SMS also comes in mighty handy in libraries, at parties, or at religious services where talking is not possible or a no-no. (Just make sure your phone SMS notification is set to vibrate!)

## Quick Start Guide for SMS Beginners

To send an SMS, create a new message and add a recipient from your mobile's address book. Sending a message to an SMS-capable phone only requires the recipient's phone number in the To field. Then, to type the body of your message, use the numeric keys on your phone. Press each several times to cycle through the possible letters each number represents; stop when you've reached the one you need. For example, if you want the letter B, press 2 twice. You can see the key you're pressing scroll through all the letters associated with it — 2, for example, scrolls through A, B, and C.

Is this an insanely inconvenient way to type out text? Absolutely. But there are ways to make it more bearable.

## Save Your Thumbs

Here are a couple of ways to make typing text on a numeric keypad easier and less time-consuming.

- **Use message templates** — After awhile you'll notice you send the same kinds of messages over and over, like *Running late, be there in..., On my way home,* and *Give me a call when you get a chance.* Set up templates for your most-used messages to avoid repetitive thumbing. The exact instructions on how to do this vary, so consult the user guide for your phone's model.

- **Turn on predictive text** — Many modern phones offer a predictive text feature, which precludes the need to press each numeric key multiple times to get the letter you want. Thumb out the numbers that contain the letters in your desired word by pressing each just once, and your phone will automatically predict the word you intend, saving dozens of key presses over time. See a short video demonstration of predictive text in action courtesy of Nokia at `http://nokia-asia.com/ nokia/0,,79355,00.html`. (If your phone supports predictive text, it may look different, depending on your model.)

When you get the hang of it, text messaging is a convenient way to communicate when you're not at your computer with easy access to IM or email. But there are also ways to use SMS from your desktop computer as well.

## SMS from Your Computer

Several software applications and web sites can deliver text messages to phone numbers:

- **Send text messages from AOL Instant Messenger (AIM) to a phone** — Add a new contact to your Buddy List whose name is a phone number preceded by a plus sign (that is, +7185551212). An instant message sent to that buddy will be delivered as an SMS to that mobile phone.

■ **SMS from the web** — Yahoo! Mobile (`http://mobile.yahoo.com/sms/sendsms`) sends text messages to a mobile phone number of your choice from the web.

■ **SMS via email** — Many mobile service providers allow you to send a text message to a phone via email using a specific email address consisting of the phone number @ the service provider's email domain. If you don't know the domain, free service Teleflip (`http://teleflip.com`) will route your email message for you. Simply send your message to `7185551212@teleflip.com`, substituting your destination phone number before the @ sign.

**WARNING** Check how much text messages cost on your particular mobile phone plan. Many include unlimited SMS messages, but others can charge up to 10 cents a message, which can add up over time. You don't want to be surprised by a big cell phone bill the month after you start texting!

# Hack 29: Batch Resize Photos

Level. . . . . . . **Easy**
Platform. . . . **Windows XP**
Cost . . . . . . . **Free**

Everyone likes to email digital photos, but no one likes to receive pictures that are so huge they take forever to download and require you to scroll left and right and up and down to see the entire image. Luckily there's an easy way to resize a large group of photos freshly downloaded from your digital camera with two clicks.

Microsoft ImageResizer PowerToy is a free utility that plugs into Windows Explorer. Download and install ImageResizer from the right side of the page at `http://microsoft.com/windowsxp/downloads/powertoys/xppowertoys.mspx`. Then, browse to the folder where you stored your digital photos.

Select the photos you want to resize, right-click, and choose Resize Pictures from the context menu to get the ImageResizer dialog box. Click the Advanced button to see all of the options, as shown in Figure 4-6.

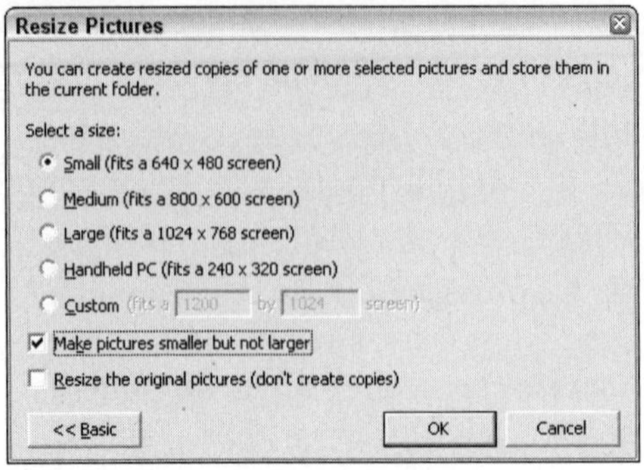

**Figure 4-6** The ImageResizer options dialog box.

From there, choose one of the ImageResizer suggested dimensions, or enter your custom width and height. Be sure to select the Make Pictures Smaller But Not Larger option if you don't want to size up — and you won't, because making digital photos larger degrades quality. Click OK.

By default, the ImageResizer creates copies of the files and adds the chosen size to the filename. For example, if your original photo filename was `Jeremy001.jpg`, and you resized it using the Small setting, the new version will be named `Jeremy001 (Small).jpg`.

Alternately, if you're looking for a complete photo manager that can do more extensive photo processing including batch resizing, red-eye reduction, photo rating, keyword assigning, search and lots of fun effects, download and install a copy of Google's free Picasa (`http://picasa.com`). After Picasa indexes all of your photos, select the ones you want to resize so they appear in the Picture Tray on the bottom left. Then click the Export button on the lower right. Here you can copy the photos at a new size to another folder on your hard drive for emailing, publishing online, or burning to CD.

# Hack 30: Send and Receive Money on Your Cell Phone

Level....... **Easy**
Platform.... **Cell phone (text messaging optional)**
Cost ....... **Free**

Popular online payment service PayPal (`http://paypal.com`) is a quick and easy way to email money to friends and co-workers — to cover your share of the dinner bill or to pitch in on a shared gift or to make a payment for work done. PayPal's new mobile service now enables you to send and receive money directly from your cell phone when you're out and about.

Mobile-to-mobile payments can come in handy in lieu of cold, hard cash when purchasing something from someone you don't know (say from Craigslist, `http://craigslist.org`) or when you can't find an ATM and your buddy's covering you. This hack explains how to initiate cash transactions via PayPal on your cell phone.

## PayPal Mobile

You'll need a free PayPal account to get started. To add money to your PayPal account, link your checking account or credit card to it. To enable cell phone payments, you need to activate your mobile phone number within your PayPal account. Do so by entering your cell phone number on the PayPal web site in the mobile area (`https:// paypal.com/cgi-bin/webscr?cmd=xpt/ cps/mobile/MobileOverview-outside`) and set up a mobile PIN (separate from your PayPal password). PayPal calls your phone on the spot and asks you to verify the PIN. When the PIN is matched, your phone is PayPal-enabled.

Then, to send someone else's phone $5.50 in cash, text message PAYPAL (or 729725) the following message:

```
send 5.50 to 7185551212
```

where the recipient's phone number is (718) 555-1212.

The first time I tried this with my Nokia phone using Cingular, I got a text message back immediately saying that the recipient was invalid. Turns out only certain carriers — Alltel, Sprint, T-Mobile, and Verizon — support the SMS function.

Luckily, there's a plan B for folks not on those plans: You can call PayPal's automated voice system to send cash as well. Dial 1-800-4PAYPAL and follow the instructions to send money to the destination cell phone number.

Either method results in a text message to the recipient's phone with instructions for picking up the money. In short, the recipient has to go to the web site and link her mobile phone number to her PayPal account to claim the payment.

The obvious question is: Why wouldn't a thief just steal your phone and text himself a few Benjamin Franklins? If you treat your PayPal mobile PIN the way you do your ATM PIN, that isn't possible because every single transaction initiated from your phone gets an immediate callback from PayPal asking that you enter your mobile PIN to proceed.

## Send Money to an Email Address

If the payee doesn't have a cell phone (or doesn't want to associate it with his PayPal account), you can also text message money to someone's email address. Just make your text message *send 5 to editor@lifehacker.com* instead (substituting an email address for the phone number). In this case the recipient doesn't get immediate notification of the payment on his phone, but it also means he doesn't have to associate his mobile number with his PayPal account, either.

You cannot use PayPal with someone's email address if you're using the 800 voice number — only if you're sending PayPal a text message (which means PayPal supports your mobile carrier). If you do use the voice system to send a payment to someone's phone and she doesn't want to link her mobile to PayPal, you can cancel the pending payment and re-initiate it through the PayPal.com web site.

The following table lists examples of all the PayPal Mobile SMS commands.

| COMMAND | DESCRIPTION |
| --- | --- |
| send 10.99 to 2125551981 | Send $10.99 to (212) 555 1981 phone number. |
| send 5 to name@example.com | Send $5.00 to name@example.com. |
| s 10.99 t 2125551981 | Use the shortened s and t for send and to. |
| s 10.99 t 4150001234 note thx 4 dinn | Add a *thx 4 dinn* note with your payment. |
| send 5.43 EUR to 3105551212 | Send your payment in Euros (CAD for Canadian dollars, GBP for British pounds, AUD for Australian dollars, or JPY for Yen also work). |
| send 10.99 to 4150001234 share address | Share your address with someone to have him ship you an item. |
| send 10.99 to 3105551212 share phone | Share your phone number with recipient. |
| send 5 to 2125551981 share info note send asap | Share your phone and address and send a note *send asap* to recipient. |
| Bal | Check your current PayPal balance. |
| Cancel | Cancel a pending payment. |

## PayPal Alternative

TextPayMe (http://textpayme.com) offers a service similar to PayPal Mobile Payments. TextPayMe's SMS payment address is a regular email address, so usage isn't limited to cell phone carriers. However, consumers are more likely to have a PayPal account than a TextPayMe account because PayPal's service has been established for many years and is linked with popular auction site eBay (http://ebay.com).

# Hack 31: Bypass Free Site Registration with BugMeNot

Level . . . . . . . **Easy**
Platforms . . . **All**
Cost . . . . . . . **Free**

Ever more web sites require you to register on them for free and sign in with a username and password to view their contents. An active surfer can easily accumulate dozens of logins for various sites across the Web. But what about when you don't want to go through the whole rigmarole of registering for a web site — you simply want inside?

Web site BugMeNot (http://bugmenot.com) maintains a public database of shared usernames and passwords for free web sites. If you come across a site that prompts you to log in to view its content, bypass the registration process by heading to BugMeNot to search for an already-created username and password. Not all BugMeNot logins will work, but you can see the percentage success rate for a particular login and report whether it worked for you as well. If you can't find a BugMeNot login that works? Create one and share it with the BugMeNot community.

There are three ways to use BugMeNot:

- Enter the address of the site you want to log into on BugMeNot.com to get a list of possible logins.

- Drag and drop the Bugmenot bookmarklet to your web browser's links toolbar. When you come onto a site you'd like to log into, click the bookmarklet and get login detail suggestions in a pop-up window, as shown in Figure 4-7.

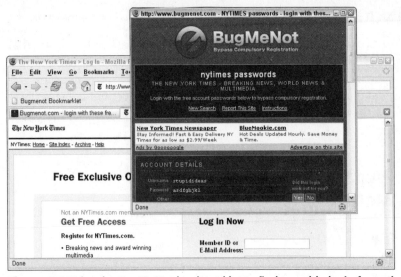

**Figure 4-7** Using the BugMeNot bookmarklet to find a usable login for nytimes.com.

> Copy and paste the suggested login — in this example, username stupidideas and password asdfghjkl — into the nytimes.com login page to view a password-protected article.

■ Download and install the BugMeNot Firefox extension, available at `http://roachfiend.com/archives/2005/02/07/bugmenot`. Restart Firefox. Next time you are presented with a username and password prompt, right-click inside the username text box and choose Login with BugMeNot as shown in Figure 4-8.

The extension is the fastest way to log in with a BugMeNot account because it doesn't require you to copy and paste the username and password into the login fields, but it only works in Firefox (`http://mozilla.org/firefox/`).

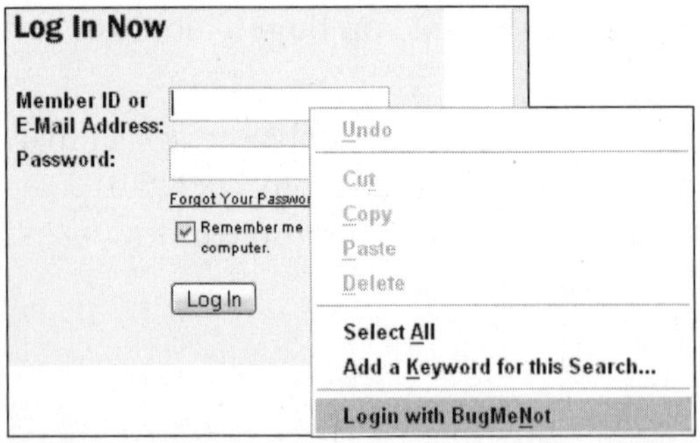

**Figure 4-8** Log in with BugMeNot details directly from the context menu using the BugMeNot Firefox extension.

**NOTE** See Hack 71, "Extend Your Web Browser," for more on how to install a Firefox extension.

BugMeNot does not work on web sites that require a paid subscription to view, and some sites block BugMeNot. The most popular BugMeNot sites include *The New York Times* (http://nytimes.com), *The Washington Post* (http://washingtonpost.com), and IMDB (http://imdb.com), the Internet Movie Database.

## Hack 32: Speed up Web Pages on a Slow Internet Connection

Level....... **Easy**
Platform.... **All**
Cost ....... **Free**

It may feel like centuries have passed since the last time you heard the unmistakable mating call of your computer's modem dialing into an ISP. But even in today's broadband-saturated world, dialup remains an affordable and sometimes necessary connectivity alternative while traveling or when your high-speed connection isn't available.

When you're surfing the Web on a slow connection, it can seem like grass grows faster than the download progress meter on your web browser turns. But it's not difficult to optimize your browsing setup for the fastest way to log on, get what you need done, and get off. This hack covers some strategies for squeezing the most productivity out of a limited flow of bytes over a slow internet connection, be it via an analog dialup line or a cell phone modem connection.

**NOTE** See Hack 41, "Turn Your Cell Phone into a Modem," for more on dialing into the internet from your mobile phone on the go.

### Configure Your Web Browser for a Slow Connection

Chances are that your web browser's setup assumes your internet connection is fast and ever-present. A couple of small changes for your dial-in session can make a big difference:

- Increase the size of your browser's cache so that you re-download the same web page elements less often. The default cache size in Firefox, for example, is 50 MB. Your hard drive probably has plenty of free space, so consider increasing this number to 100 MB or more. To do so in Firefox, select Tools → Options → Privacy, and set the number on the Cache tab, as shown in Figure 4-9.

- If you want real speed and your inner aesthete won't be too offended, under Web Features uncheck Load Images. This, of course, takes away the pretty pictures on web pages, but it significantly speeds up page load on a slow connection. You can also specify sites that should be exceptions to the no-images rule using the — you guessed it — Exceptions button, as shown in Figure 4-10.

- To disable images in Internet Explorer, select Tools → Internet Options; go to the Multimedia section on the Advanced Tab and deselect everything. Unlike Firefox, Internet Explorer does not allow for exceptions to the rule.

**TIP** Advanced users can employ the Firefox Profile feature to set up slow-connection preferences separate from your default profile, and switch to it as necessary. See more on how to manage profiles in Mozilla's Help section (http://mozilla.org/support/firefox/profile).

**Figure 4-9** Increase the size of the cache to decrease the number of repeated downloads.

**Figure 4-10** Set Firefox to not download images or Java applets to speed up page load.

## Block and Disable Bandwidth Hogs

Five minutes on a dialup connection and you begin to resent every unnecessary pixel, advertisement, and Flash movie on the Web. Install an ad blocker such as AdBlock for Firefox (`https://addons.mozilla.org/firefox/10`) or FlashBlock (`http://flashblock.mozdev.org`) to avoid losing minutes of your life so some web page can suggest you shoot the turkey and win an iPod in one of its banner ads.

Speaking of bandwidth hogs, if your podcasting software (like iTunes) is set to automatically download new episodes when you connect to the internet, you'll qualify for Social Security before you can view your browser's home-page. Be sure to disable automatic podcast downloads when you're on a slow connection.

## Use Tabs to Load Pages While You Work

The real beauty of tabbed browsing shows its efficient self in the face of a slow internet connection. When searching the Web for information or clicking links from your RSS aggregator, click your mouse scroll wheel or Control-/Command-click to open up each page in a new tab. This way you can read one page while others load in a background tab.

**NOTE** The web browsers that feature tabbed browsing are Firefox, Internet Explorer 7 (default in Windows Vista), and Opera. Internet Explorer 6 on Windows XP does not have tabbed browsing.

If the amount of time you're on the phone line is an issue, log on, open up a bunch of pages in multiple tabs, disconnect, and read offline.

Speaking of offline...

## Work Offline Wherever Possible

Yes, always-online web applications are popular these days, but the fact is you're not always online. The capability to work offline makes a huge difference in productivity when you're dependent on a slow connection. Here's a quick list of offline work examples that can help you get things done when you're dialing in:

- Use a desktop RSS reader and download all unread articles for offline reading. (See Hack 69, "Subscribe to Web Sites with RSS," for more on using RSS.)

- Save web pages to your hard drive for reading later. (Chapter 9, "Master the Web," provides many hacks for improving your web experience.)

- Webmail users, install a desktop email client like Mozilla Thunderbird (http://mozilla.org/products/thunderbird) and download your messages for offline reading and responding.

- Download bank transactions to Quicken or Microsoft Money instead of connecting to your bank's web site to pay bills.

A slow connection to the internet can be an exercise in utter frustration, but tweaking your tools to fit the task can make it a lot more bearable.

## Hack 33: Securely Save Web Site Passwords

Level . . . . . . . **Easy**
Platform . . . . **All (Firefox)**
Cost . . . . . . . **Free**

One of the most convenient features in Firefox is its capability to save the passwords you use to log on to web sites — like your web mail and online banking — so you don't have to type them in every time. Those saved passwords automatically fill in as asterisks in the password field, but did you know how easy it is to see what they are? In Firefox, select Tools → Options. In the Passwords tab, click the View Saved Passwords button. Then click Show Passwords — and there they are, all your high-security passwords in plain text and full sight.

Now consider how easy it would be for your Firefox-loving housemate to log onto your Gmail, or the computer-sharing temp at the office to get into your checking account, or for a laptop thief to log into your PayPal account. Not such a great feature anymore, eh? But you don't have to go back to re-typing in your passwords every time you visit a login-only site.

This hack describes how to secure your saved passwords in Firefox without requiring you give up the convenience of those auto-filled login details.

In Firefox, select Tools → Options and, on the Passwords tab, click the Set Master Password button, as shown in Figure 4-11.

The master password is a single password that will lock the rest of your saved passwords away from prying eyes. It's a password you'll have to enter once a session — each time you restart Firefox.

When you set your master password, Firefox has a neat Password Quality Meter that displays how difficult your password is to crack. Try different combinations of words and numbers and symbols to get this secure-o-meter as high as possible. For example the password lifehacker scored low on the quality meter, but *l1f3h4ck3r* registered about 90% (see Figure 4-12), making it fairly hard to crack.

**Figure 4-11** Set your master password in the Firefox Options dialog box.

Now, the trick is to pick something you will always remember because if you forget your Master Password, you won't be able to access any of your saved passwords. That would be bad. (Hack 55, "Choose Secure, Memorable Passwords," offers help in creating great passwords you won't forget.)

After you've set your Master Password, close Firefox. When you reopen and go to a page where you've saved a password — like Yahoo! Mail — you'll get a security prompt as shown in Figure 4-13.

Enter your master password, click OK, and your Yahoo! Mail login details will fill in automatically.

The master password prompt is a bit of an inconvenience, but much less than entering a password every time you visit login-only sites. It buys you the expediency of saved passwords with the security that you must be authorized to access them.

**NOTE** The Firefox Master Password is difficult — but not impossible — to crack. If there are passwords to web sites you absolutely don't want stored on your computer, when you enter it and Firefox asks if it should save it, just click No.

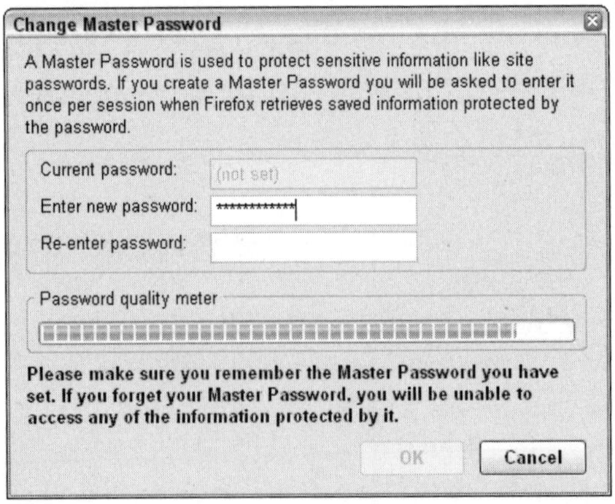

**Figure 4-12** The master password quality level.

**Figure 4-13** The master password prompt.

# Get Your Data to Go

Computers are everywhere, but your data isn't. You will travel, relocate, switch jobs, use more computers, and generate larger quantities of data in your lifetime than any previous generation.

Ten years ago an average person might have been able to store all the data she needed on a 1.44MB floppy disk. Now, in the age of MP3 players, ubiquitous broadband, personal camcorders, and digital cameras, the average person generates and collects dozens of gigabytes of data per year. Laptop sales have surged over desktop computer sales in recent years because more people require mobility and computing power wherever they go. Modern web applications enable data storage and access from any Internet-connected computer with a web browser installed.

Every day you create a digital trail that details your life. Your sent mail folder describes your professional and personal relationships. Your digital photo and video archive documents family vacations, graduations, births, and the car accident you got into last year. You've got your college papers, your resume, and professional documents created at your last three jobs stowed away on your hard drive. Your data is your life. Secure, easy access to it — no matter where you are — is a must.

Whether it's taking it with you, storing it up in the cloud, connecting to your home server from anywhere, or using your cell phone to get online, this chapter's hacks cover several ways to get your data on the go.

# Hack 34: Carry Your Life on a Flash Drive

Level . . . . . . . **Medium**
Platform . . . . **Windows XP and Vista (with a flash drive)**
Cost . . . . . . . **Free**

Portable hard drives such as USB flash drives and iPods get cheaper, smaller in size, and larger in capacity by the day. Instead of lugging around your laptop, or emailing yourself files, store your favorite software applications and important data on a thumb (flash) drive about the size of a car key. Then plug it into any computer for quick and easy access on the go.

This hack covers popular portable applications and some practical uses for these small drives.

A few scenarios where a USB drive loaded with your favorite applications and important documents might come in handy:

- You work on a set of files on several different computers (like at the office and at home, on the laptop and the desktop) and you want easy access to them from one place.

- Your IT department doesn't give you administrative rights to install your favorite software on your office computer.

- You'd like to back up your files and store them offsite, like home files at the office or work files at home. (You can store USB drives in a safety deposit box or mail one to Mom in Florida every few months, too.)

- You don't want to download and install your favorite application at every computer you use.

- You want to avoid using your in-laws' hijacked web browser to download virus scanners and spyware cleaners; instead you want to take the tools you'll need to fix their computer along on your flash drive.

- You want to bring the latest episode of *The Sopranos* with you on the airplane, or create a digital music mix to DJ a friend's party. (USB drives are more portable and durable than DVDs, CDs, or VCR tapes.)

**NOTE** Later in this chapter, Hack 40, "Backup Files to Your iPod," shows you how to use the iPod as an external hard drive from which you can also run portable applications and store your data.

## Portable Applications

When you install software on your computer, the setup program makes changes to Windows' registry and stores special files (called DLLs) throughout your PC's file system so that the program can run. Portable apps — software programs meant to run from a single hard drive — don't require any changes to the operating system. They are self-contained and stand alone on one drive. Portable applications meant for use on flash drives are often stripped down to the bare essentials to take up the least amount of disk space possible. However, program size becomes less of an issue for software makers as larger-capacity drives become cheaper and more available. (As of this writing, thumb drives up to 16 GB in size are available on the market.)

When purchasing a flash drive, keep in mind that size does matter. The more space you have, the more programs and information you can store.

Some popular portable software applications include:

- **Web browser** — Portable Firefox, 7.55MB installed. Includes all Firefox profile information such as bookmarks and extensions.

  `http://portableapps.com/apps/internet/browsers/portable_firefox`

- **Office suite** — Portable OpenOffice.org, 90.6MB installed. Spreadsheet, word processor, and presentation software.

  `http://portableapps.com/apps/office/suites/portable_openoffice`

- **Email** — Portable Thunderbird, 21.7MB installed. Email, address book, and mail filters.

  `http://portableapps.com/apps/internet/email/portable_thunderbird`

- **Instant messenger** — Trillian Anywhere; about 34 MB installed, depending on the size of your Trillian profile. Multi-protocol instant messaging client works with AIM, Yahoo! Messenger, MSN Messenger, ICQ, and IRC.

  `http://trilliananywhere.com`

- **Virus scanner** — Portable ClamWin, about 15 MB installed (with definitions). Open source Windows virus scanner.

  `http://portableapps.com/apps/utilities/antivirus/portable_clamwin`

- **Remote login** — TightVNC (viewer executable only), 159 KB installed. Log in to your remote VNC server with the TightVNC viewer. (See Hack 36, "Remote Control Your Home Computer," for more information on using the TightVNC viewer.)

  `http://tightvnc.com/download.html`

What kind of space are we talking about? Those six portable programs total 327.85 MB, or about 33 percent of a 1 GB flash drive, which leaves plenty of space for work files.

For a constantly updated directory of software fit for toting around on a thumb drive, keep an eye on John Haller's web site, Portable Apps (`http://portableapps.com`).

The Portable Apps site also offers an entire suite of software packages for your flash drive in a single download. The suite includes a web browser, email client, web editor, office suite, word processor, calendar/scheduler, instant messaging client, and FTP client, ready to save to your flash drive and use. Two flavors are available for download: Standard and Lite (smaller file size). Download it for free at http://portableapps.com/suite. The Standard, unzipped and installed, takes up 206 MB; the Light, a mere 68.6 MB.

Several other software applications discussed in other hacks in this book are small enough to fit on a thumb drive or offer a portable version:

- **KeePass password manager** — See Hack 56, "Securely Track Your Passwords," for more on using KeePass.

- **TrueCrypt data encryption utility** — See Hack 58, "Encrypt Your Data," for more on making your files inaccessible in case your thumb drive is lost or stolen.

- **AutoHotkey text replacement** — See Hack 27, "Save Time with Text Substitution," for more details on creating custom abbreviation replacement and common misspelling correction programs with AutoHotkey.

## Useful Data to Store on Your Thumb Drive

Software is worthless without data. Store your important files on your flash drive for access on any computer. That includes your:

- To-do list
- Address book
- Passwords (Be sure to encrypt this file for security! See the following section, "Secure Your Drive," for more information.)
- Multimedia — photos, music, and video (depending on the size of your drive)
- Office documents
- ReturnIfLost.txt file with your contact information
- Web site bookmarks
- Web browser configuration (see Hack 76, "Take Your Browser Configuration with You," for more information)

## Secure Your Drive

Flash drives are tiny and convenient, which means they're easily lost, damaged, stolen, and transported. More and more cases of stolen laptops and hard drives have spelled disaster for companies and individuals who handle sensitive customer data or private company documents.

Here are a few strategies for securing the data on your thumb drive.

### Lock Sensitive Text Files

Free software LockNote, freely available at `http://locknote.steganos .com`, is a standalone text file encryption program. Save the `LockNote.exe` file to your thumb drive. Launch it, and enter any textual information you'd like to secure — passwords, addresses, phone numbers, account numbers, and so on — and then close the document. LockNote prompts you for a password and scrambles the file so that anyone without the password can't open it.

The `LockNote.exe` file weighs in at about 296 KB — about 0.29 MB — and is worth the space if you're dealing with sensitive, confidential material.

### Encrypt Your Data

If you have different types of existing files, you can create a password protected ZIP archive of them. Using free software 7-Zip, available at `http://7zip.org`, add the files you want to save on your flash drive to a new ZIP archive, and set a password to open them, as shown in Figure 5-1.

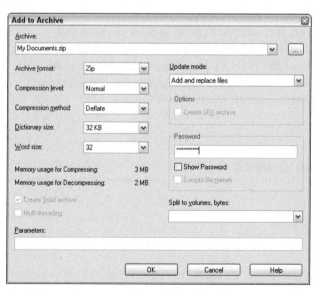

**Figure 5-1** Set a password on the zipped files for security.

Make sure you change the Archive Format from 7z to Zip so that Windows can extract the file without 7-Zip. Finally, move the resulting archive (.zip file) to your thumb drive.

You can browse the file and folder names within a password-protected ZIP file, but the individual files cannot be extracted or the contents viewed without entering the password. A stronger, alternate encryption method employs the free software TrueCrypt (http://truecrypt.org/downloads.php). For detailed instructions on how to encrypt an entire thumb drive — or just a particular folder or set of files with TrueCrypt — see Hack 58.

### Make Your Drive Returnable

Place an "If found, please return" text file with contact information on your flash drive to increase the chances that it'll be returned in case of loss. But don't encrypt this file — it should be readable by anyone!

### Using Your Thumb Drive

When your flash drive is loaded, plug it into any computer with a USB drive and access like any other internal hard drive. All the usual Mac/PC compatibility issues apply (for example, an .exe file won't launch on a Mac), but Office documents, PDFs, and text files are cross-platform.

> **WARNING** If you're not sure the computer you're using is spyware and virus-free, assume that it is not. USB drives are the perfect way to spread computer nasties, so be extra cautious with a promiscuous thumb drive. For this very reason, network administrators sometimes disable the capability to mount a thumb drive on public computers (such as at libraries).

# Hack 35: Run a Home Web Server

Level....... **Advanced**
Platform.... **Windows XP and Vista**
Cost ....... **Free**

A web server is software that continuously runs on a computer and allows other computers to download documents from it. Any web page you view has traveled over a network connection from the site's hosting web server to the browser on your computer. Web servers are usually loud, scary, headless machines in cold windowless rooms, but you can run one under your desk at home.

Why would you want to run a home web server? Maybe you want to download files — perhaps some of your digital music collection — on your home computer from anywhere. Maybe you want your friends and family to have access to your music or photo collection from anywhere, too.

In this hack, you set up a home web server that enables anyone (with the right password) to connect to your computer and download your MP3 files from it, for an easy way to share your music collection with friends, or play a song from your home machine for co-workers at the office.

There are tons of uses for your personal web server beyond a password-protected jukebox: you can publish your weblog at home, host a personal wiki, and share video files and photos. Basically any file you want to publish as read-only is a good candidate. A home web server has the advantage over special server/client software because it only requires a web browser to connect to it.

**WARNING** Running a server on your home computer is a risky undertaking. Before you start, ensure that your computer has all the latest patches and security updates (visit `http://windowsupdate.microsoft.com` to make sure) and that you've done a thorough spyware and virus scan. This hack is for advanced users who feel comfortable editing textual configuration files and exposing port 80 on their home computers to the Internet. You should be running a strong firewall with explicit user-set rules.

Here's what you need to get started:

- A Windows PC
- An always-on broadband (DSL or cable) Internet connection

## Step 1: Disable Other Servers or Firewall Software

First, disable and stop any firewall or server software you may have running, including Windows Firewall, Skype, Trillian or any other instant messaging applications. This is extremely important, and if it's not done, can cause the server installation and startup to fail miserably. These programs and services can be started and used again as usual once you're done setting up the web server.

## Step 2: Install Apache HTTP Server

Download the Apache HTTP server, available at `http://httpd.apache.org/download.cgi`. Use the link under Best Available Version next to Win32 Binary (MSI Installer). If the Windows binary is not available on the homepage, click the Other Files link and go to the binaries folder; and from the win32 folder, download the most recent `.msi` file. As of writing, that file is `apache_2.2.3-win32-x86-no_ssl.msi`.

Click the downloaded file to start the installation wizard. Accept the license agreement and use the default location for the Apache files, which is `C:\Program Files\Apache Software Foundation\Apache 2.x\`. When you reach the screen prompting for server information, enter your own email address and `homeip.net` as the domain information, as shown in Figure 5-2.

It doesn't matter what domain you put here. I chose `homeip.net` because it's descriptive, and one of the DynDNS home domains. (See Hack 37, "Give Your Home Computer a Web Address," for more information on DynDNS.)

### Complete the Installation

Complete the installation wizard using the Typical Installation setting. Set the server to run on port 80 for all users. If Windows' Firewall (or any other firewall you may be running) asks what it should do about the server running on port 80, choose to unblock or allow Apache to run on it.

When the installation is complete, open your web browser and go to `http://localhost/`. If the page you see reads something along the lines of: "If you can see this, it means that the installation of the Apache web server software on this system was successful" — or, more simply, a page that declares, "It works!" — you're golden.

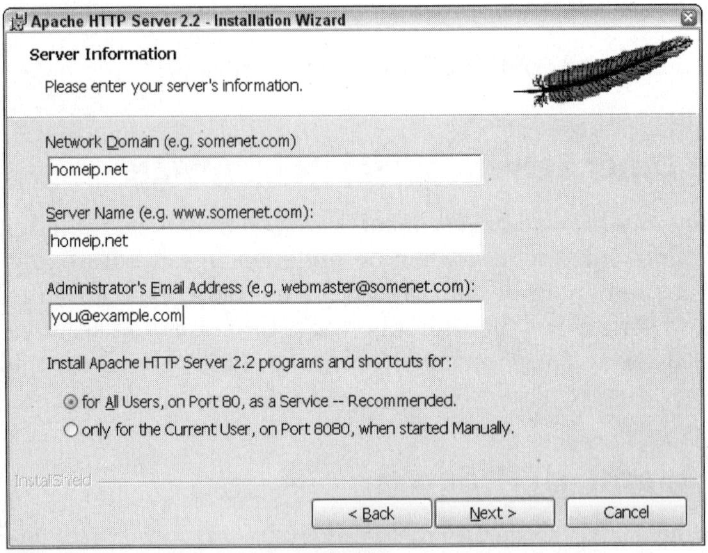

**Figure 5-2** Set the web server options.

### Common Problem

A common installation error with Apache reads, "Only one usage of each socket address (protocol/network address/port) is normally permitted. : make_sock: could not bind to address 0.0.0.0:80 no listening sockets available, shutting down. Unable to open logs." This means that some other server program (like Skype) is interfering with Apache. To figure out what program it is, open a command prompt and type:

```
netstat -a -o
```

Find the PID (Process ID) of the program running on your local machine on port 80 (or http.) Then open the Windows Task Manager (Ctrl+Alt+Delete). Choose View → Select Columns, and check PID. Match the PID to the running process to find out which server program is running, and stop the program. Then retry the Apache installation.

## Step 3: Configure Apache to Share Documents

Now you want to make your music collection available via your new web server. To do so, browse to the folder that contains Apache's configuration files, located at `C:\Program Files\Apache Software Foundation\Apache 2.x\conf\`. Then, make a copy of the main configuration file, `httpd.conf`, before you make any changes — just in case. Save the copy as `httpd .backup.conf` in that same directory.

Then, using a plain text editor like Notepad, open the `C:\Program Files\Apache Software Foundation\Apache 2.x\conf\httpd.conf` file. The contents of this file look long and scary, but most of the defaults will work just fine. You just have to change a few things.

First, comment out the line that starts with `DocumentRoot` and add another with your directory, like this:

```
#DocumentRoot "C:/Program Files/Apache Group/Apache2/htdocs"
DocumentRoot "C:/Documents and Settings/penelope/My Documents/My Music"
```

where `C:/Documents and Settings/penelope/My Documents/My Music` corresponds to the location of your music files.

**NOTE** While Windows directory structure normally uses backslashes, Apache's default `httpd.conf` uses forward slashes, so that's what's used in this hack.

Then, comment out the line that starts with `<Directory "C:/Program...”` and add another with your directory, like this:

```
#<Directory "C:/Program Files/Apache Group/Apache2/htdocs">
<Directory "C:/Documents and Settings/penelope/My Documents/My Music">
```

Last, about 20 lines later, there's a line that reads:

```
AllowOverride None
```

Change it to:

```
AllowOverride All
```

When you're done, save `httpd.conf`. Then, click the Apache icon in your taskbar and choose Restart. If Apache restarts successfully, you edited your the file correctly. Visit `http://localhost/` in your web browser. This time you should see a listing of your music files.

> **NOTE** If Apache doesn't start correctly, it's because it can't read the `httpd.conf` file, which means you probably had a typo in your changes. Check your changes carefully, save, and restart Apache to try again. If necessary, copy `httpd.backup.conf` to `httpd.conf` to start all over again.

## Step 4: Password-Protect Your Web Site Documents

You don't want just anyone to be able to download your music. Your bandwidth and files are private and precious, so you want to secure things a bit. Begin by creating a password prompt:

1. Open a command prompt (go to the Start menu, choose Run, then type cmd and press Enter). Change to the Apache bin directory by typing:

   ```
   cd "C:\Program Files\Apache Software Foundation\Apache 2.x\bin"
   ```

   Where Apache 2.*x* matches the version you installed (Apache 2.2, for example).

2. Create a password file by typing:

   ```
   htpasswd -c "C:\Documents and Settings\penelope\My Documents\↩
   web-server-pass-file" penny
   ```

   Replace the path with wherever your password file should be located (which can be any folder *except* the web server's document root that you set up above). Replace `penny` with your preferred username.

3. When prompted, enter the password you want to set up. After you've done that, a password file will be created.

Now, follow these steps to apply that login to your music directory:

1. Open a new file in a plain text editor such as Notepad. Enter the following text into it:

```
AuthType Basic
AuthName "This is a private area, please log in"

AuthUserFile "C:\Documents and Settings\penelope\My Documents\⊃
web-server-pass-file"
AuthGroupFile /dev/null

<Limit GET POST PUT>
require valid-user
</Limit>
```

Make sure you replace C:\Documents and Settings\penelope\My Documents\web-server-pass-file in the text with the path to the password file you created above.

2. Save this new file in your web server's document root you set earlier (in this case, C:/Documents and Settings/penelope/My Documents/My Music) and name it .htaccess. Don't forget the dot in the beginning, before htaccess. In other words, you are saving the file as C:\Documents and Settings\penelope\My Documents\My Music\.htaccess.

**NOTE** If you're using Notepad to create your .htaccess file, put quotes around the filename — ".htaccess" — when you save the file so that Notepad doesn't automatically put a .txt extension on the file. (If there's a .txt file extension, your password won't work!) Alternatively, choose All Files from the Save as Type drop-down.

3. Point your web browser to http://localhost/. You are prompted to log in as shown in Figure 5-3.

4. Enter the username and password you set up in your password file, and you're in.

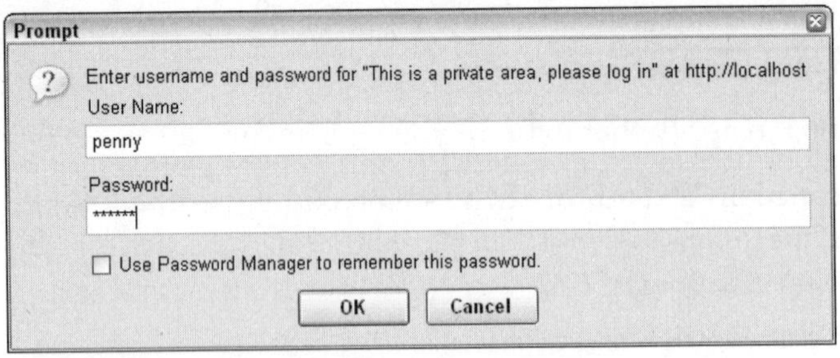

**Figure 5-3** The password prompt for your local web server.

Congratulations! You've got a home web server running.

If you are not behind a firewall, you can access your web server from other computers by typing your computer's IP address into a web browser's address bar. (If you're not sure what your IP is, visit What Is My IP at http://whatismyip.com to find out.) If your IP is 12.34.567.890, then type http://12.34.567.890 into a browser's address bar.

**NOTE** Depending on your internet service provider, your computer's IP address may change, but there's an easy way to set up a memorable name that doesn't change. See Hack 37, "Give Your Home Computer a Web Address," for more information.

If you are behind a firewall (like a wireless router), you'll need to open up port 80 on the firewall and forward it to your computer. Consult your router's manual or, for more information on port forwarding go to http://lifehackerbook.com/links/portforward.

In the meantime, enjoy accessing the files on your home computer from anywhere via your home web server!

## Hack 36: Remote Control Your Home Computer

Level....... **Advanced**
Platform.... **Windows XP and Vista, Mac OS X**
Cost ....... **Free**

Ever been at a friend's house and wanted to show off a photo you left saved on your home computer? Want to check from the office that your daughter's doing homework and not instant messaging with friends at home? Need to grab a file on your home hard drive when you're miles away? With a relatively old protocol called VNC (Virtual Network Computing) and some free software, you can remotely control your home computer from anywhere.

In this hack, you set up a VNC server on your home computer, which will enable you to connect to your desktop and drive it from any Internet-connected computer.

**WARNING** As mentioned earlier, running a server and opening up a port on your home computer to the Internet is a risky undertaking. Make sure your computer has all the latest security patches, has been checked for spyware and viruses, and that you're using strong passwords. The VNC protocol is not inherently secure. This hack assumes you're comfortable with basic networking concepts. If this fine print has scared you off, LogMeIn (`http://logmein.com`) is a web-based application that also provides remote desktop control, which may be a better option for some folks. VNC is preferable because it's free, it doesn't require third-party intervention, and it works across operating systems.

The VNC protocol remotely controls another computer over a network. Think of it as a window into your home computer's desktop from any other computer, as shown in Figure 5-4.

**Figure 5-4** An open VNC connection to a Windows PC from a Mac.

Your key presses and mouse clicks travel over the network and happen on the remote computer — your home computer — in real time, and anyone at the remote computer can watch the action as it happens.

A few things you can do with a VNC server running at home:

- Start downloading a large file, like a movie, in the morning so it's there when you get home in the evening
- Search your home computer's IM logs, address book, or file system for important information from the office.
- Help Mom figure out why Microsoft Word doesn't start without having to go to her house (even though Mom would like to see you more often).
- Control a headless (monitor-less) machine like a media center or file server in another room in the house from the laptop on the couch.

VNC requires two components for a successful connection: the server on your home computer and the viewer on the remote computer. Ready to set them up?

## Step 1: Install the VNC Server

There are several free VNC servers for Windows and Macs, so pick the section that you need.

### Windows

TightVNC (http://tightvnc.com) is a free Windows VNC server and client software package. TightVNC is a nice choice because it also allows for file transfers and high compression levels for slow connections. Download TightVNC from http://tightvnc.com/download.html and run the installation on your home computer. Start the server, and set a password for incoming connections.

If you're running a firewall, it may prompt you about whether to allow the VNC server to run: allow it.

TightVNC can be set to run as a Windows service, which means your Windows usernames and passwords can be used to authenticate on the VNC server connection. If you choose this option, be sure all your Windows passwords are set and strong, and that any password-less guest accounts are disabled.

### Mac

OSXvnc (http://redstonesoftware.com/vnc.html) is a free Mac VNC server. Download, install, set up a password, and start the server.

### *About the Server*

If your VNC server is connected directly to the Internet, it is now listening for internet requests on port 5900, VNC's default port (which is also configurable). Visit WhatIsMyIP (http://whatismyip.com) from your home computer to determine its IP address and write it down.

If your home computer is behind a home network router with a firewall, remote computers cannot connect. You must open up a port on your router's firewall and forward requests to your computer. Consult your router's manual for more information on how to do that, or check out the article "How to access a home server behind a firewall" at http://lifehackerbook.com/links/portforward.

## Step 2: Install the VNC Client

On the remote Windows computer, also download and install TightVNC (http://tightvnc.com), but this time, start the viewer instead of the server. If you're on a Mac, download the free Chicken of the VNC (http://sourceforge.net/projects/cotvnc) Mac viewer to connect to your home PC. Enter your home computer's IP address and password to connect.

> **NOTE** Alternately, you can enter your home computer's domain name. Then, when connecting using the VNC viewer, you can enter a URL like pennyscomputer.dyndns.org **instead of an IP address.**

Once connected, you're virtually sitting at your home desktop from any-where in the world.

## More Tips

A few extra VNC tips to consider:

- For slower network connections, set the compression to Best. The window image quality will be lower, but the connection response will be snappier.

- Bring a VNC viewer with you on a USB memory stick so you don't have to download and install on every computer you want to use to connect to your server.

- Avoid having to install a server on Mom's computer; email her the 166 K self-extracting SingleClick UltraVNC server, available at http://ultravnc.sourceforge.net/addons/singleclick.html for your next tech support phone session.

# Hack 37: Give Your Home Computer a Web Address

Level....... **Advanced**
Platform.... **All**
Cost ....... **Free**

Accessing your home computer from the Internet is a lot easier if a memorable, permanent web address such as yourname.com points to it.

Depending on your ISP, the IP address assigned to your home computer can change over time, which means you need to keep track of the current one. Instead, a permanent web address made up of words instead of numbers, which automatically resolves to a dynamic IP, keeps accessing your home server simple.

Why would you want to assign a domain name to your home web server? Maybe you want to start a blog that you're going to host at home instead of buying a web-hosting plan and you want the URL to be unforgettable. Maybe you want to set up a personal home page at yourname.com for business purposes or so that folks can easily find your web site. Or, maybe your home computer's IP address changes and you don't want to have to worry about keeping track to access your server.

> **NOTE** This tutorial assumes you already have a web or VNC server running at home. If you don't, check out the preceding two hacks for getting one set up.

A dynamic DNS service, like DynDNS (http://dyndns.com), is a constantly updated database of IP addresses and domain names. For free, you can get one of the available DynDNS domain names plus a custom subdomain (like lifehacker.getmyip.net), or for a small fee you can register your own domain (like joesmith.com) and set it to resolve to your home computer web server with DynDNS.

> **WARNING** Some corporate and university networks and ISPs don't allow computers outside the network address internal IP addresses. To test that your home computer's IP address is accessible from the outside, visit Network Tools (http://network-tools.com) from your home computer and choose the Ping option. If the ping is successful (meaning, it doesn't time out), your computer is accessible from the outside.

Let's get started.

## Step 1: Set Up Your DynDNS Account

From your home computer, register for a free account at DynDNS (`http://dyndns.com`). Agree to the site's terms, and use a legitimate email address to complete registration. (Once in awhile, DynDNS will email asking you to confirm that you want to continue maintaining your computer's IP record, so make sure that address is one you check to maintain your service.)

Log into your new account. Go to the My Services area and, under My Hosts, click Add Host Services. There, click Add Dynamic DNS Host. DynDNS will autofill your current IP address. Choose a domain and type in a custom subdomain, which can be anything from `lifehacker.dyndns.org` or `john.is-a-geek.com` or `gtrapani.homeip.net`, as shown in Figure 5-5.

## Step 2: Set up Your Computer to Update DynDNS

Now that your computer is registered with DynDNS, each time its IP address changes, it will let DynDNS know. This can be done either with a free updater client software or through your router.

If your computer is connected directly to the Internet, download the DynDNS updater client for Mac or Windows, available at `https://dyndns.com/support/clients`. Install and enter your DynDNS information so that your computer can send its current IP address to the DynDNS database when it changes.

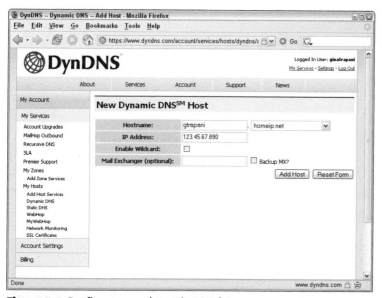

**Figure 5-5** Configure your dynamic DNS host.

If you are behind a router, you're in luck: most modern routers support dynamic DNS services. Consult your router's manual on how to set the dynamic DNS service provider (in this case, DynDNS.com), the host name (whatever you chose at DynDNS.com), and your DynDNS.com username and password.

### Step 3: Give Your New Domain a Spin

Enter your new domain name (like `http://gtrapani.homeip.net`) in your web browser's address bar, and your home web server's home page should appear. From here you can publicize or bookmark your server's new domain name no matter how often your IP address changes.

### DynDNS Options

DynDNS has a couple of options to consider.

- **Enable Wildcard** — Allows you to set up sub-subdomains. For example, `blog.johnsmith.mine.nu` can resolve to a weblog, while `jukebox.johnsmith.mine.nu` can resolve to a music directory. Virtual hosts must be configured for your Apache web server to display the right site when addressed by different subdomains. Get more information on setting up virtual hosts at `http://lifehackerbook.com/ch5/`.

- **Custom domain name** — Upgrade your account to use a custom domain name like `yourname.com`. Assign a domain name you've purchased to your home server for about 25 bucks a year (DynDNS's fee) plus the cost of the domain registration. See more info on Custom DNS at `https://dyndns.com/services/dns/custom`.

## Hack 38: Search the Web from Your Phone

Level....... **Easy**
Platform.... **A mobile phone with text messaging**
Cost ....... **Dependent on your mobile phone plan**

You're out and about town and you need to call a local cab, find out movie times at theaters nearby, or check the weather forecast. You don't need a laptop or even a tricked-out PDA to search the Web: you can do it directly from any phone that can send text messages. Major web search engines Google and Yahoo! — and a smaller new company, 4INFO — offer SMS search results to your cell phone on the spot.

Here's how it works: you send a text message that contains a short code —
like w 90210 or m 11215 — to the service address to get the weather or movie
times in a particular ZIP Code sent back to your mobile phone immediately.

**NOTE** For more on how to send a text message from your SMS-enabled
phone, see Hack 28, "Text Message Efficiently."

This hack covers the services and short codes you need to get information
sent to your cell on the go. The following table provides a list of common tasks,
the numbers to call, messages to send, and example replies.

| TASK | TO | MESSAGE | REPLY |
| --- | --- | --- | --- |
| Find a Wi-Fi hotspot | YAHOO (92466) <br> 4INFO (44636) | wifi 11215 <br> wifi 90210 | Naidre Miller Incorporated <br> 718-965-7585, <br> 382 7th Ave, Brooklyn, NY |
| Find a local business | GOOGL (46645) <br> YAHOO (92466) | taxi Marietta, OH <br> pizza 11215 | Ohio Valley Cab Co <br> 330 Franklin St # B <br> Marietta, OH 45750 <br> 740-374-8294 <br> 0.4 mi, SW |
| Check flight status for American Airlines flight 810 | 4INFO (44636) <br> GOOGL (46645) | AA 810 <br> AA 810 | American Airlines #810 <br> Landed <br><br> D:SAN <br><br> A:ORD-115p |
| Sports scores, stock prices, and horoscopes | GOOGL (46645) <br> 4INFO (44636) <br> 4INFO (44636) <br> 4INFO (44636) | yankees <br> mlb <br> yhoo <br> virgo | MLB <br> *Minnesota*: 6 <br> NY Yankees: 1 <br> Final, Sep 2 <br><br> Recent game: <br> Sep 1 <br> Minnesota: 1 <br> *NY Yankees*: 8 |
| Dictionary definitions | GOOGL (46645) <br> YAHOO (92466) | d philomath <br> d philomath | Glossary: * philomath: a lover of learning |
| Drink recipes | 4INFO (44636) | drink cosmo | Cosmo <br><br> 2 oz. Vodka 1 oz. Triple Sec 1 oz. Cranberry Juice Juice 1 Lime <br><br> Shake with ice and strain over ice into your favorite cocktail glass and serve. |

*(continued)*

*(continued)*

| TASK | TO | MESSAGE | REPLY |
|------|-----|---------|-------|
| Weather | GOOGL (46645)<br>4INFO (44636)<br>YAHOO (92466) | w asbury park, nj<br>w seattle,wa<br>w york, pa | Weather:<br>Asbury Park, NJ<br>66F,Overcast<br>Wind: E 5mph<br>Hum:73%<br>Sa:63-66F,Rain<br>Su:59-75F,Showers<br>M:60-77F,Mostly Sunny<br>Tu:63-76F,Showers |
| Movie times | Specific movies:<br>  GOOGL (46645)<br><br>Movies in a<br>ZIP code:<br>  4INFO (44636) | pirates 92037<br><br>m 11228 | * Pirates of the Caribbean:<br>Dead Man's ...<br>2hr 31min,PG-13,<br>Action/Adventure/Comedy,<br>3.4/5<br>AMC La Jolla 12<br>11:50am 3:00pm 6:45<br>10:00<br>8657 Villa La Jolla Dr.<br>La Jolla, CA<br>858-558-2262 x087 |
| Translations | GOOGL (46645) | translate<br>beautiful in<br>italian | Google Translation:<br>'beautiful' in English<br>means 'bello' in Italian. |
| Comparison<br>shopping | GOOGL (46645) | price buffy<br>season 7 dvd | Froogle:<br>* Buffy the Vampire<br>Slayer: Season 7 - DVD,<br>$34.99, Circuit City<br>* Season 7 [DVD],<br>$39.98, Newbury Comics<br>* Season 7 [DVD],<br>$56.98, The Electric Fetus |
| Look up location<br>of a ZIP or<br>area code | GOOGL (46645)<br>YAHOO (92466) | 718<br>92037 | 718: area code for<br>Brooklyn, Queens,<br>Staten Island, New York. |
| Driving directions | GOOGL (46645) | San Francisco ca<br>to Santa Cruz ca | (See text following<br>table.) |
| Currency<br>conversion | GOOGL (46645) | 5 usd in euro | Currency Conversion:<br>5 U.S. dollars =<br>3.89650873 Euro |

Driving directions messages are long and may come in multiple message installments. Here's the reply to the example message:

```
(1/3)Directions:
Distance: 72.5 mi (about 1 hour 9 mins) 9 steps.
1. Head SE from 11th St (0.3)
2. (L) at Folsom St (0.1)
3. (R) at 10th St (0.2)


(2/3)4. Bear (L) into US-101 S entry ramp to San Jose (35)
5. Take CA-85 S ramp to Cupertino/Santa Cruz (13)
6. Take CA-17 ramp to San Jose/Santa Cruz (0.2)
(3/3)7. Take CA-17 S ramp to Santa Cruz (23)
8. Bear (L) at Chestnut St (0.2)
9. (L) at Church St (0.1)
```

**TIP** Add GOOGL, YAHOO, and 4INFO to your phone's address book for quicker message addressing.

## Get Help

No one expects you to remember all of the search codes listed in the preceding table. Luckily each service provides a help command that returns a listing of all the possible commands it supports. Text GOOGL, 4INFO, or YAHOO the word `help` to get a command reference texted back to you. Save the message to your phone so that you can refer to it any time you want to SMS search.

## Test Drive SMS Search on the Web

All three mobile search services offer web-based demonstrations of SMS search via phone. Test drive text message search at the following locations on the Web:

- 4INFO — `http://4info.net/howto`
- Yahoo! SMS — `http://mobile.yahoo.com/search/smsdemo`
- Google SMS — `http://google.com/sms`

## Pre-Schedule Search Result SMS Alerts

4INFO offers a particularly useful feature: pre-scheduled automatic search results that come to your phone on a regular basis. For example, if you want to get a text message whenever the status of your FedEx package changes, you could set up alerts from 4INFO to do just that. Get fantasy sports team updates, your horoscope, stock prices, or scores texted to your phone automatically on a schedule. Visit `http://4info.net/waysto/waystoalert .jsp` to set it up.

# Hack 39: Optimize Your Laptop

Level....... **Easy**
Platforms ... **All**
Cost ....... **Free**

You just got a shiny new laptop to use on your commute to the office, on business trips and vacations, and at the coffee shop down the street. You'll be a productivity powerhouse! But hold your horses for a minute there, bucko.

More folks than ever are hitting the pavement with a notebook computer under one arm, but any road warrior can tell you that life with a lappie isn't always easy. This hack provides some hints and tips for extending the life of your laptop and easing the pain of the never-ending outlet and hotspot hunt.

## Extend Your Battery Life

Laptop productivity on the cold, cruel, and often electrical outlet-less road depends entirely on how much juice your battery's got left. Here are a few ways to increase the life of your laptop battery when there's no outlet in sight:

- **Dim the display.** The screen draws the most power from your laptop's battery. Dim it to the lowest setting you can stand to preserve battery life.

- **Turn off unnecessary processes.** If you don't need them, disable Wi-Fi and Bluetooth detection, spyware and virus scanning, and desktop search file indexing (like Google Desktop) while you're on battery power. Eject any CD, DVD, or other unneeded disk to prevent your computer from spinning or scanning for them for no reason.

- **Enable the power-saver profile.** Use the Microsoft Windows Max Battery Power Option (in Control Panel) and Mac OS X Energy Saver (in System Preferences), which sets your computer to use resources as sparingly as possible when battery life is most important.

- **Re-calibrate your battery's fuel gauge.** Do a deliberate full discharge of your laptop's lithium-ion battery every 30 charges or so, then recharge to calibrate the battery life gauge. If it isn't recalibrated, the gauge can read inaccurately and cut off your laptop's operation prematurely because it thinks the battery is depleted when it's not.

## Save Your Keyboard and Screen

There are crumbs at the coffee shop, sand at the beach house, and right now your fingers are covered in Doritos dust. Use a protective cover on your keyboard to prevent stray crumbs from getting into the cracks. It will do double duty by also protecting your laptop's screen from scratches caused by the keys when the top is closed. The iSkin (http://iskin.com) is a thin rubbery cover that fits Apple laptops (iBooks and PowerBooks) and stays on while you type.

Alternatively, you can cut a piece of rubberized shelf liner to fit inside your laptop when you close — sort of like the bologna in a sandwich. Some people also use a thin piece of cloth cut to fit the keyboard.

If your laptop keyboard is already a hideout for crumbs and pet hair, purchase a can of compressed air to blow out any debris stuck between the keys.

## Keep It Cool

After an hour or so of usage, a laptop computer can burn one's unprotected thighs and wrists. In fact, the Apple User Guide for the new MacBook Pro model states, "Do not leave the bottom of your MacBook Pro in contact with your lap or any surface of your body for extended periods. Prolonged contact with your body could cause discomfort and potentially a burn."

If laptop heat is a problem, get material that doesn't conduct heat well between your skin and your lappie, like a lap desk or your laptop sleeve. Long-sleeved shirts with big cuffs help on wrists when the top of your keyboard gets hot to the touch, too.

Additionally, overheating is one of the most common reasons for laptop hardware failure. Be aware of how hot your machine gets.

## Set Yourself up to Work Offline

You have 10 hours to kill on that transatlantic flight without Internet access. Or your favorite coffee shop's wireless network is down. It's not always easy or possible to get online with your laptop, so be as prepared to work offline as much as possible.

For example, don't depend entirely on web-based email on your laptop. The Mozilla Thunderbird email client (http://mozilla.org/products/thunderbird) is must-have software that enables you to download your email locally and work with it offline. Thunderbird 1.5 also has excellent SMTP server management so you can quickly switch which server you send your mail through when you *do* get online. Using a NetZero dialup account that requires you use smtp.netzero.net? Need to use the secure SMTP server at the office for work mail? No problem. You can set up multiple SMTP servers and associate them with different email accounts with Thunderbird.

## Secure Your Data

While you're out and about and on open wireless networks, make sure you've got a secure firewall installed on your laptop and that its settings are extremely restrictive. (See Hack 85, "Firewall Your Computer," for more on running a software firewall.)

Also, turn off folder sharing and any local servers you have running (like a web, FTP or VNC server) to keep others from peeking in on your data. Make sure your laptop's logins have strong passwords assigned.

Lastly, consider encrypting the data on your disk in case of theft; you can use a utility like Mac OS X's FileVault to do so.

> **NOTE** Hack 58, "Encrypt Your Data," and Hack 83, "Truly Delete Data from Your Hard Drive," provide practical methods of making your documents inaccessible to laptop thieves and snoops.

## Carry with Care

Your laptop spends a lot of time swinging over your shoulder, banging around on your back, bumping into the guy next to you on the subway, and sliding around on your car's back seat. Wrapping it up in that spare Linux tee-shirt and shoving it into your messenger bag full of gadgets probably isn't a good idea, either. Make sure your laptop is snug as a bug in a rug. Invest in a padded sleeve or bag made to carry laptops that'll protect it if your bag falls over or is accidentally kicked.

## Back Up

Portable computers deal with a lot more wear and tear than desktops, which increases the risk of hard drive failure. Make sure you back up the data on your laptop regularly — and often. Create a lappie docking station space at home where you can plug in to recharge the battery and hook up an external drive to back up your data.

## Pack Helpful Extras

If you have a CD-R or DVD-R drive in your lappie, keep a few spare blanks or a USB drive for easy backup on the road. A two- to three-prong electrical plug adaptor, an extra battery (charged), an Ethernet cable or phone cord, and an extra mouse might all be helpful additions to your portable arsenal.

## Find a Hotspot

A few web sites will find wireless hotspots while you're online and off, including:

- JiWire (`http://jiwire.com/search-hotspot-locations.htm`). Results include pay-for and free hotspots all over the country. JiWire also offers a downloadable Wi-Fi directory that's accessible when you're offline and looking for a hotspot, available for Windows and Mac OS X at `http://jiwire.com/hotspot-locator-frontdoor.htm`.

- ILoveFreeWifi (`http://ilovefreewifi.com`). Includes only free wireless hotspots for a select number of cities.

# Hack 40: Back up Data to Your iPod

Level....... **Easy**
Platforms ... **Windows XP and Vista, Mac OS X (with Apple's iPod music player)**
Cost ....... **Free**

Your iPod isn't just a music player — it's a giant external hard drive that can store any kind of digital data in addition to music. That makes it a convenient place to back up and store your important files. You can carry around your documents along with several dozen CDs' worth of music on that little white music player by enabling what's called disk mode.

Here's how:

1. Connect iPod to your computer, and open iTunes.

2. In the iTunes Preferences pane's iPod tab, select Enable Disk Use at the bottom of the page (see Figure 5-6).

   If you're an iPod Shuffle owner, you can use a storage allocation slider to set the amount of space you want to use for music, and the amount for other files.

3. Your iPod will appear in Windows Explorer or Mac Finder, as shown in Figure 5-7.

Now you can save and read files to your iPod as if it were any other disk drive. When you're finished, be sure to eject the iPod disk before disconnecting it from your computer. Then, you can connect the iPod to any other computer with disk mode enabled to access the files on it there, too.

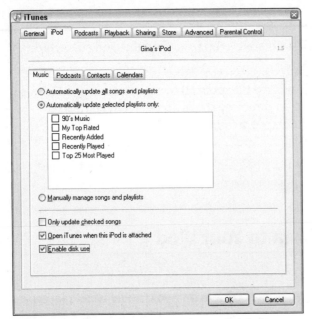

**Figure 5-6** Setting the iPod to work as a disk in iTunes.

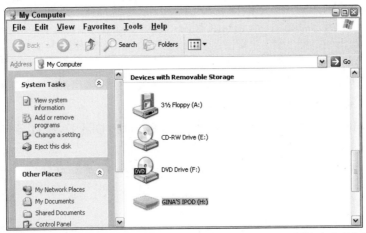

**Figure 5-7** The iPod named Gina's iPod appears as an additional disk in Windows Explorer.

## Encrypt Your Data

iPods are a hot commodity that get smaller and more easily lost — and more stolen — with each new model. You don't want your data to drive off in that cab without you or make it into the hands of a mugger, so do encrypt the data you store on it.

### Mac OS X

Using OS X's built-in Disk Utility, make an encrypted, password-protected disk image of your home directory, and then drag and drop it onto your iPod. If it's got enough space on it, the iPod can preclude a need to back up to an external hard drive because it is one. Be sure to exclude your music collection from the disk image; iTunes put that on your iPod once already.

### Windows

See Hack 58 for how to password-protect sensitive files you want to store on your iPod.

## Take Your Software with You on the iPod

Not only can you back up your data and take important documents with you on the iPod, you can also run software from it. Hack 34 points out several portable software applications that you can also copy and run from an iPod mounted as an external disk drive.

## Hack 41: Turn Your Cell Phone into a Modem

Level . . . . . . . **Medium**
Platform . . . . **Windows XP and Vista, Mac OS X (with mobile phone)**
Cost . . . . . . . **Dependent on your mobile phone plan**

You're stuck with the laptop in the land of no internet, but you have unlimited minutes or a great data plan on your cell phone. What to do? Plug that phone into your laptop, of course, and get surfing!

In this hack you transform your cell phone into a modem that gets you online even when there's not a Wi-Fi hotspot, landline, or Ethernet jack in sight.

## What You'll Need

You will need the following items for this hack:

- A PC or Mac.
- A mobile phone with built-in modem. Most newer mobile phones can be used as internet modems; check your model's user guide for more information.
- A cell phone plan that includes data transfer.

- ▪ (Optional) A phone to computer data cable (if your phone and computer don't both support Bluetooth).

## Configure Your Cell Phone as a Modem

Here's how to get online with your mobile phone:

1. Connect the phone to your laptop using a USB cord or through Bluetooth.

   If your phone didn't come with a cord, check Froogle (`http://froogle.com`) or Cellular Factory (`http://cellularfactory.com/data_cable.jsp`) for the right cable, which most likely will set you back between $10 and $40. If your phone's Bluetooth-enabled but your laptop is not, you can purchase a USB Bluetooth adapter for about $15.

2. If necessary, install the phone's modem driver.

   When the phone is connected, Windows knows you just plugged in something new and wants to know what it is, so the Add New Hardware wizard appears, eager to get the question settled. If you're lucky, your phone came with a handy CD that contains your drivers. Alternately, you can download them from your phone manufacturer's web site. Point the Add New Hardware wizard to the location of the drivers. When the drivers are installed, your cell phone modem will appear in the modems list in Control Panel.

   **NOTE** When I tried this with a Samsung A920 and a Nokia 6682, Mac OS X recognized the phone as a modem right away, without the need for additional drivers.

3. Connect to your ISP through the modem.

   You'll need connection software provided by your carrier. Again, this might be on that CD that came with your phone, or you can download it from your plan's web site (like Sprint PCS Connection Manager or Nokia PC Suite). When the software is installed, it's probably a matter of pressing the Go or Connect button and you'll be online using your provider's data network.

   If you don't have connection software or you're on a Mac (and the software isn't available for you), simply enter the phone number for your mobile phone's network in the modem's dial up properties. The Sprint data network can be reached by dialing #777 from a Sprint phone. Check with your provider for your details if you have a data plan. Alternatively, you can dial into an AOL or NetZero or Earthlink account as well for regular old 56 K dialup speeds.

If software isn't available, you can set up your connection manually. Here's how:

1. When the mobile is installed as a modem on Windows, select Start → Control Panel → Network Connections.

2. Click the Create a New Connection link in the left panel.

3. In the New Connection wizard:

   Choose Connect to the Internet, and click Next.

   Select Set Up My Connection Manually, and click Next.

   Choose Connect Using a Dial-Up Modem, and click Next.

   Check off your newly installed cell phone modem (see Figure 5-8).

4. Click Next. Then enter your ISP's access number, username, and password. Consult with your cellular provider to obtain these details.

5. Click Finish.

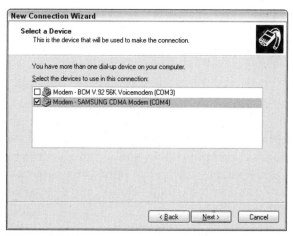

**Figure 5-8** Select your cell phone modem in the dialup connection wizard.

## Keep an Eye on the Meter

Some data plans provide connections that don't come near broadband speeds but beat out classic 56 K dialup any day — like the Sprint Power Vision network, which reaches speeds of about 230 K.

> **WARNING** Check your mobile plan to avoid insane charges for downloading data. If you are paying per megabytes of data transferred, the cost can quickly become exorbitant. Some wireless service providers quote in terms of cents per kilobyte of data, but remember, a seemingly low 2¢ per kilobytes equates to a hefty $20 per megabyte. Spend any amount of time surfing the internet or downloading large emails with attachments, and in no time you'll have to pay for multiple megabytes of data.

Before you go disconnecting your home broadband connection in favor of using your cell phone modem all the time, be warned: cell connection speeds will vary based on your location, and will slow you down when sending large attachments or downloading bigger files. For casual surfing and email-checking on the road, however, your cell phone can provide all the connectivity you need. (See more ways to optimize your cell connection in Hack 32, "Speed up Web Pages on a Slow Connection.")

# Hack 42: Use Gmail as an Internet Hard Drive

Level. . . . . . . **Easy**
Platform. . . . **Windows XP and Vista, Mac OS X (with Gmail)**
Cost . . . . . . . **Free**

Google's web-based email service, Gmail (`http://gmail.google.com`), offers more free storage space for messages and attachments than any other service does (2.6 GB as of this writing — and rising). An easy way to make files available from any internet-connected computer is to simply email them to yourself (at Gmail or any other web-based email service.) But a free software application makes keeping your files up in the Gmail "cloud" and accessible from any web browser even easier.

## Windows: Gmail Drive Extension

The Gmail Drive shell extension accesses your Gmail web-based email account as if it were another hard drive on your computer.

Download the Gmail Drive shell extension, available at `http://viksoe` `.dk/code/gmail.htm`. Extract the files and run `setup.exe`. The shell extension will add a disk called Gmail Drive to your computer (see Figure 5-9).

To access files on the Gmail Drive, double-click it. You will get a prompt for your Gmail username and password, as shown in Figure 5-10.

After you've logged on to your Gmail account, you can create folders and drag and drop files to the Gmail Drive as if it's any other hard drive. The files are whisked away to your Gmail account and appear as attachments to new email messages from yourself in your inbox, as shown in Figure 5-11.

**Figure 5-9** The Gmail Drive appears as an additional disk in My Computer.

**Figure 5-10** Gmail Drive login prompt.

**Figure 5-11** Gmail Drive shell extension files appear in your Gmail inbox as new messages with attachments.

The Gmail Drive extension (and Gmail itself) doesn't support message attachments 10 MB in size or greater, so this works well only for photos, Microsoft Office documents, and other small to medium-sized files. In an attempt to stop email viruses, Gmail also does not allow attachments with an .exe extension, so if you save an executable file to your Gmail Drive — say, setup.exe — it appears in your Gmail account as setup.exe_renamed. To use an executable file that's been renamed as such for storage in Gmail, download it and change the name back to its original (by removing the _renamed from the file extension).

> **TIP** Configure a Gmail filter that archives and labels incoming Gmail Drive files. To do so, set the search criteria to any messages with the GMAILFS:/ in the subject line. See Hack 48, "Master Message Search," for more information.

## Mac OS X: gDisk

Mac users can find similar functionality in the free software gDisk, available for download at http://gdisk.sourceforge.net. Create folders inside the gDisk interface that map to Gmail labels. For example, if you create a *photos* label in gDisk, the files stored there automatically appear in *photos.gDisk* label in your Gmail inbox. Like the Gmail Drive extension, gDisk is slower to copy files, but unlike the shell extension, it is not integrated into the OS X Finder.

For more on using email as data backup, check out Hack 22, "Automatically Email Yourself File Backups."

# Control Your Email

An enormous Doberman straining against his leash turns a corner, his petite owner following behind with exaggerated steps. A neighbor calls out the inevitable joke: "Are you walking the dog or is the dog walking you?"

The next time you let a new email message interrupt your work, or you can't find your way out of an overstuffed inbox, think of the dog and his walker. Are you controlling your email or is your email controlling you?

Email has become an indispensable method of communication in the modern office. As more business is done around the world and telecommuting, outsourcing, and collaboration over vast distances become even more common, about 150 *billion* email messages are sent daily. But it's not just for long-distance communication anymore. Email is so commonplace that many of those messages are between people who work a few feet away from one another.

Unlike paper correspondence, in which the onus is on the sender to create, print, and mail a letter, the ease with which an email can be sent puts the burden on the recipient. Suddenly it's up to you to read and respond to enormous amounts of email every day — but to what effect on your work and your sanity?

It's easy to let the email take the reins of your workday. All you have to do is leave your email software open while you perform your regular job functions. Each time it notifies you of a new message, stop what you're doing immediately, no matter how important it is or how involved you are, and switch to your inbox. Scan the new message. If it's something you feel like dealing with, do it. If not, switch back to the task at hand. Try to remember where you were before that email arrived. At the end of the day, wonder how all those read messages accumulated in your inbox, what you're supposed to do about them again, and where the day went.

There is a better way.

You can process your email in prescheduled increments throughout the day, send out messages that are most likely to elicit the response you're looking for, and keep your inbox free of a festering pile of unfulfilled obligations. Managing the daily onslaught of information, messages, and other interruptions vying for your attention is a skill lifehackers hone over time. This chapter provides practical strategies for getting your email under control and keeping it there.

# Hack 43: Craft Effective Messages

Level . . . . . . . **Easy**
Platform . . . . **All**
Cost . . . . . . . **Free**

The old computer science adage, Garbage in, garbage out (GIGO) means that if you give a computer the wrong input, it returns useless output. Humans are a lot more forgiving than computers, but in many ways GIGO applies to email correspondence as well. The clearer your email messages are, the more likely you are to get the result you want in a more timely fashion — whether it's a response, a completed task, or an informed recipient.

A recent survey of workers at big companies reveals that employees waste anywhere from half an hour to three hours a day processing poorly written messages.[1] In an ineffective email message, the sender's expectations aren't clear, the most important information is hard to find, and the body of the message is too long and difficult to read.

You spend at least a couple of hours a day reading and responding to email. How much of that time could be saved if all the messages you sent and received were to the point and free of any unnecessary information?

This hack covers ways to get the most out of email you send with the least amount of time, energy, and work.

## Composing New Messages

Keep in mind the following simple strategies for whittling the messages you send down to their most effective state.

### Determine Your Purpose

Every email message has a very specific purpose. Either you are conveying information or requesting action from the recipient. Before you click that

Compose button, know what you expect to get out of the exchange. If you don't know your message's purpose, don't write it.

If you need to flesh out your thoughts by writing, send the email to *yourself.* Then follow up with anything you need to ask or tell others.

### Use an Informative Subject Line

First impressions are pretty important in a world where two dozen different things are already competing for your email recipient's eyeballs and attention. The first thing your correspondent will see is the subject line of your message. Boil that line down to a few words that convey your message's purpose. Think of yourself as a newspaper headline writer, tasked with telling the whole story in just a few words to grab the reader's attention.

Remember that your recipient will use subject lines to scan and sort her inbox, to track conversations, to prioritize tasks, and to absorb information at a glance, so make your subject lines amenable to that.

Here are some examples of bad subject lines:

```
Subject: Hi!
Subject: Just wanted to tell you...
Subject: Can you do me a favor?
Subject: IMPORTANT!!!
```

None of those subject lines gets specific about the content of the message. Yes, this message may be IMPORTANT!!!, but what is it regarding? A "favor" might range from lending the sender your stapler to donating your kidney. One might want to "just tell you" a lot of things, from "I like your tie" to "I hear you're getting fired tomorrow."

Some examples of good subject lines include:

```
Subject: Tomorrow's managerial meeting agenda
Subject: Questions about Monday's presentation
Subject: QUESTION: May I quote you in an article?
Subject: FYI: Out of the office Thursday
Subject: REQUEST: Pls comment on the proposed redesign layout
Subject: IMPORTANT: Must fax contract before 3PM today
```

Notice the optional use of prefixes (FYI, Request, Important) that convey the message type before addressing the content in the rest of the line. You can even shorten them to Q: for Question, REQ: for Request, and IMPT: for Important.

If your message contains several requests for action or info related to different topics entirely, break it down into separate messages. This will help get each point addressed in specific, relevant conversation threads.

## Be Succinct

The purpose of writing an email isn't to hear yourself think; it's to elicit the desired response from the recipient.

The shorter your email, the more likely it is to be read and your request filled. No one wants to muddle through a long, wordy missive picking out the questions, task requests, and important points. Respect your recipient's time and expect that your message will be skimmed quickly. Get right to the point and hit send. Everyone appreciates brevity.

> **NOTE** Lots of email-savvy folks send subject-only messages to convey very short bits of information. For example, a blank email with the subject line,
> `FYI: Out of the office for the rest of the afternoon [EOM]`
> **(where EOM stands for End Of Message) says all that it has to.**

## Put Your Messages on a Diet

If you're sending messages to people outside your corporate network, where download speeds and email software may differ from your environment, eliminate unnecessary attachments and HTML elements that may weigh down the message. Here are some tips:

- If you're attaching photos, be sure to rotate them to the correct orientation and resize them. (See Hack 29, "Batch Resize Photos," for a quick way to make your photos better suited for email.)

- Don't assume everyone has HTML email enabled; lots of folks (including myself) disable HTML email to avoid marketing trackers and long message downloads.

- Don't assume that your message looks the same way in your recipient's software as it did in yours; all email applications format messages differently.

- In some email software, a long web site address that wraps in the message may be unclickable. Use a service like TinyURL (`http://tinyurl.com`) to shorten that address before you send your message.

## Facilitate a Complete Response

A few line breaks can go a long way in a message that contains a set of questions, important points, or task requests. Use line breaks and bullet points liberally to make your message easy to read and respond to.

For example, the following message intersperses information with questions in one continuous paragraph:

```
Hi Becky,

Got your message about Tuesday, thanks! What's the conference room
number? Turns out I'm going to drive instead of take the train. Will I
need a parking pass? Also, I have the Powerpoint presentation on my
laptop. Is there a projector available I can hook it up to, or should I
bring my own?
```

It would be a lot easier for Becky to see the bits of the message that require a response if it were formatted this way:

```
Hi Becky,
I'm all set for Tuesday's meeting. A few questions for you:
* What is the conference room number?
* If I drive, how should I get a parking pass?
* Is there a projector available that will work with my laptop?
```

The second version clearly delineates what questions the sender needs answered, and makes responding inline to the questions a lot easier on Becky.

## Make It Clear Why Everyone Got the Message

Messages that have several recipients in the To: field can spread accountability too thin across a group of people. If everything thinks, "Someone else will take care of it," nothing will get done. As a sender, include multiple recipients on a message only when you absolutely must — and then make it clear in the body of the message why everyone is receiving it. For example:

```
To: Victor Downs, Lorrie Crenshaw, Kyran Deck
Subject: Staff luncheon confirmed for June 18th

We reserved a room for 40 at Lottie's for 1PM on Tuesday, June 18th.

LC: FYI, we'll have to cancel our weekly meeting.
KD: Please send out staff-wide email invite with directions and shuttle
information by the 4th.
VD: Will the shuttle be available for transportation that day? Please
let Kyran know.
```

## Don't Forget the Attachment

It's too easy to dash off a message saying "the file's attached" and then never actually attach the file. The Bells and Whistles plug-in for Microsoft Outlook (free trial, $20 a license, available at `http://emailaddressmanager.com/outlook-bells.html`) notifies you when you try to send a message with the word "attached" or "attachment" in it and no file is attached. The Gmail Attachment reminder Greasemonkey user script, available at `http://userscripts.org/scripts/show/2419`, does the same for Gmail users.

## Replying to a Message

Nothing's worse than sending an email with three questions and getting back the answer to only one. To avoid unnecessary email back and forth, answer all the messages that require a response as thoroughly as possible.

### Respond to Individual Points Inline

For email that includes lists of questions or response-worthy points, press the reply button and include your comments inline — that is, interspersed within the original email — to ensure you address every point. For example, Becky might reply to the earlier message this way:

```
Hi Rich,

Rich Jones wrote:
> * What is the conference room number?
It's room 316 in B Building.

> * If I drive, how should I get a parking pass?
Park in the west lot and give your name at the booth. The guard will
issue you a guest pass there.

> * Is there a projector available that will work with my laptop?
Yes there is - a member of our tech team will be there to help set you up.

See you then,
Becky
```

### Task Requests

When you receive a request for action, don't wait to respond until you're ready to complete the action. Review the request and respond with any questions you need answered before you can get it done right away.

For example, if you receive the following email:

```
Subject: REQUEST: Please comment on the redesign layout proposal

Let us know what you think about the new font choice and background color.
```

You might respond right away:

```
Subject: Re: REQUEST: Please comment on the redesign layout proposal

Tamara Smith wrote:
> Let us know what you think about the new font choice and background
color.

Can you send me a link to the new proposal?

Also, when is the deadline for final comments?
```

## Lead by Example

You may be a master at writing effective email, but communication's a two-way street. Lead by example when you receive poorly written messages. When you respond, edit an email's unspecific subject line so that further correspondence on the topic is easily identifiable in your inbox. Break up someone's run-on message into chunks and respond inline. If the purpose of the message is unclear to you, respond with the question: "What's my next step regarding this?" If someone sends you a rambling, five-screen description, reply briefly: "Sounds good." These strategies train others to not expect long messages from you in real time and to craft better subject lines and task requests.

## Don't Respond in Real Time

Although some folks may live and die by the "Bing! You have new mail!" of their email client, email was never meant to be instant, real-time communication, and shouldn't be used as such. If someone needs to engage you at this moment in time, he can call. Otherwise, create the expectation that email to you will not get answered on the spot.

Even if you are checking your email real time (and you shouldn't be unless you don't want to get anything else done), don't respond to non-emergency messages right away, especially from co-workers. It sets an impossible expectation for the future. Settle on a reasonable maximum response time goal; for example, commit to responding to email within 4 to 6 hours on business days, at most within 24 to 48 hours.

## Get Outside the Inbox

Tone-deafness is the biggest pitfall of textual communication — especially quick, off-the-cuff methods like email. The sender's facial expression or tone of voice doesn't come inside her email messages, and feelings can be hurt, recipients can be offended, and messages can be taken the wrong way when tone doesn't come across in email missives. In fact, the American Psychological Association published a study that shows emailers overestimate their ability to convey their intended tone by about 25 percent when they press the Send button, as well as their ability to correctly interpret the tone of messages others send to them.[2]

Some issues are too complex or sensitive to be communicated via email. Know when it's appropriate to just pick up the phone and call someone or visit in person to convey a message and answer questions on the spot.

### Know When Not to Say a Thing

Even though email correspondence *seems* private, it's not. Copies of every message you've ever sent out were made on servers across the Internet, and business email is saved on your employer's server as well. A recent study shows that about one-third of large companies in the United States actively monitor their employees' email.[3] This number will only go up as liabilities and privacy issues related to email increase.

Keeping that in mind, never write email when you're upset, emotional, stressed, tired, hungry, drunk, or otherwise impaired. After an email is sent there's no taking it back, and every email you send is written documentation that can be used in court or to support a case for promotion or firing. Never say something in an email that you wouldn't publish in a company newsletter, say to a newspaper reporter, or announce at a meeting.

If an email upsets you or you're feeling a rant coming on, write it out in a text file, save it, and give yourself time to think things over. Later, go back and edit or start all over on a more composed note.

## Hack 44: Highlight Messages Sent Directly to You

Level . . . . . . . **Easy**
Platform . . . . **Windows XP and Vista (Microsoft Outlook)**
Cost . . . . . . . **Free**

When faced with an inbox full of new, unread email, it's nearly impossible to determine which messages need to be dealt with right away, and which can be put off until later. You get CC'ed on memos and included on large mailing lists or receive company- or department-wide notifications. When you're pressed for time, those types of messages are all good candidates for later reading. But what about those few messages addressed *only* to you?

Email overload expert Itzy Sabo says[4]:

*Such messages are most likely to be more important than the rest of the stuff that fills up my inbox, because:*

\*    *They have not been sent to a bunch of people, but specifically to me.*

\*    *They are therefore more likely to relate to my area of responsibility.*

\*    *They are also more likely to require action.*

\*    *If I don't answer, nobody else will.*

## Color Me Blue

Using Microsoft Outlook, you can make those important to-me-only messages jump out of your inbox with one simple setting. Select Tools → Organize, and in the Using Colors section, click the Turn On button next to Show Messages Sent Only To Me In Blue, as shown in Figure 6-1.

Then, blue messages will pop in your inbox during email processing sessions, and you'll do well to check on those first. (Of course, you can use the color drop-down to select a different color for your only-to-me emails if you want.)

## All Other Email Programs: Create a Not-to-Me Filter

Most modern email applications have a rule or filter feature that matches incoming messages against criteria you define and performs some action. Create a not-to-me filter that de-highlights lower priority messages or even moves them to an Inbox - Low Priority folder.

(See Hack 12, "Filter Low-Priority Email Messages," for more on using email filters to clean out and prioritize your inbox.)

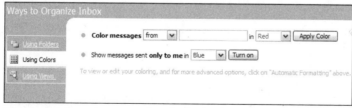

**Figure 6-1** Organize your Inbox by highlighting messages addressed only to you.

# Hack 45: Use Disposable Email Addresses

Level . . . . . . . **Easy**
Platform . . . . **All**
Cost . . . . . . . **Free**

Much of the junk email you receive is from spammers who bought or scraped your email address from a web site where you registered for membership. Most registration-based web sites require that you use a legitimate email address; often you have to retrieve an email from that address's inbox to complete registration.

If you hate the idea of giving your email address to any web site that asks for it, and you want to protect your email address from junk mail and spam, use a disposable email address instead.

## Web-Based Public Email Addresses

Several services, such as Mailinator (http://mailinator.com) offer free, public, disposable email addresses. Choose any email name at the mailinator .com domain — like goaheadspamme@mailinator.com or joe@mailinator.com — and use it to register at a web site. Then, visit Mailinator.com to check the public inbox, which doesn't require a password.

**CAUTION** Remember, anyone can check the joe@mailinator.com inbox, so make sure nothing too personal winds up there!

Dodgeit (http://dodgeit.com) offers a service similar to Mailinator, with the capability to check all public email accounts at dodgeit.com via RSS. If you use the Bloglines (http://bloglines.com) RSS reader, you can also create unlimited disposable email addresses there to receive newsletters, mailing list messages, and other low-priority mail inside your newsreader.

For more on RSS, see Hack 69, "Subscribe to Web Sites with RSS."

## Multi-Domain Email Addresses

If you host your email at your own web site domain (see more on in Hack 49, "Future-Proof Your Email Address" later in this chapter), you have a limitless supply of email names available to you; really anything @yourdomain.com. Each time you sign up for a web site, use a unique name that you can block or filter later if you start receiving spam.

For example, if my real email address is gina@example.com, I might register at Amazon.com using the amazon.com@example.com email address, which also comes to me. If Amazon sells my address and I start receiving spam at amazon.com@example.com, I can block further email to that address and I'll know it was Amazon who sold me out. (This is just an example. In all the years I've been a registered Amazon.com user, I've never received spam at the unique address I use there.)

**NOTE** For more on how to avoid signing up for a web site at all, see Hack 31, "Bypass Free Site Registration with BugMeNot."

# Hack 46: Decrease Your Email Response Time

Level....... **Easy**
Platform.... **All**
Cost ....... **Free**

Responding to your email in a timely, professional manner is one of the best things you can do for your career. But no one emerges from the womb with a natural talent for parrying a constant stream of new messages popping up in front of your face all day long. Email responsiveness is an acquired skill — the one that just may differentiate you from everyone else in the world overwhelmed by an overloaded inbox.

Michael Hyatt, CEO of Thomas Nelson Publishers, agrees. He said: "The truth is, you are building your reputation — your brand — one response at a time. People are shaping their view of you by how you respond to them. If you are slow, they assume you are incompetent and over your head. If you respond quickly, they assume you are competent and on top of your work. Their perception, whether you realize it or not, will determine how fast your career advances and how high you go. You can't afford to be unresponsive. It is a career-killer."[5]

While it's not easy to maintain a high rate of email responsiveness in an age of hundreds of new messages per day, you can increase your rate without becoming a slave to your inbox. This hack provides strategies for responding to your email in a timely fashion without killing your entire workday.

## Respond in Batches

Your inbox dictates the ebb and flow of your work if it interrupts you every time it has a new message. Don't let it.

The explosion of email communication and proliferation of email-enabled PDAs has led a lot of Americans to non-stop inbox monitoring. In fact, 41 percent of respondents in a recent survey said they checked their email in the morning before going to work. More than 25 percent said they had never gone more than a few days without checking email, 60 percent said they check it on vacation, and 4 percent look at email in the bathroom.[6]

The reality is that checking email adds up to a whole lot of time, much of it wasted. The world will not end if an email sits in your inbox for a few hours.

Schedule two or three "meetings" with your inbox each day at predetermined times to process email. If your job requires that you keep your email program running at all times, set it to check for new messages every few hours instead of every five minutes. (For more on protecting your sanity from the insidiousness of constant email checking, see Hack 9, "Reduce Email Interruptions.")

## The One-Minute Rule

When you've begun an email processing session, start at the oldest message you received and work up. Follow the one-minute rule: if a message will take less than one minute to process and respond to, do it on the spot. One minute doesn't sound like a lot of time, but in reality a whole lot can happen in 60 seconds. Dash off quick answers to questions, follow up with questions on requests, and knock down any "Sounds good" and "Let's discuss on the phone; when's a good time" and "Received the attachment, thanks" type of messages. If you think that a message needs a lengthy, complicated response, consider taking it offline and making a phone call instead.

Most of your new messages will fall under the "can respond in less than a minute" umbrella, so go ahead and do it.

## Respond to Task Requests — Even When It's Not Done

If someone asks you to complete a project or task, it's natural to think, "I don't have time to deal with this right now, so I'll just leave it in my inbox to handle later." There the message atrophies for weeks, and a month later, you've never gotten back to the sender and the task still isn't done. That's the quickest route to Irresponsibleville.

When asked to do something via email, respond right away with:

Questions you may need answered to get started.

A request for the task completion deadline.

How busy you are and when you think you'll be able to get started.

The next time the requester can expect to hear from you regarding the task.

An immediate response that says, "I'm booked solid for the next three months. What's your deadline? Drop me a note in September if you're still interested in having me work on this" — effectively, "no can do" — is much more professional and appreciated than no response at all or a three-week delay.

## Don't Leave It in Your Inbox

Touch a message once in your inbox and commit yourself to taking it to the next step: whether that's dashing off a reply, or moving it into your queue for a next step. But whatever you do, don't scan messages in your inbox and just leave them there to scan again later. It's a waste of time to repeat the same action again (and again).

## Hack 47: Empty Your Inbox (and Keep It Empty)

Level....... **Easy**
Platforms ... **All**
Cost ....... **Free**

When you can consistently reduce the contents of your inbox to zero messages, you've reached the ultimate level of email control. Think of your inbox as a temporary holding pen for unprocessed email. An unprocessed message is one you haven't decided what to do about yet. Clearing the inbox imbues you with a sense of control and the feeling that you have no unfulfilled email obligations that you haven't put into motion using a trusted filing system.

However, folders alone aren't the answer. You don't want to waste time dragging and dropping messages into a complex filing system — you want to make a quick decision and move forward. The more folders you create over time in your email application — either by sender, topic, urgency level, task — the less useful your email organizing system becomes. This hack introduces a simple, three-folder system to keep your inbox clear and ensure that every single message you receive is both findable and actionable without cluttering your inbox.

### The Trusted Trio

The three folders you need to keep your inbox empty and your messages in process are, as shown in Figure 6-2, Action, Archive, and Hold.

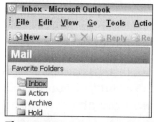

**Figure 6-2** Action, Archive, and Hold folders clear your inbox.

### The Action Folder

Messages in your Action folder represent tasks you must complete, whether that's a response that will take more than one minute to write or another type of action. Each of these messages represents an item on your to-do list.

Examples of emails for this folder include a request to update the web site or a message from a long-lost high school friend who you haven't spoken to in years that you want to spend some time updating on your life.

Review this folder on a regular basis and clear it out as tasks are completed.

### The Archive Folder

The Archive folder is your long-term email reference library. It's where you place all the messages that contain information you may want to retrieve at some point in the long-term future, including any completed threads, completed requests, memos you've read, questions you answered, and completed project email. Basically, any email that's closed but that you may to refer to at some point in the future belongs in Archive.

It may seem scary to those who enjoy organizing information into specifically named folders to dump everything directly into Archive. However, the archive is completely searchable, and any message you place there will be retrievable using advanced search operators. For more on plucking messages out of Archive (without a complicated folder scheme), see the next hack, "Master Message Search."

### The Hold Folder

The Hold folder is a temporary holding pen for important messages you'll need quick access to within the next few days. If you're waiting on someone else to get back to you with crucial information, or you're maintaining a thread about a time-sensitive topic, keep it in the Hold folder.

Examples of messages that would go in Hold are a FedEx confirmation number for a delivery that's on its way, or a message from a co-worker that says, "I'll get back to you Tuesday re: The Big Project."

This folder should be reviewed on a regular basis and cleared out as the message contents are no longer needed (such as when that FedEx package gets delivered or when your co-worker gets back to you).

## What to Do

Now that your three folders are in place, it's time to empty your inbox. Whether you're starting with an overstuffed inbox with months' worth of messages or the two dozen that arrived since your last processing session, the method is the same. Beginning with the oldest email in your inbox, open the message, and:

- If it requires a response that will take less than one minute to write, respond on the spot, then move the message to Archive.

- If it requires an action on your part that will take more than one minute to complete, move it to the Action folder.

- If it's a piece of information you'll need within the next few days, move it to Hold.

- If it's an informational message you may want to refer to later, move it to Archive.

- If it's of no use, delete it.

Wash, rinse, and repeat for every message in your inbox until it is completely empty.

**NOTE** This exact folder scheme may not work for everyone, but it's a good start on the road to a simple, well-defined processing system. If you tweak and modify this method, just remember: the fewer folders, the less thought has to go into dealing with each individual message.

## Keep It Empty

Once you've got your inbox down to zero messages, keeping it that way is a matter of repeating the preceding process a few times a day. Schedule times for processing email into your schedule — like once first thing in the morning, once after lunch, and once in the late afternoon. Train yourself to follow the golden rule:

*Never leave a read email in your inbox.*

Commit to making a decision about the fate of every message you read in the inbox on the spot. Whether you respond immediately or file it in Action, Archive, or Hold, never leave a message in your inbox; you want that space for future incoming mail — because there will always be more.

## The Catch

Now, just because you have all your messages filed neatly away in Action, Archive, and Hold doesn't mean you're free and clear. The hard part of this system is consistently reviewing Action and Hold and completing the "open loops" stowed away there. To keep yourself from getting lulled into a total sense of completeness, mark all the messages in Hold and Action as unread so you can keep an eye on the number of outstanding items.

> **NOTE** Special thanks to Merlin Mann, author of the Inbox Zero series (`http://inboxzero.com`) and "The Inbox Makeover" which appeared in MacWorld (available at (`http://macworld.com/2005/04/features/tipsinbox/index.php`), which greatly influenced the methods outlined in this hack.

## Hack 48: Master Message Search

Level. . . . . . . **Easy**
Platforms . . . **All**
Cost . . . . . . . **Free**

Paper is the paradigm that we still use to understand digital documents. Manila folder icons, for example, represent digital folders when, in reality, those so-called folders are just pointers to data on a disk that never actually changes location.

Transitioning from a paper-based world into a digital document scenario, filing digital documents like email messages (represented by tiny envelopes) is a natural thing to do. But your email messages are already indexed and searchable without the work of dragging and dropping them into these illusory folders.

In the previous hack, you created an archive of closed messages to reference later without any subfolders in it. As long as you know what it is you need, a well-crafted query can pluck out the message you're looking for immediately — without traversing a six-folder-deep hierarchy.

In the physical world you can't throw years' worth of letters, cards, and memos into a drawer and then pick out the one Tom sent you about that fabulous rental he got in Key West back in 2003 in seconds. However, that is absolutely possible with an email folder containing thousands of messages.

### Search Criteria

Most email programs have message search built right in. Not surprisingly, Google's web-based email product Gmail has the strongest searching capabilities on the market and undoubtedly other email software makers will follow suit in the near future.

For example, your search for Tom's message might look like Figure 6-3 in Gmail's Search Options area:

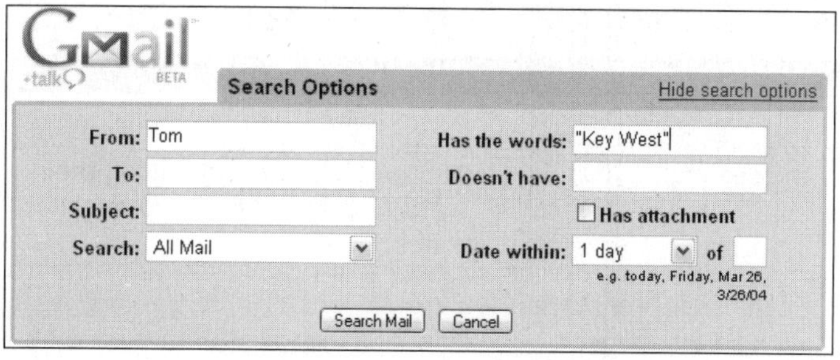

**Figure 6-3** Searching for a message from Tom that contains the phrase "Key West."

You can do even more complex queries with Gmail's advanced search operators. For example, if you wanted to search for messages from Tom or Kelly that have the phrase "Key West" or the word "rental," use the `or` operator (also signified with the pipe |). Like Google web search, enclose phrases in quotes. The entire query can go into one search box also. It would look like this:

```
From:(Tom | Kelly) ("Key West" OR rental)
```

You can exclude terms as well. For instance, if you wanted to see all the messages from people at a specific company (at the example.com domain) except for Joe, you could search for:

```
From:(*@example.com AND -joe@example.com).
```

A summary of all of Gmail's searching operators is available at `http://mail.google.com/support/bin/answer.py?answer=7190`. Here's a sampling:

| OPERATOR | DEFINITION | EXAMPLE |
|---|---|---|
| `from:` | Specifies the sender. | `from:Amy` returns messages from Amy. |
| `to:` | Specifies the recipient. | `to:Jonah` returns messages addressed to Jonah. |
| `subject:` | Searches the subject line. | `subject:lunch` returns: Messages with the word *lunch* in the subject line. |
| OR | Searches for messages with either term A or term B. OR must be in all caps. A pipe (\|) works in place of OR. | `from:Jonah OR from:Amy` returns messages from Jonah or from Amy. |

*(continued)*

*(continued)*

| OPERATOR | DEFINITION | EXAMPLE |
|---|---|---|
| `-` | Excludes a term from the search. | `Java -coffee` returns messages containing the word *Java* but not the word *coffee*. |
| `has:attachment` | Searches for messages with an attachment. | `from:david has:attachment` returns messages from David that contain any kind of file attachment. |
| `filename:` | Searches for an attachment by name or type. | `filename:poem.doc` returns messages with an attachment named `poem.doc`. |
|  |  | `filename:jpg` returns messages with JPEG photo attachments. |
| `" "` | Searches for an exact phrase (capitalization isn't considered). | `"Nice job"` returns messages that contain the phrase *nice job* or *Nice job*. |
|  |  | `subject:"dinner and a movie"` returns messages containing the phrase *dinner and a movie* in the subject. |
| `()` | Groups words; used to specify terms that shouldn't be excluded. | `from:amy (dinner OR movie)` returns messages from Amy that contain either the word *dinner* or the word *movie*. |
|  |  | `subject:(dinner movie)` Returns Messages in which the subject contains both the word *dinner* and the word *movie*. Note that AND is implied. |
| `after:` `before:` | Search for messages sent after or before a certain date (date must be in `yyyy/mm/dd` format). | `after:2001/09/11` returns messages sent after September 11, 2001. |
|  |  | `before:1997/05/17` returns messages sent before May 17, 1997. |
|  |  | `after:2006/06/01 AND before:2006/06/03` returns messages sent after June 1, 2006, but before June 3, 2006. (Or messages sent on June 2, 2006.) |

Using these operators, a well-crafted query can turn up messages with specific attributes from your Archive folder — or entire email archive — in seconds.

**NOTE** To search your Outlook or Thunderbird email messages using operators like Gmail's, consider using the free Google Desktop Search (`http://desktop.google.com`) to do so. See also Hack 53, "Instantly Retrieve Files from Your Hard Drive" for more on using Google Desktop Search.

## Saved Search Folders

Another efficient digital filing technique is saving a search as a folder. No more dragging and dropping messages by hand; you can create a virtual email folder defined by search criteria.

For example, during the writing of this book I created a `Book` email folder that contained all the correspondence between myself and my publishing company, Wiley.

To do this in Thunderbird, execute a search from the upper-right corner search box. Then, from the drop-down choose Save Search as a Folder and edit your criteria. In my case, any message where the sender or recipient contained the word `wiley.com` or my agent's email address should be included in my `Book` folder. The query is defined in Thunderbird as shown in Figure 6-4.

Then, the Book folder appears in my folder list as usual, except a small magnifying glass over the folder icon indicates it's a saved search. Click on the folder and Thunderbird updates its contents with all the messages that match the search.

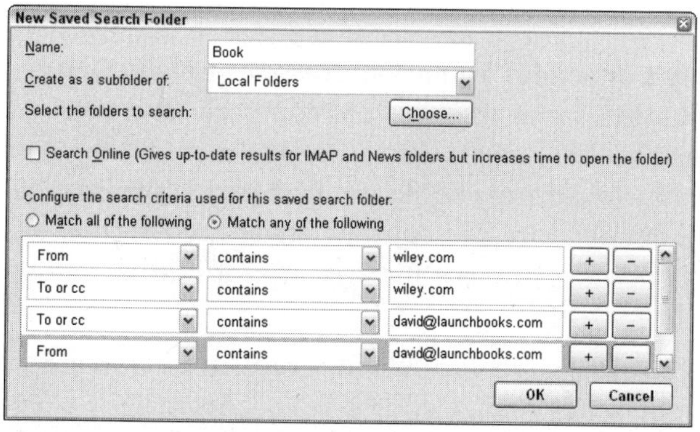

**Figure 6-4** Creating a folder from saved search criteria.

The advantage of saved search folders is that one email can live in any number of saved searches, as long as it fulfills the criteria. Folder deletion just removes the query — not the messages themselves.

After this book is completed, I'll delete that folder — but all the messages will remain in their original locations.

# Hack 49: Future-Proof Your Email Address

Level....... **Easy**
Platform.... **All**
Cost ....... **Free**

You've probably got as many email addresses as you do pairs of socks, but you don't want to change them as often. In fact, switching your primary email address can be a big inconvenience that leads to missed messages and lost relationships. You give your email address to countless friends, relatives, and web services, and publish it on mailing lists, web sites, and documents forever cached in search engine indexes. But if your email address is tied to a former ISP, the company you used to work for, the university you attended, or the embarrassing handle you chose in college, switching to a new address can become a necessity.

If you're thinking about changing your primary email address, chances are you've got lots of choices. Before you commit to your next unique identifier on the Internet, check out some do's and don'ts for future-proofing your email address.

## DON'Ts

- **Don't use your company's or school's email address for personal use.** Someday you will graduate or leave your current company, and you don't want to leave your email messages behind, not to mention try to make sure all of your contacts' address books are updated. Certainly your company or school email address is appropriate to use for company and school correspondence, but as your primary individual address, not so much.

- **Don't use the address your ISP gave you.** You upgrade to broadband and RoadRunner gives you a free name@yourstate.rr.com email account. Nice, right? Wrong! Someday you will live in another state, and use another ISP, and that address won't work anymore. Pass.

## DO's

- **Use an address that is accessible from anywhere.** More and more you will use multiple computers at home, at work, and in public places. Make sure you can securely access your email from anywhere, so choose an address that enables you to do so. Many popular web-based email services use SSL logins and have fancy dynamic interfaces (like Google's Gmail), so use an address at one of them or that works with one of them. You can even use email forwarding to, say, send a copy of every email you receive and send to a web-based account for online searchable archives from anywhere.

- **Choose an easy-to-remember name you won't regret down the road.** Remember when qtGrrl81 was an email handle that made you proud? Well, now that you're a freelancer soliciting business or applying for jobs, you want something a bit more grown-up. Choose an email address that will be easy to remember, to recognize, and that won't make you cringe when you have to recite it over the phone to your mutual fund company.

## Bottom Line

You want an email address that will stick with you for years to come. The most ideal (and most costly) solution is to register a domain name and set up an email address at a provider (such as yourname@yourname.com). Your provider goes away and you can move that domain to a new provider, no address change required.

> **NOTE** **Lifehacker.com readers make email hosting service recommendations at** `http://lifehackerbook.com/links/emailhosts`.

For those who don't want to plunk down the cash for their own domain and email provider, any of the popular free web-based mail services are a great option. Gmail and Yahoo! Mail are two free, take-it-with-you web-based email providers. Your best chance for getting the handle you want is probably highest at Gmail, which was most recently launched.

The problem with depending on a free web-based service for your email is loss of control. If Gmail changes its domain, decides to start charging, has server problems, or goes away (all unlikely but possible scenarios), you're affected without much recourse. In a pay-for situation with your own domain name, you can change providers and only you own your own data if something goes wrong.

# Hack 50: Script Repetitive Responses

Level....... **Medium**
Platform.... **Windows XP and Vista, Mac OS X, Unix (Thunderbird)**
Cost ....... **Free**

Is there an echo in your Sent email folder? Do you consistently receive messages that ask the same questions or require the same type of information in response? To knock down repetitive email quickly, build up a set of scripted email responses that you can drop into emails quickly, personalize if necessary, and send off without spending the time composing the same information every time. With a set of trusty scripted templates, you can whip through tedious, recurring email like an expert air traffic controller in the busy airport of your inbox.

The Quicktext Thunderbird extension saves collections of reusable text snippets that help you compose personalized replies to those tiresome email messages with a few keystrokes.

> **NOTE** For more on text substitution — or if you don't use Thunderbird — see Hack 27, "Save Time with Text Substitution."

Unlike other text saver utilities, Quicktext is specific to email because it recognizes variables that reference message details — like the recipient's first or last name, the subject line, or attachment filenames. Quicktext replaces these variables with the right info for speedy, yet personalized responses. Easily reply to Lucy Wood's message with a "Dear Ms. Wood" or to Robin Cullen's email with "Hi Robin" using one keyword or click, no name-typing required.

Here's an example: you have a computer for sale and you post an ad on a message board or in the local newspaper. Within a day you have an inbox full of messages inquiring about it. You can dash through those messages with Quicktext. Just follow these steps:

1. Download Quicktext from `http://extensions.hesslow.se/quicktext`. Save the `.xpi` file to your computer.

2. From the Thunderbird Tools menu, choose Extensions. Click the Install button and browse to the `.xpi` file you saved. Click Install Now. When installation is complete, shut down Thunderbird and start it up again.

3. Click the Compose button to start a new email message, and then select Tools → Quicktext.

4. Click the Add button, choose Group, and enter **computer sale**.

5. Click Add again, and choose Text. Call this script **lowbid** and in the Text section on the right, enter your snippet (see step 6). Also set the keyword to **lowbid**, as shown in Figure 6-5.

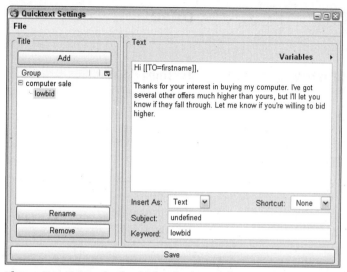

**Figure 6-5** Create the lowbid script in Quicktext.

6.  Set the text to the following:

    ```
    Hi [[TO=firstname]],
    Thanks for your interest in buying my computer. I've got several
    other offers much higher than yours, but I'll let you know if they
    fall through. Let me know if you're willing to bid higher.
    ```

7.  Create any more Quicktexts that might apply to computer inquiry
    responses. Say one called **more info** with the keyword **moreinfo** that
    reads:

    ```
    Hi [[TO=firstname]], thanks for your interest in buying my computer.
    It's a 700Mhz IBM Thinkpad with 32MB of RAM and a 3GB hard drive. Let
    me know if you need any more information.
    ```

8.  After you've set up your scripts, go to a message about the computer.
    When you press the Reply button, you see a dropdown list of the
    Quicktext groups you set up — computer sale and greetings are shown
    in Figure 6-6.

9.  Insert the appropriate reply either by selecting it from the dropdown
    menu or by typing the keyword — lowbid, in this example — and
    pressing the Tab key. Your response, complete with the recipient's first
    name, is automatically inserted into the message body.

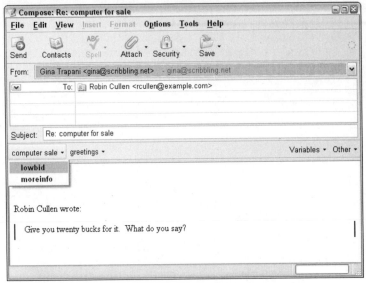

**Figure 6-6** Composing a message using a Quicktext script.

Quicktext can also reference snippets within other snippets. For example, you could set up a group called **greetings** that contains two snippets:

- **personal**, which is set to:

  ```
  Hi, [[TO=firstname]],
  ```

- **business**, which is set to:

  ```
  Dear [[To=firstname]] [[To=lastname]]:
  ```

Then, in other snippets, you can reference one greeting by using the `[[TEXT=greetings|personal]]` variable. See the Quicktext homepage (`http://extensions.hesslow.se/quicktext/#variables`) for the full list of variables.

> **NOTE** Thunderbird is available as a free download at `http://mozilla.org/thunderbird`.

## Hack 51: Encrypt Private Email

Level.......**Advanced**
Platform....**Windows XP and Vista (Thunderbird)**
Cost .......**Free**

Most email messages you send travel vast distances over many networks, secure and insecure, monitored and unmonitored, passing through and making copies of themselves on servers all over the Internet. In short, pretty much anyone with access to any of those servers or sniffing packets along the way can read your email.

Now more than ever, you may want to encrypt your email to protect it from prying eyes. Not only do a large number of big companies monitor their employees' email, [7] but phishing and other email scams increase by the day.

Pretty Good Privacy (PGP) technology isn't foolproof, but it can stop efforts to harvest credit card numbers and commit identity theft. Email encryption with PGP requires that both the sender and recipient have it enabled; and when they do, it offers strong protection against email snoops.

## How PGP Email Encryption Works

Sam wants to send Jane a secret email love letter that he doesn't want Joe, Jane's jealous downstairs neighbor who piggybacks her Wi-Fi connection, to see. Jane uses PGP, which means she has a *public* key (which is basically a bunch of letters and numbers) that she's published on her web site. Jane also has a *private* key that no one else — including Joe the Jealous Wi-Fi Piggy-backer — has.

So Sam looks up Jane's public key. He composes his ardent profession of love, encrypts it with the public key, and sends Jane his message. In transit, copies of that message are made on Sam's and Jane's email servers — but that message looks like garbled nonsense. Joe the Jealous Wi-Fi Piggybacker shakes his fist in frustration when he sniffs Jane's email for any hint of a chance between them. He can't read Sam's missive.

However, when Jane receives the message in Thunderbird, her private key decrypts it. When it does, she can read all about Sam's true feelings in (pretty good) privacy.

You can get PGP set up in a few simple steps using the free Mozilla Thunderbird email program (`http://mozilla.org/thunderbird`).

## Configure PGP in Thunderbird

Here's what to do:

1. Download the free GNUPGP software for Windows, available at `http://lifehackerbook.com/links/gnupgpwin`, and run the installer.

2. Download the Enigmail extension for Thunderbird, available at `http://enigmail.mozdev.org/download.html` and save it to your computer.

3. In Thunderbird, select Tools → Options → Extensions → Install New Extension, and then choose the Enigmail extension file.

4. With Enigmail installed, restart Thunderbird. From the new OpenPGP menu, select Preferences, and set the location of the GnuPGP binary, which is most likely `C:\Program Files\GNU\GnuPG\gpg.exe`.

5. To generate your public/private key pair, select OpenPGP → Key Management. From the Generate menu, choose New Key Pair. Choose the email address you want to create a key for, and set a passphrase. Press the Generate Key button, and relax — it can take a few minutes.

6. After key generation is complete, create and save a revocation certificate, which can invalidate your public key if your private key is ever compromised.

You're all set to send encrypted mail. To find someone's PGP key, select OpenPGP → Key Management. From the Keyserver menu, choose Search. Search for another PGP user by name or email address and add his or her key to your key manager. When it's in there, you can encrypt mail to that person.

Compose your message as usual. Encrypt it by clicking the little key at the lower right of your compose window. You can also cryptographically sign your message to prove it's you; that's the little pencil. Both of these buttons turn green to show that they're active. Then send your message.

To anyone who uses your computer and doesn't authenticate in Thunderbird with the passphrase — or anyone looking through your email files on your ISP's server — the message will look like nonsense, as shown in Figure 6-7.

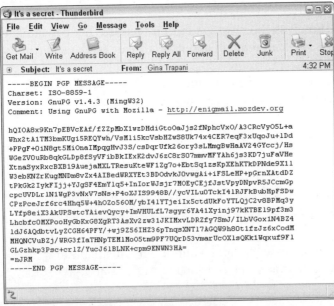

**Figure 6-7** A message in its encrypted state.

Only your private key can decrypt the message and display its contents.

**NOTE** This hack was written by Lifehacker.com feature writer and computer professional Jason Thomas, whose patience for silly questions about how encryption works knows no bounds.

# References

1. Center for Media Research, Research Brief (`http://centerformedia research.com/cfmr_brief.cfm?fnl=050921`).
2. American Psychological Association (`http://apa.org/monitor/feb06/egos.html`).
3. Forrester Research as reported by Reuters (`http://wired.com/news/wireservice/0,71071-0.html?tw=rss.index`).
4. Itzy Sabo, "Small Change Makes Big Difference to Email Prioritization: How to Color-code Your Messages," Email Overloaded weblog (`http://itzy.wordpress.com/2005/12/27/how-to-color-code-your-messages/`).
5. Michael Hyatt, "What's the Secret to Your Success?," Working Smart weblog (`http://michaelhyatt.com/workingsmart/2006/02/whats_the_secre.html`).
6. "Got Two Extra Hours For Your Email?," *The New York Times*, November 2005 (`http://nytimes.com/2005/11/10/fashion/thursdaystyles/10EMAIL.html?ei=5090&en=eb222acdf706a35d&ex=1289278800&partner=rssuserland&emc=rss&pagewanted=print`).
7. "Companies Read Employee E-Mail," Reuters (`http://wired.com/news/wireservice/0,71071-0.html?tw=rss.index`).

# Organize Your Stuff

The more findable your stuff is, the more effective you can be.

Every day you add to a personal library of stuff on your computer's hard drive and in your physical workspace — email, business cards, bookmarks, receipts, documents, news items, magazine clippings, photos, and files. The more organized you keep your personal information library — which represents hours of your work and life — the faster you'll be able to draw from it and act on it in the future.

Create a system that makes it easy — and fun — to shuttle your digital (and paper) bits and pieces into their right place for instant retrieval in the future. Clear away the amorphous piles of stuff that spring up around you on your physical and digital desktop. Your personal library will have ample space to accommodate every type of item it stores. Your personal "librarians" will fetch what you need when you need it with a quick keyword search. When you receive a new piece of information you may need later — such as a co-worker's change of address or web page you may use in next month's report — where to place that new data will be immediately obvious, so that moving it into your system is an automatic act that requires no thought or effort.

This chapter's hacks contain strategies for structuring, securing, and quickly retrieving items from your personal reference library. It provides filing techniques as well as methods for plucking what you need from a teetering pile of unorganized documents. Instant storage and retrieval is possible if you set up the right buckets and tools for doing so.

Everyone's personal organization system differs, and these hacks cover just a few ways you can organize your stuff efficiently. Take from these suggestions the bits that work for you, and modify them for your own purposes. However, while you design your personal system for dealing with information, keep in mind these guiding principles:

- Every item has its place. Every item goes into its right place immediately.

- Those places are large, generic buckets, each with a specific purpose.

- Those places aren't split up into complex, multiple subfolder trees that make you stop and have to think hard about what should go where or how to navigate to what you need.

- Every item is highly findable and instantly retrievable.

- Unneeded information is purged regularly. Old information is archived out of sight.

Whether it's a computer desktop or a physical tabletop, clutter represents procrastination, distraction, and unprocessed information. Let's clear it away.

## Hack 52: Organize My Documents

Level....... **Easy**
Platforms ... **All**
Cost ....... **Free**

If you've had a computer for any length of time you know that your documents folder gets disorganized really fast. If your current file organization system works for you, congratulations. But if you frequently find yourself letting files clutter your computer's desktop, or if you spend time arranging files in a deep, complicated hierarchy of folders, it's time for a revamp.

Now, you don't want to waste time dragging and dropping files into intricate, multi-level folder systems all day long. But you can create a simple set of folders that will accommodate every type of file you need to store in an organized way. The system keeps the files you need to work with right at your fingertips.

My friend and inspiration Merlin Mann says that when you're a short-order cook, "you have to remember you're in the business of making sandwiches — not deciding the prettiest way to stack the customers' orders."[1] You don't want a filing system that makes you spend a lot of time deciding what folder that file should go in. You want to make your stuff as accessible and retrievable as possible with the least amount of effort — so you can focus on making sandwiches.

There are a million and one ways to arrange files and folders on disk. Some might argue that spending a moment even thinking about it in the age of desktop search is unnecessary. That may be true, but some semblance of order clears your desktop and your mind and prepares you for anything.

Over the years I've developed a six-folder structure for My Documents that are created on every computer I use without fail. This scheme accommodates every file you will accumulate, clears the desktop, smoothly fits in with an automated backup system (see Hack 18, "Automatically Back up Your Files"), and makes command-line file wrangling a breeze.

In alphabetical order, the six main folders are called bak, docs, docs-archive, junkdrawer, multimedia, and scripts, as shown in Figure 7-1.

Here's a quick rundown of what each does and what it might contain:

- bak — Short for backup, this is your backup destination of first resort. Your actual data backups should reside on external disks but bak is where you store your Quicken backup file, your address book exported to CSV, or a dump of your web site's database.

> **NOTE** I spend a lot of time at the command line, so I prefer the short name bak, **but there's no reason you can't name your folder** backup **— or any name you prefer.**

- docs — docs is the Big Kahuna of all six folders. It's the place where all the working files for your current tasks, projects, and clients go. Its contents change frequently, and the folder should be purged often.

  You can keep subfolders in docs — finance, clients, or creative-writing, for example. The clients folder might have subfolders, too, like acme and book-in-progress. That gets you three subfolders into the hierarchy, however, and that's usually as deep as you can go before your file tree gets in the way of your work.

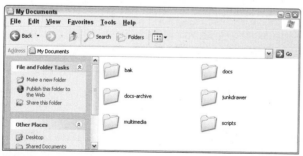

**Figure 7-1** The six core folders of a My Documents organization system.

- docs-archive — Purge your docs folder of closed working files — those for completed projects, a former employers, or past tax years, for example — every few weeks. These go into your docs-archive folder. The archive exists for reference and search, but the separate folder keeps all that extra stuff from cluttering up docs, which is your working task dashboard. The files in docs-archive don't change much, if ever, so you can back them up on a different (less frequent) schedule.

- junkdrawer — The junkdrawer (or temp or tmp) is a temporary holding pen for files you're working with this moment but don't need to save long-term. Your web browser and email program should both save downloaded files and attachments to junkdrawer by default. If you're checking out a video, just testing out a script, or need a place to store a software's setup.exe program, place those files into junkdrawer. junkdrawer files you want to keep should graduate into docs; otherwise, the automated hard-drive janitor (see Hack 20, "Automatically Empty Your Digital Junk Drawer") comes sweeping through and deletes anything older than a couple of weeks from junkdrawer while you sleep.

- multimedia — Here's where your music, video, and photos folders go. The benefit of having all those space-hogging files under one umbrella parent folder is backup. Chances are your multimedia backup scheme is different than your documents backup because of the sheer amount of disk space required. Drop them all in the multimedia folder and you can easily exclude them from your backup scheme. Keep in mind that sharing your media with a home web server (see Hack 35, "Run a Home Web Server") works nicely with an all-encompassing multimedia folder, too.

**NOTE** Most multimedia managers let you specify where you'd like it to store your files. However, particularly pushy programs such as Apple's iTunes insist on storing files in a My Music folder in your My Documents folder. For software oblivious to the user's preferences, one must make an exception.

- scripts — Any executable script or shortcut lives in scripts. This is the place for your weight logger, the janitor script, and any other batch scripts and Windows shortcuts for quick launching programs (see Hack 26, "Quick Launch Software Applications").

## A Word About the Windows XP Default Home Directory

Anyone who works at the command line appreciates short, to-the-point file paths. The Windows XP default user documents directory is something like:

```
C:\Documents and Settings\username\My Documents\
```

Which makes you wonder what Microsoft was thinking at the time. (In fact, Microsoft rethought things in Windows Vista and made the users' default home directory something along the lines of `C:\Users\username\`, similar to the Mac OS `/Users/username/` home directory path.)

You can change the Windows XP `My Documents` directory to `c:\home\username\documents\` or something similar — a consistently lowercase path without spaces is much easier to remember, type, and script.

Here's how:

1.  Right-click the My Documents icon and select Properties. The My Documents Properties dialog box opens.

2.  Click the Move button, and choose the new location.

3.  Windows politely asks if you'd like to move all your documents from the old location to the new one. Go ahead and confirm so Windows can transfer your documents to the new location for you.

4.  Click OK until you've exited the dialog box.

## Beyond the Big 6

These may not be the only folders that live in your home directory. For example, a programmer may keep a `code` or `dev` directory as well. Just make sure any additions don't truly belong within one of the core six. Remember, with simplicity comes effortlessness; the more folders you have, the more easily things get scattered and disorganized — so add to your system sparingly.

## Hack 53: Instantly Retrieve Files from Your Hard Drive

Level....... **Medium**
Platform.... **Windows XP and Vista**
Cost ....... **Free**

Every minute you spend on your computer, you're collecting more and more data, documents, and information to do your job and get on with your life. Instant retrieval of the bit or byte that you need right this very second is an essential requirement in the digital age.

The built-in file search in Windows XP simply doesn't get the job done well. However, the company that provides the best web search tool, Google, offers free software with technology that indexes and searches your hard drive as well as it indexes and searches the Web. Google Desktop is like your own personal librarian, who fetches the data you need immediately using keywords and advanced search operators.

> **NOTE** The Windows Vista interface focuses on an improved file search capability. The first item on the Start menu is a search box, which is also built into every Explorer window. With Vista, you have the capability to create dynamically populated smart folders based on search terms, like files most recently accessed, or Word documents that contain the phrase *life hack*. Therefore, Google Desktop may not be as beneficial on PCs powered by Windows Vista.

This hack covers the installation, configuration, and use of Google Desktop to make every file — even ones you created years ago and forgot about that contain your keyword — instantly retrievable with a query using Google's advanced search operators.

## Google Desktop Installation

The best time to install Google Desktop is just before you go to bed or leave the office for lunch because it takes time for the program to index the email, files, and web pages that are already stored on your computer. The polite Google Desktop only indexes your files while you aren't using your computer so it won't slow you down, but it may take several hours of idle computer time to build a complete index, depending on how much data you have stored. (You can search your computer before the index is complete, but you won't get full results.)

When you're ready to let Google Desktop build a complete index, download it from `http://desktop.google.com`, install as usual, and get it started.

## Configuration

Google Desktop has several options to consider. To access them, right-click the Google Desktop icon in your system tray and select Preferences. In the Local Indexing tab, set the drives (including network drives) and file types you want indexed, whether or not secure web pages and password protected office documents should be included, and if your index should be encrypted for increased security. If you use Gmail and want Google Desktop to index your messages, enter your Gmail login in the Google Account Features tab.

You can also enable the controversial Search Across Computers feature, which enables you to search the documents on your home computer from, say, the office. (Before you do, please read the sidebar about security implications.)

**SECURITY IMPLICATIONS OF THE GOOGLE DESKTOP SEARCH ACROSS COMPUTERS FEATURE**

Google Desktop includes a Search Across Computers feature that stores your computer's files on Google's servers so you can search them from other computers. If you use this feature, your desktop files are only searchable by you, but storing them on Google's servers brings up a lesser-known privacy issue: The Electronic Communications Privacy Act (ECPA), enacted by Congress in 1986, states that while a search warrant is required to seize files on your home computer, a subpoena is enough to get access to files stored on the server of a service provider (like Google.)

For these reasons, the Google Desktop Search Across Computers feature made privacy advocacy groups skittish. In February 2006, the Electronic Frontier Foundation (EFF) advised consumers not to download and use Google Desktop version 3 because its default setting was to copy the files on your hard drive onto Google's servers.[2]

At the time, an EFF attorney said, "If you use the Search Across Computers feature and don't configure Google Desktop very carefully — and most people won't — Google will have copies of your tax returns, love letters, business records, financial and medical files, and whatever other text-based documents the Desktop software can index. The government could then demand these personal files with only a subpoena rather than the search warrant it would need to seize the same things from your home or business, and in many cases you wouldn't even be notified in time to challenge it. Other litigants — your spouse, your business partners or rivals, whoever — could also try to cut out the middleman (you) and subpoena Google for your files."

Version 4 of Google Desktop turned off the Search Across Computers feature by default, and requires you explicitly to turn the feature on to store your files on Google's servers.

Although the Search Across Computers feature is admittedly convenient, I recommend that you keep it turned off and use your own server to keep your files accessible, private, and in your own control. (See Chapter 5, "Get Your Data to Go," for several free ways to make your documents available from anywhere without a "man in the middle" like Google.

Google Desktop offers many features, like mini-applications called Gadgets, but this hack focuses on its most important and useful feature: search.

## Files Google Desktop Indexes

As of version 4.0, Google Desktop Search indexes:

- Email from Gmail, Outlook 2000+, Outlook Express 5+, Netscape Mail 7.1+, Mozilla Mail 1.4+, and Thunderbird.

- Files on your computer, including text, Word, Excel, PowerPoint, PDF, MP3, the contents of ZIP files, and image, audio, and video files.

- Media files' metadata. For example, MP3 song files by artist name and title, not just the filename.

- Web pages you've viewed using Internet Explorer 5+, Netscape 7.1+, Mozilla 1.4+, and Firefox.

- Instant messenger logs from Google Talk, AOL Instant Messenger 5+, and MSN Messenger.

When your file index is complete, Google Desktop provides a search box in your task bar (or floating, or in the Sidebar, depending on your choice in the Display section of the Preferences page). Now you're ready to start finding information.

## Search Operators

Like Google Web search, Google Desktop search displays search results using your web browser. The results from your computer are included at the top of the regular Google Web search results page, as shown in Figure 7-2.

**TIP** Press the Control key twice to summon a Google Desktop search box; press the Control key twice again to dismiss it.

Also like Google Web search, you can use advanced operators when searching your file system to narrow down results by all sorts of criteria. Advanced Search operators currently include:

| OPERATOR | DESCRIPTION |
| --- | --- |
| "..." | Enclose all or part of your query in quotation marks and Desktop returns only items that contain that *exact* quoted phrase. For example, the query `"Copyright 2007"` would not return an item containing that phrase "In 2007, I filed for copyright'" because it is not an exact match. |
| – | Used directly in front of a word causes searches to not return items containing that word. For example, results for the search `bats -baseball` would include all items in the Desktop cache that contain the word *bats*, *except* for the items that also contain the word *baseball*. |

| OPERATOR | DESCRIPTION |
|---|---|
| `site:` | Limits Desktop search to results from the web site you specify. For example, a Desktop query of `help site:www.google.com` returns only pages you've visited on `www.google.com` that contain the word *help*. Important: there can be no space between the `site:` operator and the specified web site. |
| `filetype:` | Restricts the type of files Desktop returns. The argument is either a file type extension or the full name of an Office application. For example, a search for `tax filetype:xls` or `tax filetype:excel` results in only Excel files that have the word *tax* in them. Do not put any spaces between `filetype:` and the extension or type argument. |
| `under:` | Restricts the folder from which your file search results can come. For example, results for the search `basketball under:"C:\Documents and Settings\username\My Documents"` include only files found in the `C:\Documents and Settings\username\My Documents` folder. |

Email searches can be restricted to matches within email message headers. The available search operators are `Subject:`, `To:`, `From:`, `Cc:`, and `Bcc:`. You can combine any of these operators in a single query, and you also can include either or both of the `" "` and `-` operators.

See the full list of Google Desktop advanced search operators and the details of how to use them at `http://desktop.google.com/features.html#advancedsearch`.

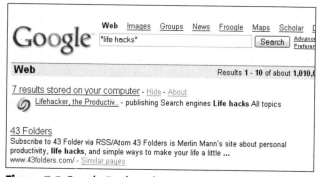

**Figure 7-2** Google Desktop incorporates results for files on your own computer in regular Google Web searches.

# Hack 54: Overhaul Your Filing Cabinet

Level . . . . . . . **Easy**
Platform . . . . **All**
Cost . . . . . . . **Free**

One of the main clutter culprits in most offices is the To File pile. Often this heap spontaneously appears right on top of or next to the filing cabinet, which is pretty silly. Instead of adding stuff to the pile, why wouldn't you just file it? The reason is generally an unworkable, messy, overflowing file cabinet.

This hack explains how to revamp your overstuffed, under-labeled file system and turn it into a neat, breezy and pleasurable place to organize your important paperwork.

## Give Your Paperwork a Spacious Place to Live

Face it: That plastic file box or enormous binder held shut with a rubber band just isn't going to cut it. You have personal, financial, insurance, car, client, tax, and medical paperwork to track.

If you've been using an undersized filing cabinet that can't possibly accommodate your stuff — or no filing cabinet at all — invest in a spacious, well-designed file drawer or cabinet that leaves you room to spare. Lots of room. In fact, *Getting Things Done* author David Allen says your file drawer should be only three-quarters full: "If you want to get rid of your unconscious resistance to filing, then you must keep the drawers loose enough that you can insert and retrieve files without effort."[3]

If you're out to buy a new filing cabinet, he also advises you not to skimp on quality.

"Nothing is worse than trying to open a heavy file drawer and hearing that awful *screech!* that happens when you wrestle with the roller bearings on one of those $29.95 special-sale cabinets. You really need a file cabinet whose drawer, even when it's three-quarters full, will glide open and click shut with the smoothness and solidity of a door on a German car."

It's true. A tool that's easy and fun to use is a tool you *will* use.

## Limit One File Folder Per Hanging Folder

As soon as things start to get crowded inside filing cabinet land, your first instinct is to start putting several manila folders into one hanging folder. Bad idea. Allocate one single manila folder to one single hanging folder. This cleanly separates your folders and makes them easy to ruffle through them. (Using hanging folders at all is a matter of preference.)

Keep a supply of both manila folders and hanging folders within reach so that creating a new one is as easy as possible.

## Choose a Simple, Logical Naming Scheme

You may be a plain A-to-Z–type person, but there are more ways than one to alphabetize file folders. One great method breaks things up into categories, like Car, Client, Taxes, Bank Account; then you preface a folder name with that word. For example, one folder might be `Car: Honda Accord` and another is `Client: Acme`, and another `Bank Account: ING Direct`.

Whatever method you choose, make sure it is obvious and consistent throughout your files to make retrieving paperwork as simple and thoughtless as feasible.

## Use a Label Maker

You may be tempted to save money and space and skip getting a label maker. That's understandable. But don't underestimate the value this inexpensive small tool provides. Neatly labeled folders make a file drawer look sharp, accessible, organized, and professional. Making a new label is a lot more fun and satisfying than scribbling onto a tab with a pen and running out of room, or having to cross something out (or white out!) and start all over. Printed labels also make your folders legible, and presentable at meetings with clients and co-workers.

The Brother P-Touch Home and Hobby Label Maker, for example, gets the job done and it'll only set you back about 20 bucks.

## Purge and Archive

Over time it's easy for your filing drawer to get out of control and filled with stuff that doesn't matter anymore or that you simply don't need on hand at all times. In fact, according to the Small Business Administration, 80 percent of filed paperwork is never referenced again. Purge your paperwork every few months — get rid of the irrelevant stuff, like user guides you can get on the web or for gadgets you no longer own, past project research, and former employer paperwork.

Archive old stuff you don't want to trash but don't need immediate access to by packing it into cardboard file boxes and putting it in storage. Closed bank account records, old credit reports, and your 1996 taxes are good candidates here.

# Hack 55: Choose Secure, Memorable Passwords

Level....... **Easy**
Platform.... **All**
Cost ....... **Free**

A good password is easy for you to remember and hard for others to guess.

Everywhere you turn you have to come up with a password to register for something or another. Whether it's the dozens of web sites that require you to log in to use them, or your ATM card PIN, or your wireless network login, how do you decide on a new password? More importantly, how do you remember it?

## Don't Use the Same Password for Everything

The problem with using the same password for everything you do is that if it's compromised and someone finds it, the rest of your identity is at risk. If your mutual fund company, for example, has a security breach that exposes user-names and passwords, and you use the same login details there as your online banking and at Amazon.com, the thieves could not only compromise your mutual fund account, but your bank account and the credit card details stored at Amazon.com as well. If you give your roommate your wireless network password and it's the same as your email password, it wouldn't be difficult for your roomie to snoop into your private messages. The trick is to keep a unique password for each service you use.

## Remember 100 Different Passwords with One Rule Set

Remembering a unique password for the dozens of logins you have may sound impossible, but it's not. You don't need to remember 100 passwords if you have one rule set for generating them.

Here's how it works: create unique passwords by choosing a base password and then applying a rule that mashes in some form of the service name with it. For example, you could use your base password with the first two consonants and the first two vowels of the service name. If your base password were asdf (see how easy that is to type?), for example, then your password for Yahoo! would be ASDFYHAO, and your password for eBay would be ASDFBYEA.

Something simpler — but along the same lines — might involve the same letters to start (say, your initials and a favorite number) plus the first three letters of a service name. In that case, my password for Amazon would be GMLT10AMA and for Lifehacker.com GMLT10LIF. (Include obscure middle initials — like your mother's maiden name or a childhood nickname — that not many people know about for extra security.)

Before you decide on your single password generation rule, keep in mind that while password requirements differ for each service in terms of length and characters allowed and required, a good guideline is a password at least eight characters long that includes both letters and numbers. To make a password even more secure — or applicable for services that require special characters — add them around or inside it, like #GMLT10LIF# or GMLT10#LIF.

One problem with rules-based passwords is that some sites have their own rules that conflict with your own, such as no special characters. In those cases, you have to document or remember the exception to your rule for those services. The next hack explains how you can keep track of your passwords.

**TIP** A clever password generator bookmarklet, available at http://angel .net/~nic/passwd.html, generates a random password based on a web site URL. View a video demonstration of this bookmarklet in action at http:// weblog.infoworld.com/udell/2005/05/03.html.

---

### CHOOSING YOUR BASE PASSWORD

Here are some options for choosing your base password:

◆ **The first letter of a phrase or song refrain.** For example, if you wanted to use the famous Jackson 5 song "I Want You Back," your base password might be IWUB. Remembering the password is a matter of singing the song to yourself.

◆ Use a pre-established keyboard pattern, like yui or zxcv. Just look at your keyboard to remember it.

◆ Use your spouse's initials and your anniversary, like TFB0602. (This one guarantees you won't forget an anniversary card, either.)

◆ For extra security, choose an easy-to-remember base, like your spouse's initials or the word *cat*, and then shift your fingers up one row on the keyboard when you type it. In the case of cat, you'd get dq5.

Then combine this base with some extra information unique to the service.

# Hack 56: Securely Track Your Passwords

Level. . . . . . . **Advanced**
Platform. . . . **Windows XP and Vista**
Cost . . . . . . . **Free**

Hack 55 covers how to choose memorable passwords, but what about the passwords you already have? Or passwords that were assigned to you that you can't change? Or passwords for systems with special requirements that your usual password scheme doesn't work for?

Sometimes you just *have* to write down a password to remember it. Don't do it where others can read it, like on a Post-It note or in an easy-to-read text file or Word document. You can keep a secure and searchable database of those hard-to-remember passwords using the free, open source software application KeePass (`http://keepass.sourceforge.net`).

## One Master Password to Rule All

A KeePass database stores all your passwords in an encrypted state, and uses one master password (and optionally a special file called a key-file) to access that database. KeePass has fields for username, password, URL, and notes associated with each login, and you can create login groups — such as Windows, web sites, Wi-Fi networks — to organize your passwords. KeePass is very secure; if you keep it running, it will lock its workspace after a certain amount of idle time and require you enter the master password again to access the database.

Here's how to set up KeePass:

1. Download KeePass from `http://keepass.sourceforge.net` and install.

2. To create your KeePass database, select File → New. The Set Master Kay dialog box opens, as shown in Figure 7-3.

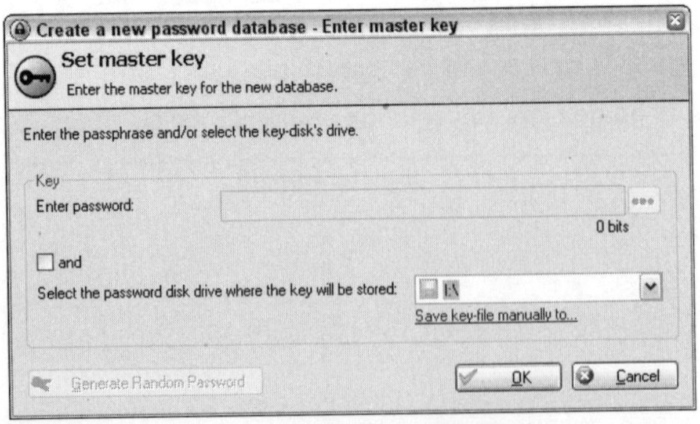

**Figure 7-3** The KeePass database dialog box.

3. To use a master password to access your database, just enter one into the password field. (You'll have to enter it one more time to confirm.)

    To use a key-file stored somewhere on your computer, either choose a disk from the drop-down, or choose Save Key-File Manually To and place the key-file somewhere other than the root of the drive. (A thumb drive is a great place to store a key-file so you can take it with you like one of your house keys.)

    For extra security, use both a key-file and a master password to secure your KeePass database. If you associate a key-file with your password, anyone who somehow gets your master password (perhaps using key-logging software) still can't access your database without the key-file.

    If you choose to use a key-file, KeePass employs random mouse movement or random keyboard input (see Figure 7-4) to generate the file. Press OK when you're done.

4. KeePass creates your database, and then you add entries to it. KeePass suggests some default groupings for your passwords — Windows, Network, Internet, Email, and Homebanking — as shown in Figure 7-5.

5. To add an entry, right-click in the right pane and choose Add Entry. Assign your login a title (for example, Gina @ Home computer). (The title will be displayed in your list of logins inside KeePass, so make it as descriptive and unique as possible so you can scan the list and pick it out quickly.) Enter your username, a password, and optional URL, notes, expiration date, and file attachment to the entry, as shown in Figure 7-6, for each of your existing logins. Toggle the . . . button next to the password field to display the contents of your password or obscure it with asterisks.

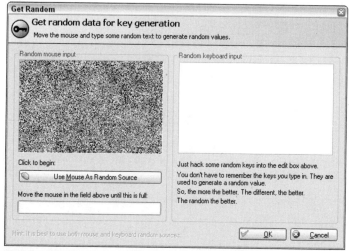

**Figure 7-4** KeePass generates a secure key file.

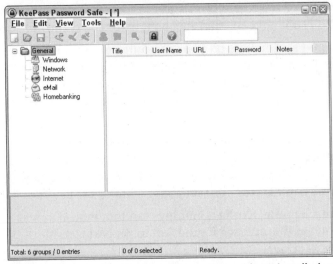

**Figure 7-5** A new KeePass database comes with preinstalled groups.

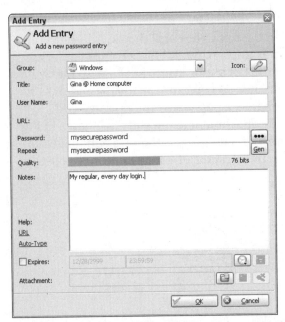

**Figure 7-6** Adding a new password entry into your KeePass database.

KeePass displays how secure your password is with an as-you-type quality meter, just below the Repeat field.

6. Click OK and your login is entered into the KeePass database. Repeat the process for every login you want to track in the database.

## Find and Use Your Passwords with KeePass

After you have entered all your username and password information into KeePass, you can find and use your login information whenever you need it. For example, you can set up a `Wifi networks` password group that lists your logins at all the networks you use, including school, home, friends' houses, and coffee shops, as shown in Figure 7-7.

When you're at your friend Mark's house, you can then either browse to the `Wifi networks` folder or simply enter **Mark** in the search box on the upper right to retrieve the `Mark's house` entry. Right-click the entry, choose Copy Password to Clipboard, and then drop it into Mark's Wi-Fi login prompt.

Configure other useful KeePass features for instant password retrieval in the Options panel in the File menu, including:

- Start KeePass with Windows automatically.

- Clear any password copied to clipboard after a certain amount of time; or allow for only one password paste for extra security.

- Minimize KeePass to the system tray to save Windows taskbar real estate.

- Attach files to KeePass entries. This feature is useful for storing PGP signature files (see Hack 51, "Encrypt Private Email") or even pass-worded Word documents or encrypted text files (see Hack 58, "Encrypt Your Data," later in this chapter).

- Install KeePass on a thumb drive with your database for instant, secure access to your passwords from any computer with a USB port.

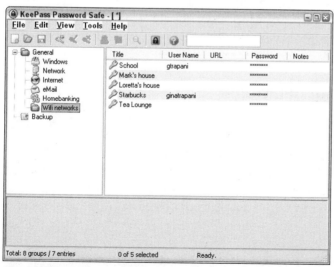

**Figure 7-7** A Wi-Fi network group of saved passwords in KeePass.

> **NOTE** For web site passwords, you can securely save login information directly in Firefox. The advantage of that method is that copy and paste isn't required — Firefox autofills the login box with your details. However, this only works for web-based passwords — not Wi-Fi, network, email, or Windows login information. See Hack 33, "Securely Save Web Site Passwords," for more information.

You can encrypt a text file with your passwords saved in it, but that method doesn't provide the structured password detail entry that a KeePass database does.

## Hack 57: Tag Your Bookmarks

Level....... **Medium**
Platform.... **Web**
Cost ....... **Free**

The Web gets bigger every day, and so does your bookmark list. A social bookmarking service called del.icio.us (`http://del.icio.us`) stores your bookmarks online and associates keywords (called *tags*) to each bookmark for easy retrieval. Storing your bookmarks online also makes them accessible from every computer you use.

The bare bones interface and peculiar URL of the del.icio.us service hides the feature-rich, highly hackable nature of this web application. Recently acquired by Yahoo!, del.icio.us is a fantastic option for any web researcher or power bookmarker who wants to quickly access and organize web content that matters to him. This hack covers just some of the ways to use del.icio.us to manage your bookmarks, create a personal index of web content, and tap into the community to find even more useful resources on the Web.

### Getting Started with del.icio.us

Register for a free account at `http://del.icio.us`. When you're signed in, your del.icio.us bookmarks will be available at `http://del.icio.us/username`. A social bookmarking service, by default, means that all your bookmarks are public and viewable by other members of the del.icio.us community. You can enable private bookmark-saving in the settings area of your del.icio.us account, at `http://del.icio.us/settings/username/privacy`.

## Add a Bookmark

The basic way to add a bookmark to del.icio.us is to use the `post` link at `http://del.icio.us/post`. But that's also the least efficient way. For faster bookmarking, go to the del.icio.us browser buttons area at `http://del.icio.us/help/buttons`, and drag and drop a quick post link to your browser toolbar. Then, when you browse to a page you want to save, just click the button to add your bookmark.

## Tags, Not Folders

Most web browsers organize your bookmarks in folders and subfolders. Arguably the best feature of del.icio.us is the use of tags: labels or keywords that let you view your bookmark list based on single or combined keywords.

For example, to bookmark a web page that describes a foolproof technique for slicing a ripe mango, add it to your del.icio.us bookmarks and tag it `mango`, `howto`, `kitchen`, `fruit`, `cooking`, and `summer`. One bookmark can have as many tags as you'd like.

If you also bookmarked a page with a great smoothie recipe and you tagged it `smoothie`, `fruit`, and `recipe`, the mango page and the smoothie page would both appear under the `fruit` tag listing. However, only the mango page would appear under the `howto` tag. A list of both `fruit` and `summer` tags would only include the mango page as well, because the smoothie page was not tagged `summer`.

To enter a set of tags for a bookmark in del.icio.us, you simply type a list of words separated by spaces. So you'd enter:

```
smoothie fruit summer
```

in the `tags` field for the smoothie page bookmark. The freeform nature of the tags field makes creating and assigning new tags extremely easy, but it also leaves the door wide open for misspellings and similar tags (like `fruit` and `fruits`). After using del.icio.us for some time, you'll develop a vocabulary of tags you use often, and del.icio.us will make suggestions from your tag as you type.

In Figure 7-8, I'm bookmarking an article about Harper Lee's recent piece in *O Magazine*. I've included a description for the bookmark — a particularly good Lee quote.

As I type the letter b into the tags field, del.icio.us uses my pre-established tag vocabulary (under `your tags`) to suggest tags that could match (like `books`, `bananas`, and `beauty`). In this case, I was looking for `books`.

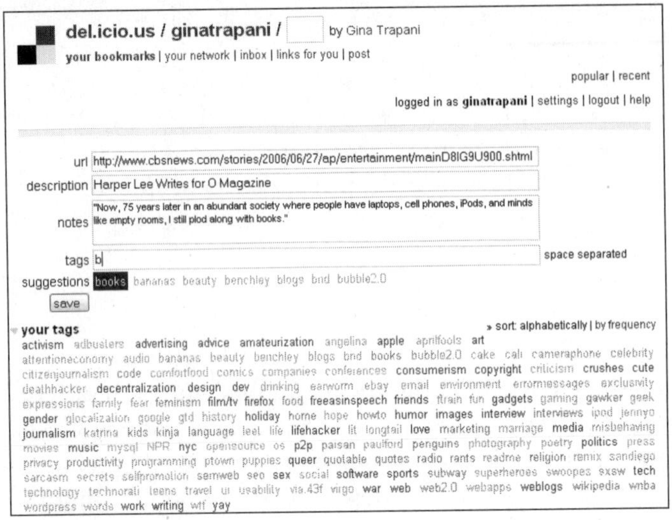

**Figure 7-8** Adding tags to a bookmark in del.icio.us.

## Navigating del.icio.us by URL

Getting around del.icio.us is easiest if you use its hackable URL scheme to get what you want. All you need to do is add what you're looking for to the end of the del.icio.us URL. For example, here's the base URL:

```
http://del.icio.us/
```

To find bookmarks tagged mango by all del.icio.us users, you simply add `tag` and `mango`, like this:

```
http://del.icio.us/tag/mango
```

To find bookmarks tagged `writing` by the user `ginatrapani`, add the username and then the tag:

```
http://del.icio.us/ginatrapani/writing
```

(Replace `ginatrapani/writing` with your own username and your tag(s) to quickly find your bookmarks.)

To find bookmarks tagged `tech` and `howto` by all del.icio.us users, combine the tags with + signs:

```
http://del.icio.us/tag/tech+howto
```

How about bookmarks tagged `tutorial`, `router`, and `linksys` by all del.icio.us users?

```
http://del.icio.us/tag/tutorial+router+linksys
```

Find all bookmarked sound files:

```
http://del.icio.us/tag/system:media:audio
```

Find all bookmarked video files:

```
http://del.icio.us/tag/system:media:video
```

Find MP3 files tagged `mashup`:

```
http://del.icio.us/tag/system:filetype:mp3+mashup
```

## Other del.icio.us Features

You can import your current browser bookmarks into del.icio.us using its import feature, located at `http://del.icio.us/settings/username/import`. You can also export your del.icio.us links at `http://del.icio.us/settings/username/export`.

To keep your del.icio.us links in sync with the Firefox web browser, use the Foxylicious Firefox extension, freely available at `https://addons.mozilla.org/firefox/342`.

## Hack 58: Encrypt Your Data

Level . . . . . . . **Advanced**
Platform . . . . **Windows**
Cost . . . . . . . **Free**

The next level in organizing your digital stuff is considering privacy and safety.

Everyone has some files the person would like to protect from intruders or others who have access to one's computer. If you use online storage, exchange sensitive information over email, or store data on an easily-lost CD or thumb drive, you may want to encrypt that data to keep it from getting into the wrong hands.

When you encrypt data, you use a special algorithm to scramble the bits that make up that file into nonsensical information, which can only be restored to its meaningful state with the right password.

TrueCrypt is a free, open source encryption application that works on Windows and Linux. Given the right credentials, TrueCrypt creates a virtual hard drive that reads and writes encrypted files on-the-fly. This hack explains how to encrypt your private files using TrueCrypt.

## Set up the Encrypted Volume Location

Here's how to set up an encrypted virtual disk with TrueCrypt:

1. Download TrueCrypt from `http://truecrypt.org`. Install and launch it.

2. Click the Create Volume button to launch a wizard that prepares the encrypted drive location. Choose Create a Standard TrueCrypt Volume and click Next.

3. On the Volume Location page, click the Select File button, navigate to the location where you want to store your encrypted files, and type a name for it. I'm going with `C:\Documents and Settings\penelope\My Documents\4myeyesonly`, as shown in Figure 7-9.

   `4myeyesonly` isn't the file you want to encrypt; it's the container that will store the files you encrypt. Click Next.

4. Choose your encryption algorithm. The curious can flip through the dropdown and view info on each option, but you can't go wrong here; the default AES selection will work for most purposes. (Hey, if it works for Top Secret government files,[4] it should work for you.) Click Next.

5. Choose the size of the virtual drive — for example, 100 MB, as shown in Figure 7-10.

   The advantage here is that the file will always look like it's exactly 100 MB, giving no hint to the actual size of its contents. Click Next.

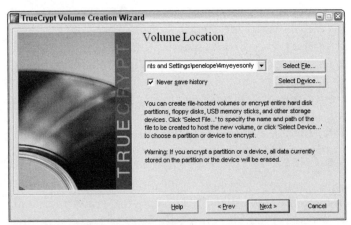

**Figure 7-9** Create an encrypted volume with TrueCrypt.

**Figure 7-10** Set the size of your encrypted container.

6. Choose your volume password. TrueCrypt wants something hard to crack, like 20 characters with letters and numbers mixed together. The whole point here is to keep snoopers at bay, so make your password a non-dictionary word that's difficult to guess. Alternately, you can use a key-file to lock your volume. Keep in mind that if you forget your password or your key-file gets corrupted or lost, the files on your TrueCrypt volume will be inaccessible — forever.

7. Format the volume. This part is fun: TrueCrypt gathers random information from your system — including the location of your mouse pointer — to format the file drive location with random data to make it impossible to read. Click the Format button to go ahead with this operation, which may slow down your computer for a few seconds. (Don't let the word *format* scare you; you're not erasing your hard drive, you're just formatting the drive location file — the 4myeyesonly file in this example — you just created.)

When the formatting is complete, your encrypted volume location is ready for use.

## Store and Retrieve Files from the Encrypted Volume

Your TrueCrypt file can hold your highly sensitive files locked up tight as a drum. Here's how to get to it:

1. From TrueCrypt, choose Select File and navigate to the volume file you just created.

2. Select an available drive letter such as Z: from the list in TrueCrypt (see Figure 7-11).

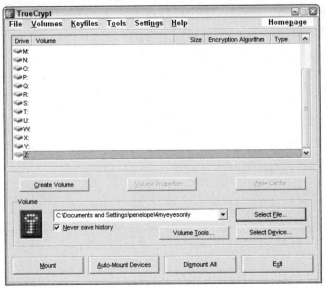

**Figure 7-11** To mount a TrueCrypt drive, select the file container and an available drive letter.

3. Click the Mount button, and enter the your volume password. If you enter the correct password, the virtual drive Z: will be mounted.

4. Go to My Computer. Listed alongside all the other drives on your computer is a new one: Local Disk Z:. Drag and drop all your sensitive data to this drive and work from it as you would any other disk.

5. When you're finished working with the data, in TrueCrypt, select the mounted drive (Z: in this example) and click the Dismount button. The Z: drive will no longer be available; all you'll have left is the 4myeyesonly file you created, which can be dropped onto a thumb drive, emailed to yourself, burned to CD, or placed on your iPod, totally encrypted.

If someone manages to open this file, its contents would be meaningless, indecipherable nonsense. Only a user with TrueCrypt installed and the password or key-file would be able to mount the drive and access the files on it.

**TIP**   Using TrueCrypt you can secure an entire drive — like a USB thumb drive. To do so, click Select Device instead of Select File, and choose your thumb drive. You can also install TrueCrypt to the thumb drive itself.

---

**MULTI-PLATFORM ALTERNATIVE: OPENSSL**

The downside to TrueCrypt is that it's not compatible with Mac OS X. For those of you comfortable on the command line, there's an alternative way to password a file that works with the Unix emulator Cygwin (`http://cygwin.com`) **on Windows, OS X, and Linux: the free utility OpenSSL.**

To password protect a tar archive of documents called `unencrypted-data.tar`, **for example, type the following at the command line:**

```
$ openssl des3 -salt -in unencrypted-data.tar -out encrypted-
data.tar.des3
enter des-ede3-cbc encryption password:
Verifying — enter des-ede3-cbc encryption password:

$
```

**That command encrypts the** `unencrypted-data.tar` **file with the password you choose and outputs the result to** `encrypted-data.tar.des3`.

**To unlock the encrypted file, use the following command:**

```
$ openssl des3 -d -salt -in encrypted-data.tar.des3 -out unencrypted-
data.tar
enter des-ede3-cbc encryption password:

$
```

---

# Hack 59: Design Your Own Planner

Level....... **Easy**
Platform.... **All**
Cost ....... **Office supplies**

There are lots of good reasons to ditch your expensive, electronic PDA for a paper-based planner system: cost, portability, and maintenance, to name a few. Paper-based planners never run out of battery juice or memory; they never crash or refuse to work the way you expect. Lots of even the most tech-savvy are going retro with paper calendars and to-do lists. This hack explains how to build your own custom paper planner, calendar, and project manager using your computer and your printer.

The D*I*Y Planner system (`http://diyplanner.com`) is an extensive library of PDF templates from which you can pick and choose. Then, print the pages you need and assemble your planner.

## Why Build Your Own Planner?

You can walk into any office supplies store and choose from a variety of prefab paper planners. But the advantages of a do-it-yourself planner are customization and scalability. Maybe you're thinking about giving up the Blackberry and you just want to test drive a paper solution. Maybe you don't want to have to order a new set of custom-print pages from your store-bought planner's manufacturer every time you run out. With a D*I*Y Planner you can add, replace, and reshuffle pages very easily. Refills are a matter of printing out a new set of pages.

You can also easily make D*I*Y Planners for your staff that cover custom timelines such as the duration of a particular project. Keep your D*I*Y Planner thin and portable by carrying around only the next couple of weeks' worth of information.

## How to Assemble Your D*I*Y Planner

First, decide on the size and type planner you want to create. The D*I*Y Planner site has templates available to print in several sizes:

- Classic (half pages of 8 1/2×11 inch paper, common in North America)
- Letter size (8 1/2×11 inch paper)
- A4 (the equivalent to letter size in Europe and countries outside of North America)
- A5 (half of A4 size)
- Hipster PDA (index cards)

Download the template kit you need from `http:// diyplanner.com/ templates/official`. Open and print the templates using a PDF reader like Adobe Acrobat or FoxIt (`http://foxitsoftware.com`). Depending on the size you chose, you may have to cut the paper in half (for Classic and A5), and punch holes in it to fit inside a binder. The Hipster PDA index-card–sized version can be held together with a small binder clip.

## D*I*Y Planner Templates and Sizes

The D*I*Y Planner system offers an extensive set of templates, including:

Calendar, to-do lists, and note-taking pages

Stephen Covey's priority matrix

David Allen's *Getting Things Done* system buckets (like Next Actions, Waiting, Projects)

Mind maps

A photographer release form

Book notes

Storyboard

Shopping lists

Address book

Contact logs (phone call/email/IM log of contacts)

Financial ledger

Meeting agenda

Goals tracker

Lined horizontal and vertical and graph paper

Project outline and notes forms

Only print as many pages of the forms as you need to assemble your custom planner. Later, if you decide to change the planner size you use, or need to add pages for certain kinds of information (like another address book page to accommodate contacts whose last name starts with S, or larger daily calendar pages to write your appointments), simply print out the pages and reassemble or add them to your planner.

# References

1. "Quick Tips on Processing Your Email Inbox," 43 Folders (http:// 43folders.com/2005/02/18/quick-tips-on-processing- your-email-inbox/).
2. "Google Copies Your Hard Drive — Government Smiles in Anticipation," EFF Breaking News (http://eff.org/news/archives/2006_02 .php#004400).
3. David Allen, *Getting Things Done*, (Penguin Books, 2001), 100.
4. "National Policy on the Use of the Advanced Encryption Standard (AES) to Protect National Security Systems and National Security Information" (http://cnss.gov/Assets/pdf/cnssp_15_fs.pdf).

# CHAPTER 8

# Kickstart Your Productivity

Our culture worships productivity. In any bookstore — probably not far from this volume — you'll see rows of books with toothy-grinned self-help experts on their covers, advising you to acquire more effective habits, manage your time, and get the most out of your life. The key to all of their advice — well, the good advice, anyway — has less to do with output and more to do with your mental state.

Higher productivity used to equal assembly line workers who could build more widgets per hour. In the information age, higher productivity comes from knowledge workers who can filter the wheat from the chaff and execute their most important tasks amid a tornado of distractions. As a productive knowledge worker, you deliberately decide *what* you are going to work on (and what you aren't), *why* you are going to work on it, and *how* you will proceed on it next — then do so without hesitation.

The biggest obstacles to this kind of clear-headed, focused direction are procrastination, anxiety, action-paralysis, and a feeling of being overwhelmed.

A mindful person sets goals for her life and work, and structures her day around activities that help her reach those goals. But many of us spend our days running around like a chicken with its head cut off, from one randomly assigned task to another, working in frenetic overdrive until the end of the day, when the dust settles, and our actual responsibilities reveal themselves — and by then we're spent. However, it *is* possible to move through your day, your work, and life peacefully, while finishing up your important tasks with a calm sense of deliberation.

This chapter provides concrete strategies to help you invest thought upfront when structuring your schedule and task list. You'll plot maps that guide you toward your goals throughout your work days, and avoid procrastination analysis by moving forward in small, digestible steps. You'll get the important stuff done and leave the rest behind.

# Hack 60: Make Your To-Do's Doable

Level....... **Easy**
Platform.... **All**
Cost ....... **Free**

A to-do list is an essential tool for anyone who keeps more than a handful of balls in the air on a daily basis. A good task list gets pop-up thoughts off your brain, commits you to a next move, and acts as a reference for what to do next when you're in action mode.

Still, an un-thought-out to-do list can actually prevent you from getting things done.

## Finish Thinking Before You Start Doing

A little thought *before* you add an item to your to-do list can mean the difference between procrastination and a completed task. A to-do is a set of instructions from your present self to your future self — a future self who will be in action mode, ready and willing to get something done. Instruct yourself the way you'd instruct an assistant who can't read your mind. Give your future self specific, concrete tasks with as much information as possible. That way, when your future self is ready to act, he has all the information he needs to proceed.

For example, instead of writing "Do my taxes" onto your to-do list, think through what that dreaded, anxiety-producing task really entails. "Gather tax documents into one folder," "Email Client X about missing 1099 form," or "Print tax forms from accountant" are much more specific instructions.

This requires an upfront thought investment when you construct your to-do list. Your task will require thinking either now or later, and it's better to do it now — while your present self is already considering the task — then to force your action-oriented future self to switch gears back into thought mode.

David Allen writes: "If you haven't identified the next physical action required to kick-start [your task], there will be a psychological gap every time you think about it ... When you get to a phone or to your computer, you want to have all your thinking completed so you can use the tools you have and the location you're in to more easily get things done, having already defined what there is to do."[1]

## Chunk up Your Tasks into Five-Minute Actions

Consider this to-do list:

> Clean out the garage
>
> Learn Italian
>
> Plan summer vacation

It lays out some very big plans, but no actionable items. Every journey starts with a single step, as they say, and the to-do items on this list represent destinations, not steps. Break up your to-do items into tiny, digestible actions that will move you toward your goal.

Inspirational writer SARK calls these tiny steps "micromovements." She writes: "Micromovements are tiny, tiny little steps you can take toward completions in your life. I'm a recovering procrastinator and I have a short attention span, so I invented micromovements as a method of completing projects in time spans of 5 minutes or less. I always feel like I can handle almost anything for 5 minutes!"[2]

Imagine you're at your desk, you have a spare 10 minutes before a meeting, and you pull out the preceding to-do list. Can you get anything here done? No. But you could get something done, if a little thought had been put in beforehand to breaking down the tasks.

For example, the next action on the Learn Italian task might be "Check UCSD's web site (www.whatever.edu) for Italian class offerings in the fall." That's something you could do before your meeting.

Here are some examples of to-do's that throw up roadblocks and their doable counterparts:

| ROADBLOCK TO-DO'S | DOABLE TO-DO'S |
| --- | --- |
| Find a new dentist | Email Jayne and ask what dentist she goes to |
| Replace the broken glass tabletop | Measure the table dimensions |
| | Call San Diego Glass at 555-6789 with dimensions |
| Upgrade web site | Draft a list of five web site upgrades |

As you can see, crystallizing your tasks into next actions will often create more than one task for a larger project. Replacing the broken glass tabletop involves measuring, calling and ordering a replacement, and possibly going to pick it up. Your future self knows she has to get out the tape measure to get started.

## Get Physical

Allen calls these small subtasks "next actions." He defines a next action as the next *physical* movement on a task. When you word your to-do items, get physical. Make sure you use action verbs that tell your future self exactly what to do.

For example, "Email Tom and ask to borrow his bike Labor Day weekend" is much more specific than "Contact Tom about the bike," and "Brainstorm report" isn't nearly as effective as "Draft five ideas for micromanagement report theme" or "Write 500-word introduction to annual report."

## Include as Much Information as Possible

When formulating your to-do instructions, place the onus on your present self to make it as easy as possible for your future self to get the job done. For example, if you have to make a phone call, include the name or number. Instead of "Donate old furniture," assign yourself "Call Goodwill to schedule pickup, 555-9878."

Be your own best friend. Arm your future self with as much information as possible to get the task done.

## Essential Elements of a To-Do Task

To make it dead simple for your action-oriented future self to get a to-do done, include information about where it can be completed (context), what project it moves ahead (project), and how important it is (priority).

These elements — context, project, and priority — make it easy for you to pluck the next item off your to-do list in the future. The details of each of these filters are described in Hack 2, "Manage a todo.txt at the Command Line."

## Purge Your List

When you start keeping a to-do list on a regular basis, it becomes easy to assign yourself any task that crosses your mind, especially when you're feeling particularly ambitious or passionate about a project.

However, circumstances change and priorities and interests shift. Review your working to-do list every few months and prune items that are no longer relevant, necessary, or important to you. Remember, deleted to-do items are even *better* than done to-do's because a little extra thought saved you the work.

## Keep an Auxiliary Someday/Maybe List

Sometimes you think of tasks you're just not ready to do yet. Maybe learning Italian — while an eventual goal — just doesn't fit into your life right now. Maybe upgrading the web site is low priority because your business is shifting gears in a major way, and any site overhaul will look very different — or maybe won't be needed — in six months.

Instead of letting tasks you're not quite committed to loiter on your to-do list until you're sick of looking at them, move them off to a Someday/Maybe holding area. Only concrete actions you're committed to completing should live on your to-do list.

# Hack 61: Set up a Morning Dash

Level . . . . . . . **Easy**
Platform . . . . **All**
Cost . . . . . . . **Free**

You love that sense of satisfaction and accomplishment when you check off an item from your to-do list as done, completed, out the door, in the can. But so many things can keep you from getting to that moment, from unexpected emergencies to long, dragged-out meetings to getting waylaid by a conversation with a co-worker in the hallway.

Although those spontaneous gear shifts are necessary and will happen, there is one way to ensure that you'll knock at least one thing off your list: Dedicate the first hour of your day to your most important task — *before* you check your email, paper inbox, or go to any meetings.

## Get One Thing Done First

Author of *Never Check Email in the Morning* Julie Morgenstern suggests spending the first hour of your workday email-free. Choose one task — even a small one — and tackle it first thing. Accomplishing something out of the gate sets the tone for the rest of your day and guarantees that no matter how many fires you're tasked with putting out the minute you open your email client, you *still* can say that you got something done. When you're open for business and paying attention to incoming requests, it's too easy to get swept away into the craziness. So get your day started off on the right foot, with just one thing done.

Morgenstern writes: "Change the rhythm of the workday by starting out with your own drumbeat. [...] When you devote your first hour to concentrated work — a dash — the day starts with *you* in charge of *it* rather than the other way around. It's a bold statement to the world (and yourself) that you can take control, pull away from the frenetic pace, and create the time for quiet work when you need it. In reality, if you don't consciously create the space for the dashes, they won't get done."[3]

To work this hack, you have to set yourself up for your morning dash.

## Park on a Downward Slope

The point of this technique is to remove any thought or planning from your first action of the day so you can get rolling immediately while you're fresh and not distracted by incoming requests. This means you have to choose and gather your materials for the morning dash the evening before.

Near the end of each work day, as you straighten up your desk and get ready to leave the office, deliberately decide on the next morning's most important task. Make sure it's tiny, achievable, and important. That is critical: to successfully set yourself up for the next morning's dash, you want to choose the smallest and most doable to-do item.

Keep in mind that much of your work may be dependent on information stored in your email inbox. (I've worked this trick in earnest, only to find that during my dash I had to open my email to retrieve information, and that bold number of unread messages threatened my focus and concentration.) The key is to set yourself up *the night before* with all the information you need to get your dash completed the next morning. Put all the materials you'll need to complete the task in a folder `First Thing` on your desktop or taskbar.

Write down your small, doable assignment and place it somewhere you will see it, even if it's a Post-It note on your keyboard. When you arrive the next morning, that's the first thing you're going to do — no matter what.

## Hack 62: Map Your Time

Level........ **Easy**
Platform..... **All (with a spreadsheet or calendaring program)**
Cost ........ **Free**

The busy person's perennial question is, "Where did the day go?" It's easy to get tossed from one thing to the next like a piece of driftwood caught in the tide of your crazy life. A thousand things compete for your time and attention and tug you here and there, but only you know how you really want to spend your time. You *can* take control, mindfully structure your days, and deliberately choose the activities — and time limits — that reflect your values and goals.

As with most things, the best way to start keeping your ideal, balanced schedule is to write it down. A personal time map will help you align the activities that fill your day with your personal goals more closely.

## Your Ideal Time Map

Author of *Time Management from the Inside Out* Julie Morgenstern says that the time you have in a day, week, or month is like the space in the top of your closet: only a certain amount of things can fit in it.[4] Before you start running from one appointment to the next, decide on how you want to fill the limited space of your day with a time map. A time map is a simple chart of your waking hours that displays how much time per day you devote to different areas of your life.

For example (and simplicity's sake), say you've decided you want to spend about one-third of your time on work, one third of your time on family, and save one-third of your time for yourself. Your time map might look something like Figure 8-1.

Obviously your ratios will vary and should reflect your life choices. If you're an entrepreneur, for example, work will take up more space. Family time will dominate for parents of young children. An entrepreneurial new parent? Well, you shouldn't expect too much "me" time. When constructing your ideal ratios, be realistic.

Put together your ideal time map using your favorite calendaring software (like Microsoft Outlook, iCal, or Google Calendar), or just download the Excel time map template shown in Figure 8.1. It automatically shades in your map and calculates percentages based on focus codes (A, B, C and D) and is available at `http://lifehackerbook.com/ch8/timemap.xls`.

|  | Sun | Mon | Tue | Wed | Thu | Fri | Sat |
|---|---|---|---|---|---|---|---|
| 5:00 AM |  |  |  |  |  |  |  |
| 6:00 AM |  |  |  |  |  |  |  |
| 7:00 AM | A | A | A | A | A | A | A |
| 8:00 AM | A | A | A | A | A | A | A |
| 9:00 AM | C | B | B | B | B | B | C |
| 10:00 AM | C | B | B | B | B | B | C |
| 11:00 AM | C | B | B | B | B | B | C |
| 12:00 PM | C | A | A | A | A | A | C |
| 1:00 PM | C | B | B | B | B | B | C |
| 2:00 PM | C | B | B | B | B | B | C |
| 3:00 PM | C | B | B | B | B | B | C |
| 4:00 PM | C | B | B | B | B | B | C |
| 5:00 PM | C | B | B | B | B | B | C |
| 6:00 PM | C | A | A | A | A | A | C |
| 7:00 PM | C | C | C | C | C | C | C |
| 8:00 PM | C | C | C | C | C | C | C |
| 9:00 PM | A | A | A | A | A | A | C |
| 10:00 PM | A | A | A | A | A | A | C |
| 11:00 PM |  |  |  |  |  |  |  |
| 12:00 PM |  |  |  |  |  |  |  |

| | Focus | Code | Hours | % |
|---|---|---|---|---|
| | Me | A | 36 | 32% |
| | Work | B | 40 | 36% |
| | Family | C | 36 | 32% |
| | | D | 0 | 0% |
| | | | 112 | |

**Figure 8-1** A sample time map.

Here are some guidelines for your time map:

- Keep the categories broad and generic, at least for your whole life map. You can do sub-time maps (such as a work time map) separately.

- Don't schedule things down to the minute. This is a guide, not an exercise in down-to-the-minute accounting.

- Keep overall ratios in mind, aligned with the things you deem most important in life right now. That is, if career is your top priority, the largest percentage of your map should reflect that.

Now that you've determined how you'd like to place your life's priorities into your days' space, you're halfway to making that a reality.

## Sub-Maps

After you've created your overall time map, sub-map sections of it, like your work day. Schedule in blocks of time to process email, attend meetings, write reports.

Make sure all of your job responsibilities are represented — likewise for your personal and family time.

## Your Actual Time Map

Now you're ready to see how your actual schedule lines up with your ideal. Place your time map somewhere in plain view, like at your desk or on the refrigerator. Each day for a couple of weeks, jot down how you spend your time, then compare your vision to reality. Note how close your actual time map is to your ideal. Adjust the actuals; adjust your ideal. Wash, rinse, and repeat.

The more you work with your time map, the more you'll become aware that the extra hour at work you put in because you were feeling pressured or generous or simply lost track of time means you'll spend an hour less with your family, doing things that you enjoy, or sleeping.

Most importantly, when someone asks, "Where did the day go?" you'll have the answer.

## Hack 63: Quick-Log Your Work Day

Level . . . . . . . **Easy**
Platform . . . . **All**
Cost . . . . . . . **Free**

Keeping tabs on what you actually spend your time doing is not an easy task, although keeping a daily log of your work can help and also provide other benefits.

A daily work log helps you become a better time estimator. By becoming aware of how long things actually take, you can more realistically estimate the length of future assignments, and budget your time — and in the case of people who bill by the hour — money more accurately. A work log enables you to get a real picture of your job responsibilities and how they line up with your ideal time map. A work log lets you look back at a day or week and have a concrete idea of where your time went. It can help you identify time sinks and make strategic decisions about what you can delegate, add, or simply delete from your schedule.

When you start keeping a daily work log, you might be surprised to find out what your workday really consists of.

## How to Keep Your Work Log

When keeping a work log, you have several options, from paper to a plain text file to a quick-logger script.

### Paper

A plain notebook or standard desk diary with dates on each page is an easy way to jot down what you've accomplished in a day.

For a more specialized work log form, designer Dave Seah created what he calls the Emergent Task Timer. This form uses rows of small boxes, each representing 15 minutes of time. You fill out the form as the day progresses, as shown in Figure 8-2.

Seah's Emergent Task Timer works especially well for those who work in 15-minute dashes. The Emergent Task Timer is available for download as a PDF file at `http://davidseah.com/archives/2006/04/18/the-printable-ceo-iii-emergent-task-timing`. (The Printable CEO is a trademark of David Seah.)

### Notepad .LOG File (Windows Only)

Alternatively, if you want the searchability and archiving capabilities of a digital work log, a simple text file can get the job done. One of the lesser known features in Notepad, Windows simple text editor, is log files: text files that automatically add the current date and time when you update them.

To set up your log file:

1. Open Notepad to create a new file.
2. Enter the word `.LOG` on the first line (don't forget the dot).
3. Save the file (`worklog.txt`, for example).

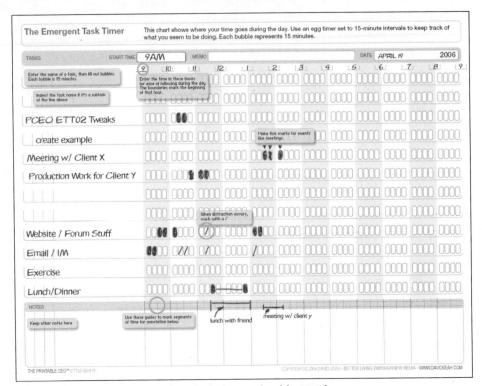

**Figure 8-2** Dave Seah's Emergent Task Timer printable PDF form.

Now, any time you open that file in Notepad, the current date and time will be added to it, and the cursor will automatically go to the next line — perfect for logging your current task or keeping any kind of journal.

> **NOTE** The Notepad .LOG file and the Quick Logger script (in the following section) both work in Windows Vista.

## Quick-Log Your Work in a Plain Text File (Windows Only)

You switch between tasks quickly during your workday, and breaking your concentration to write in a desk diary or double-click a text file may disrupt your flow. However, the process can be streamlined by using a simple script and a keyboard shortcut.

The Quick Logger VB script displays a single input box prompt where you can enter text like the description of your current task and append it to your work log (see Figure 8-3).

When you press Enter (or click OK), the text you entered is added to your work log file with the current date and time, as shown in Figure 8-4.

Quick Logger
Add to C:\Documents and Settings\penelope\My Documents\worklog.txt:
OK
Cancel
Took chapter 8 screenshots

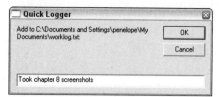

**Figure 8-3** The Quick Logger input box.

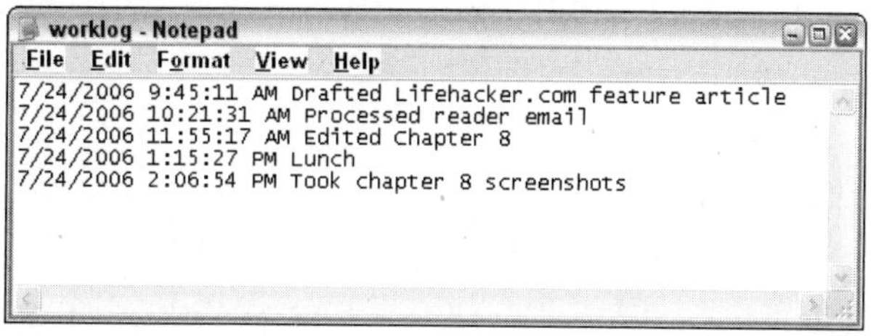

worklog - Notepad
File Edit Format View Help
7/24/2006 9:45:11 AM Drafted Lifehacker.com feature article
7/24/2006 10:21:31 AM Processed reader email
7/24/2006 11:55:17 AM Edited Chapter 8
7/24/2006 1:15:27 PM Lunch
7/24/2006 2:06:54 PM Took chapter 8 screenshots

**Figure 8-4** A work log generated using the Quick Logger script.

Here's how to get Quick Logger set up:

1. Using your favorite text editor, open a new text file and save it as `worklog.txt` in your documents folder.
2. Enter the following code into a file called `quicklogger.vbs` (or download it from `http://lifehackerbook.com/ch8/quicklogger.vbs`):

```
'-----------------------------------------------------------------
--
' QuickLogger v.0.1
' Appends the date and a line of text to a file.
' Based on code written by Joshua Fitzgerald, 7/2005.
' Modified by Gina Trapani, 7/2006.
'-----------------------------------------------------------------
--
Option Explicit

Dim filename
filename = "C:\Documents and Settings\penelope\My
Documents\worklog.txt"

Dim text
text = InputBox("Add to "&filename&":", "Quick Logger")
WriteToFile(text)

Sub WriteToFile(text)
 Dim fso
```

```
Dim textFile
Set fso = CreateObject("Scripting.FileSystemObject")
Set textFile = fso.OpenTextFile(filename, 8, True)
textFile.WriteLine Now & " " & text
textFile.Close
End Sub
```

Save the .vbs file to your documents (or scripts) folder.

3. Edit the line in quicklogger.vbs that reads:

```
filename = "C:\Documents and Settings\penelope\My⤶
Documents\worklog.txt"
```

Replacing C:\Documents and Settings\penelope\ My Documents\worklog.txt with the full path to your work log file.

(Remember, the ⤶ symbol is not part of the code. It merely indicates that the code line was too long to fit on one line in the book, and the code on the following line is actually a continuation of the first line.)

4. Right-click on quicklogger.vbs and select Send To → Desktop (Create Shortcut).

5. Right-click the quicklogger.vbs shortcut on your Desktop and select Properties. In the Properties panel, set the Shortcut Key to Ctrl+Alt+L by simply typing L (Windows fills in Ctrl+Alt for you, as shown in Figure 8-5) and press OK.

**Figure 8-5** Assign a shortcut key to the Quick Logger script.

Now, to append an item to your work log, just press Ctrl+Alt+L, enter your current task in the text box, and press Enter.

Getting into the habit of updating your workday log takes some concentration at first, but with practice the action becomes second nature. Use your work log to fill out time sheets, analyze your schedule, or explain to the boss what you accomplished that week.

> **TIP** Add special notation (like STAR!) to the best accomplishments listed in your work log. These lines will come in handy when you're in salary negotiations, getting your performance review, revising your resume, or interviewing for your next potential career move.

## Hack 64: Dash Through Tasks with a Timer

Level. . . . . . . **Easy**
Platform. . . . **All**
Cost . . . . . . . **Free**

The only way to stop procrastinating is to get to work on the task you've been putting off. In theory, this solution sounds simple; in practice, getting started on a dreaded to-do can just feel impossible. The mental blocks we throw up around daunting tasks come from an utter sense of overwhelm. Some tasks are just so big and awful you can't bring yourself to start in on them because the end seems so far in the future, and the journey there torturous.

The key is to make it as easy as possible to get started. Trick yourself into getting going by making a commitment to work on the task for just a handful of minutes — minutes that will end at the beep of a timer in a small, quantifiable amount of time.

Decide to work on your task for 10 minutes. Ten minutes! That's 1 minute for each finger on your two hands. Anyone can work on anything for 10 minutes, and that includes you and that thing you're putting off.

An entire weekend dedicated to cleaning the garage is a dreadful prospect, one you'll put off until a new species of rodent breeds under the boxes of eight-tracks stored out there. But 10 minutes of filling a garbage bag? No problem.

Productivity expert Merlin Mann writes: "By breaking a few tiny pebbles off of your perceived monolith, you end up psyching yourself out of your stupor, as well as making much-needed progress on your overdue project."[5]

This hack explains how to work your timed dash.

## Choose Your Timer

The single tool that has most helped me complete my largest and most daunting projects — like this book — is a simple kitchen timer I hijacked from the fridge and keep on my desk. Get yourself a timer — an egg timer, a digital watch, a cell phone timer, a software timer, or whatever works for you. Pick your biggest, scariest, most put-off task. Choose the next action, set your timer for 10 minutes, start it, and begin.

When the timer goes off at the end of the 10 minutes, stop. Get up, walk around, get a drink, and pat yourself on the back for what you've just done: you stopped procrastinating and got *started.*

Then, do it again.

## Adjust Your Dash

Ten minutes is a good time period to start running timed dashes. After applying the dash a few times, you'll experience something amazing: when your timer beeps: you'll want to keep working.

As you become more proficient at working the dash, you can adjust the amount of time you set yourself up to work your tasks. Depending on your energy level, available time, and total stress level around a certain task, extend — or shorten — the length of your dash. The goal is to work up to 30-minute or even 60-minute dashes, but everyone has a different workplace circumstances, and attention spans for bursts of focused activity. Find your comfort zone, set that timer, and go. You'll be amazed at how much you can get done in short, focused bursts.

## Employing Constraints

What you're really doing with a timed dash is creating and committing to a self-imposed deadline, a constraint. Constraints and limitations are often viewed as a negative thing that holds you back from achieving goals, but in reality, a constraint can be a *help*, not a hindrance. If you're one of those people who works better under pressure, a limitation puts your brain into overdrive and forces you to think quickly and creatively about the best way to spend that little time you've allotted yourself. It makes you race yourself to an imaginary finish line and gets you there more efficiently than if you had all the time in the world.

Game developer and writer Kathy Sierra says going fast can boost your creativity as well: "One of the best ways to be truly creative — *breakthrough creative* — is to be forced to go fast. Really, really, really fast. From the brain's perspective, it makes sense that extreme speed can unlock creativity. When forced to come up with something under extreme time constraints, we're forced to rely on the more intuitive, subconscious parts of our brain. The time pressure can help suppress the logical/rational/critical parts of your brain. It helps you EQ up subconscious creativity (so-called right brain) and EQ down conscious thought ('left brain')."[6]

## Timer Software Applications

If you have a choice, use a non–software-based timer (like an egg timer or stopwatch) for your dash, because it's a separate entity that won't get buried in your computer's taskbar. A physical timer forces you to look up and reset it by taking your hands off the mouse and keyboard and pressing a button. It breaks your work trance, gets your eyes off the screen, and encourages you to stand up, stretch, walk around, and not just immediately switch to browsing ESPN.com to check the Yankees' score. A change in mode is important when the timer beeps if you're dashing through intense, computer-based work.

However, if external timers make you feel silly or you don't have one readily available, some software-based timers include:

- **AleJenJes Timer** — Windows only; free download at `http://gonebowlin.com/freeware.html`.

- **Stop It!** — Mac OS X 10.4 and later Dashboard Widget; free download (donation suggested) at `http://metabang.com/widgets/stop-it/stop-it.html`.

- **The Kitchen Timer Yahoo! Widget** — Windows and Mac OS X; free download at `http://widgets.yahoo.com/gallery/view.php?widget=28040`. The free Yahoo! Widget Engine is required to run it.

You can find more timer software suggestions at `http://lifehackerbook.com/ch8/`.

## Hack 65: Control Your Workday

Level . . . . . . . **Easy**
Platform . . . . **All**
Cost . . . . . . . **Free**

Getting out of the office on time is tough when there's always another task, project, or drive-by boss request to knock out before you leave. It's easy to lose a day checking email, going to meetings, and putting out fires only to find that at 5 or 6 or 7 p.m. you haven't gotten started on something critical.

Getting out of the office is as important to your state of mind — and productivity — as getting in is. But when you're not clear and focused on your highest priority to-do items, getting out the door on a regular workday with a sense of accomplishment is impossible. Rush hour — that last hour (or two or three) of the workday — becomes your stressful closing window to get to the stuff that, a mere eight hours earlier, you thought you had all day to accomplish.

This hack presents some strategies for reigning in your workday schedule and getting out the door on time with your most important tasks completed.

## Get Your Priorities Straight

It doesn't feel like it — especially at the beginning of what seems like a long workday — but your time is limited. There are only a certain number of hours in the day, and there are an unlimited number of things you could work on. Here's what to do:

*Make sure you work on the most important tasks first.*

Say, for example, that you're an independent freelancer who volunteers your time and expertise on various mailing lists and industry events to network, make contacts, and drum up business. This strategy has worked so well, in fact, that in recent months you've acquired a full roster of clients, and getting everything done — paying and non-paying work — has become more and more difficult.

Instead of automatically volunteering at the rate you always did (whether out of habit or simply to live up to the expectations of others), actively decide what's more important: delivering your paying clients' projects on time, or volunteer work. These decisions are tricky; presumably you've built a reputation among your peers and gotten client work precisely *because* of your volunteer work. You pride yourself on being a leader in your field, and enjoy being someone others come to for advice or consultation. However, the days don't get any longer. As your work life's demands increase in one area, others have got to give.

If you're having a hard time getting out the door on time or frequently find yourself panicked at the end of the day because something critical is undone, it's time to reprioritize and reshuffle how you're spending your day. Maybe you don't have to meticulously pore over every receipt every month any more since you got yourself out of debt; instead, just skim the monthly statement and move on. Perhaps no one on staff really reads that detailed meeting summary you've typed up and emailed out every week for the past year — or maybe it could be shortened to four or five bullet points. People assign themselves duties that can become stale and unnecessary over time. Identify yours and cut them down or out completely.

Figure out what matters most and focus on that first thing. Some things may have to fall by the wayside, but you want to get the most bang for your time buck.

## Stop up Your Time Sinks

Using Hack 63, "Quick-Log Your Work Day," identify the activities that take large amounts of time to complete. Does a particularly chatty client keep you on the phone for 40 minutes? Does your group always get into extended debates over email? Do staff meetings go off the rails and drone on and on and on?

Stop any team of wild horses you're hitched to by deleting, delegating, streamlining, or constraining tasks that take longer than necessary. Be prepared to firmly but politely cut off a call with Chatty Client. Call an impromptu group meeting to discuss whatever debate they're sending long missives about over email. Excuse yourself from meetings — or work with the leader to keep them short and focused on a definite agenda.

## Make Post-Work Appointments

If your child has to be picked up at daycare at 5:30, or your buddy's waiting for you at the bowling alley, or you've got reservations with your other half for dinner, chances are you will be up and out of your desk chair on time.

Make dates with yourself or friends for the gym, a movie, or simply dinner at home at 6 o'clock sharp to get yourself out the door on time. Carpooling with a co-worker will not only cut off your day at a predetermined time, it'll save you money on gas and tolls, too.

## Wrap-up Alerts

At the beginning of the day, decide what time you're going to leave, and set a wrap-up timer. If your spouse is cooking you dinner tonight and you need to be out the door at 6 p.m., set an alert to go off at 5 p.m., 5:30, 5:45, and 5:55 (more, if necessary), saying, "Hey! Time to wrap up and get home!"

Prepare yourself mentally to start closing up shop ahead of time so you're not surprised when your other half calls at 6:30 wondering where you are. Calendar software such as Microsoft Outlook or timer software (discussed in Hack 64) generally support reminders at specific intervals before a scheduled event. Use them as your early warning system — "Head home in 30 minutes!"

# Hack 66: Turn Tasks into Gameplay[7]

Level . . . . . . . **Easy**
Platform . . . . . **All**
Cost . . . . . . . **Free**

Frequent flier miles, those stamped cards at ice cream places that earn you a free cone after you buy 10, and under-the-soda-cap promotions that get you a free song download are all examples of marketers getting you to do things they want you to do using game play.

Ever wish you could knock down the items on your to-do list with the same gusto you fit blocks together in Tetris or collect gold coins in Super Mario Bros? Granted, cleaning out the refrigerator will never be as fun as taking out a sea of grunts in Halo, but if you reframe even the most dreaded task into a game with levels, points, rewards, and a bit of friendly competition, KAZAM! You'll be done before you know it.

## Make It to the Next Level

Break your task down into chunks and track your progress to completion with a level-o-meter. Similar to a fundraiser thermometer that rises with red marker the more money raised, draw yourself a personal progress bar to track your own road to completion. This technique works especially well for group projects.

Say you have a 10-page paper due for class. Before you start writing, find a nearby whiteboard or poster board and draw out a progress bar split into 10 sections. Each time you write one page, color in one section of the bar. It's completely mental, but getting to the next level can be a huge motivator.

## Earn Points

Popular weight loss program Weight Watchers uses a points system to help its customers track their calorie/fat/fiber intakes. Ben Franklin marked which days he had failed to espouse 13 virtues he'd laid out for himself on a weekly calendar. Over time, he "had the satisfaction of seeing them diminish."[8]

Set up a personal points system to help you stay on track. Want to start going to the gym more often? Give yourself a personal point each time you go in a month. Next month, make it your business to better your total score.

## Collaborate, Compete, and Reward

The best way to knock the *dreaded* out of *dreaded task* is to work alongside someone. To help stay focused, create a friendly competition to help yourselves get through it with a reward at the end of the work.

For example, my brother and I are both chronically late people. When we used to work in the same office, we'd drive in together, picking one another up on alternate days. We chose a time to be outside for pickup, and any time one of us was late, we marked it down. As we went on, the rules of engagement intensified, with synchronized watches and 60-second grace periods — and whoever accrued five more lattés than the other had to treat for lunch. The end result? We were on time — even early — at the office more than ever. The funny thing is, it became less about the lunch or even getting in on time, and more about the bragging rights and the game of it, enjoyable even at 6:45 in the morning. (Note: this works especially well with a competitive brother.)

## Bribe Yourself

Tough tasks can be more fun when there's a reward or reason to enjoy them at the finish. For example, if you save the latest episode of "Lost" on your iPod to watch on the treadmill at the gym, you're much more likely to want to get there! If you've promised yourself a smoothie once your presentation's done, or even just a fancy coffee drink after you've finished leading that meeting you prepared for all week, you'll give yourself a much-deserved reward and create a pleasurable light at the end of the tunnel.

## Time Yourself

One of the most effective techniques is to knock down big jobs in small focused time-based chunks. Set a timer for 60 minutes and dive in, and when the hour is up, stop. Just knowing that the clock is ticking makes you try to get as much as possible done before that timer beeps. This is great for computer-based tasks such as email triage as well as for cleaning out the closet or purging your file cabinet. You can even pick a goal of several items to accomplish in that hour and work to reach it; doing it this way will hone your task/time estimation skills as well.

Whether you have to do your taxes, clean out the refrigerator, or finally sort through that monstrous pile of clothing that's been collecting in the corner of the bedroom for a month, turning any task into a game can ease the pain and psych yourself into knocking it out and checking it off your list as complete.

## Hack 67: Schedule Think Time

Level....... **Easy**
Platform.... **All**
Cost ....... **Free**

Computers are good at information storage and retrieval and performing mathematical calculations. Humans are good at thinking. You may spend your days running from one meeting to the next, signing and filing paperwork, delegating tasks, and parrying phone calls and email, but the fact is that knowledge workers are paid to think. When you create your schedule or map out your day, be sure to give yourself time to think.

Every day your brain absorbs millions of bits of information. When you're wrestling with a problem, often that *Eureka!* moment doesn't come until you've had time to stew in the details of your research and experience. Your mind needs time to let all the information it has gel before it can reveal the next step or the solution to a problem.

Microsoft founder Bill Gates is well known for his annual Think Week — one whole week a year to retreat to a lakeside cottage, catch up on reading, and ponder the future of technology. You may not have the luxury of a Gates-style Think Week, but you can take advantage of downtime in your day to give your brain time to recoup, wander, and ponder. You may be surprised at what comes out of it.

## What You Need for Think Time

The most important thing you need for think time — besides a quiet space without distractions — is some sort of capture tool. A notebook, index cards, voice recorder, computer, or a PDA should be at your fingertips so you can seize thoughts and solutions as they occur to you. A PDA or mobile phone or voice recorder will work if necessary, but they are less effective than pen and paper, requiring you to mess with thumbing in letters on a key pad or using arcane script or doing transcription later on.

If you can, just have pen and paper — lots of paper — on hand. (Or else you may be writing *on* your hand.)

## Creating Think Time

When can you schedule think time? My favorite time to ponder things is at lunch. Others more social than myself might use their commute to work, wait time at the Laundromat, or time on the subway. You might purposefully get to an appointment early to sit outside and wait and catch a few quiet minutes. Go outside and take a walk. Schedule a meeting with yourself and use that big whiteboard in the main conference room to map out your ideas.

## References

1. David Allen, *Getting Things Done* (Penguin Books, 2001), 130.
2. SARK, *The Bodacious Book of Succulence* (Simon & Schuster, 1998), 35.
3. Julie Morgenstern, *Never Check Email in the Morning* (Simon & Schuster, 2004), 97.
4. Julie Morgenstern, *Time Management from the Inside Out* (Henry Holt, 2004), 181.

5. Merlin Mann, 43 Folders (`http://43folders.com/2005/09/08/ kick-procrastinations-ass-run-a-dash`)

6. Kathy Sierra, Creating Passionate Users blog (`http://headrush .typepad.com/creating_passionate_users/2005/12/ creativity_on_s.html`).

7. The "Turn Tasks into Gameplay" hack was inspired by Amy Jo Kim's "Putting the Fun into Functional" presentation at O'Reilly's Emerging Technology conference in March 2006.

8. Benjamin Franklin. (1706–1790). His Autobiography. Available at `http:// bartelby.com/1/1/4.html#179`.

# Master the Web

Never before have human beings had ready access to such a vast repository of information in their households as we today with the World Wide Web. That storehouse of information (and misinformation) grows in leaps and bounds every day. With the proliferation of publishing tools and capture devices like digital cameras and video cameras, anyone can publish online, and millions do.

But that kind of access is useless unless you can hone your searching, filtering, and researching skills. Mastering the use of a web browser, finding what you need quickly, navigating engines and indices, determining a set of trusted sources, and judging the quality and authority of new sources are all skills anyone who uses the Web to his advantage needs. In effect, on the Web, you are your own personal research librarian.

Memorizing facts is less important than the capability to look them up quickly. The Web acts as the outboard memory of millions of people. Now more than ever you can depend on it to have the information you need, whether it's the current population of New York City or a review of that ice cream maker you're interested in. You just need to know how to fashion a query that will extract those facts from the endless virtual shelves of information.

Additionally, unlike books, film, TV, and magazines, the web is participatory media (or read/write, if you like). You not only consume it, you can just as easily produce it, and that capability becomes ever more key in an age where web search engines are the over-arching directory of topics, people, and places. (In fact, right now a potential employer or date or long-lost high school friend may be typing your name into Google. What comes up when she does?)

This chapter's hacks provide tips, tricks, and shortcuts for searching and navigating the Web; customizing your web browser for an optimal experience, and sharing and publishing information about yourself and your area of expertise most effectively.

> **NOTE** Remember, you will find updates, links, references, and additional tips and tools regarding the hacks in this book at `http://lifehackerbook.com`. Additionally, you can append the chapter number to the URL — like `http://lifehackerbook.com/ch9.` — to go directly to that chapter's updates.

## Hack 68: Google Like a Pro

Level . . . . . . . **Easy**
Platform . . . . **Web**
Cost . . . . . . . **Free**

Google (`http://google.com`) is the most powerful web search engine available right now, which can return tens of thousands of web pages that contain your search terms. Google's single, one-line input box conceals a host of functionality that can narrow your results to exactly what you need. Paging through hundreds of thousands of links to web pages that contain your keyword is time-consuming and unnecessary. Get fewer, more relevant search results with Google's advanced search operators.

There are two ways to issue queries with Google's advanced methods:

- Use the Advanced Search form by clicking the small blue Advanced Search link on the right of the Google search box.

- Use Google's advanced search operators within the single Google search box.

A page full of input boxes (the Advanced Search form) isn't the most efficient way to search. Google's operators, which usually appear in the form `operator:criteria`, and special characters such as quotes, plus and minus signs, and the tilde enable you to easily fine-tune your query from the single search box.

This hack covers only a few of the most useful Google search query formats; refer to Google's Help Center (`http://google.com/intl/en/help/basics.html`) for a Search Guide that explains all of the options.

## Exact Phrase with Quotations

To find web pages that contain an exact phrase, enclose the phrase in quotes. This functionality comes in handy when you want to only see pages that contain a specific sequence of words — especially common words.

For example, searching for the course has been set may return any number of odd results. The words are all quite common.

A search for "the course has been set" returns pages containing that exact phrase. Adding a second phrase, for example "the course has been set" "summon your courage" can zero in on exactly the result you're looking for — in this case, that swashbuckling box office disaster *Cutthroat Island*.

Some other examples of effective searching by phrase:

■ Computer error messages:

```
"cannot delete file"
"filename too long"
```

■ Quotes:

```
"I cannot tell a lie"?
```

■ Song lyrics:

```
"in a pear tree"
```

■ Names:

```
"John Smith, Ph.D" or "Anne Rice"
```

## Include and Exclude Words with + and –

Force your search results to contain or omit words using + and - signs. This is especially useful for getting more specific about context. For example:

■ Search for information on the Java programming language:

```
java -coffee
```

■ Find pages that contain the words *computer* and *virus*:

```
computer + virus
```

## Search Within a Site

Many web sites either don't have a built-in search feature, or have one that doesn't work very well. Google can search the contents of a single site with the `site:example.com` operator. Specify an entire domain name or just the suffix. For example:

■ Search the Microsoft web site for information on Windows security:

```
site:microsoft.com windows security
```

■ Search Lifehacker.com for keyboard shortcuts:

```
site:lifehacker.com keyboard shortcuts
```

■ Search only Irish web sites that mention the BBC:

```
site:ir BBC
```

■ Search only government web sites for tax forms:

```
site:gov tax forms
```

## Search Certain Types of Files

Google not only searches web pages: it also indexes PDF files, Microsoft Office documents, and other file types. To search for a specific file type, use the `filetype:ext` operator. For example:

■ Find Excel-based budget templates:

```
filetype:xls checkbook
```

■ Find PDF search engine cheat sheets:

```
filetype:pdf search cheat sheet
```

## Calculations

Google search can also perform mathematical equations and currency and other conversions. Here are some examples:

■ Find out how many teaspoons are in a quarter cup with:

```
quarter cup in teaspoons
```

■ Multiply 16,758 with 921:

```
16,758 * 921
```

■ See how many seconds there are in a year:

```
seconds in a year
```

■ Convert dollars to yen:

```
$5 in yen
```

Not sure of the international currency? This also works:

```
25 Australian money in Italian money
```

■ Compare gas prices by doing a double currency and measurement conversion:

```
$2.85 per gallon in British money per liter
```

■ Convert kb to gigabytes:

```
13233434 kb in gigabytes
```

## Synonyms

Search for synonyms using the tilde (~) next to keywords. This comes in handy when you are searching for a concept rather than for a specific word or sequence. For example:

- `~nutrition ~information muffins` returns exact matches as well as matches on Muffins Food Facts and Muffins Vitamin Information.
- `~car` turns up information on trucks and vehicles.
- A search for `~pen` yields pencils, graphite, and sketch.

## Combine Criteria and Operators

All of the preceding techniques can be combined into one query. For example:

- Search for information about privacy and Google that appears on sites *not* including google.com:

  `google + privacy -site:google.com`

- View any contributions by a one person on a site:

  `site:digitaljournalist.org "P.F. Bentley"`

- Find pages with the title of a film and the words *movie* and *review*:

  `"Inconvenient truth" + review + movie`

- Find pages with the word *lifehacker* in them not on lifehacker.com:

  `lifehacker -site.lifehacker.com`

- Find Creative Commons-licensed Excel spreadsheets on Lifehacker.com:

  `site:lifehacker.com filetype:xls "Creative Commons"`

Get pages that display directory listings of `.wma` or `.mp3` music files by the Kleptones:

```
-inurl:(htm|html|php) intitle:"index of" +"last modified" +"parent
directory" +description +size +(wma|mp3) "Kleptones"[1]
```

> **TIP** Print out the Google Search Cheat Sheet, available at `http://google.com/intl/en/help/cheatsheet.html`, and place it near your desk to help you incorporate advanced search techniques into your everyday web searching. A complete list of Google's Advanced search operators is available at `http://googleguide.com/advanced_operators.html`.

# Hack 69: Subscribe to Web Sites with RSS

Level . . . . . . . **Medium**
Platform . . . . **All**
Cost . . . . . . . **Free**

Information from web sites like newspaper sites or weblogs updates frequently throughout the day, week, or month. Like a magazine with an undetermined publishing schedule, you could spend a lot of time visiting each site you like, looking for new content, much like you might go to the newsstand to check whether your favorite magazine's newest issue is out yet.

However, checking every site you like every day is tedious and unnecessary. Like a magazine subscription that automatically brings each new issue to your door, you can subscribe to web site feeds that push information to your door.

Web site feeds are special XML documents that contain all the latest updates to a web site or to a section of it. Place the address of any number of these feeds into feedreader software (also called a news aggregator) and you can see when new items are added to your favorite sites all in one place.

This hack explains how to subscribe to feeds and lists the different types of information they can provide you.

## How to Subscribe to Web Site Feeds

To start building your subscription list to the Web, you first need a feedreader, either desktop software or a web-based application that will list the newest content available in your sites' subscriptions. Bloglines (`http://bloglines.com`) is an excellent, web-based feedreader that's used as an example in this hack. (See the following "Other Popular Feedreaders" section for other options.)

After you've registered for a free account at Bloglines (or set up your desktop or other web-based feedreader), you're ready to build your subscription list.

To subscribe to *The New York Times* Sunday Book Review, for example, go to its site (`http://nytimes.com`) and click the Add New York Times RSS Feeds link (near the bottom of the right column). That opens an entire page listing all the available feeds (one per section), as shown in Figure 9-1. (You could also go directly to that RSS feeds page: `http://nytimes.com/services/xml/rss/index.html`.)

To subscribe to the Book Review, right-click the orange RSS icon and select Copy Link Location. (If you click the feed link as if it were a regular web page, you will view the raw XML, which is meant to be read by a news aggregator, not a human.)

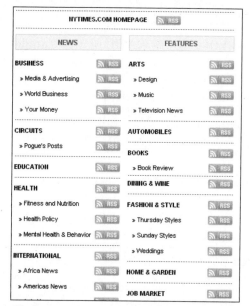

**Figure 9-1** *The New York Times* available feeds.

After you've copied the feed location to your clipboard, switch to Bloglines or your feedreader. Go to the area to add a new feed (in Bloglines, click the Add link) and paste the feed URL into the new subscription input box, then click the Subscribe button. Bloglines enables you to set a few more options for the feed, and then you can click the Subscribe button again. Repeat for any other feeds you're interested in.

In the left panel, Bloglines lists the number of unread items in each site subscription displayed next to its title (see Figure 9-2), much like an email inbox.

Click a subscription to display the latest content from that feed in the right panel.

I use Bloglines to keep up-to-date with more than 200 web sites for research purposes — an impossible feat if I had to visit each one individually.

**Figure 9-2** Tracking three web site feeds using Bloglines.

## Other Popular Feedreaders

If you already use a portal such as My Yahoo! or My AOL or the Google Personalized homepage to read news, you don't have to set up a separate feedreader. All of them display web site feed updates as well.

Additionally, some of the more popular desktop feedreaders include:

- NetNewsWire — Mac OS X only; free demo, $29.95 for a license; `http://apple.com/downloads/macosx/internet_utilities/netnewswire.html`

- Mozilla Thunderbird — Mac/Windows/Linux; free; `http://mozilla.org/products/thunderbird`

- NewsGator — Windows only (runs inside Microsoft Outlook); $29.95; `http://newsgator.com/home.aspx`

- Sharpreader — Windows only; free; `http://sharpreader.net`

## Dynamic Feeds

Web site feeds don't just contain headlines from news and blogs. Some of the more unique uses for feeds include tracking. Among them are the following:

- Weather — `http://bloglines.com`

- Classifieds — `http://bloglines.com`

- Craigslist listings — `http://craigslist.com`

- FedEx package delivery progress — `http://bloglines.com`

- Library book availability — `http://libraryelf.com`

- Sports scores and news — `http://sports.espn.go.com/espn/rss/index`

- TV listings — `http://ktyp.com/rss/tv`

- Tides — `http://tides.info`

- Deals — `http://dealcatcher.com`

- Horoscopes — `http://dailyhoroscopes.com`

- Vehicle traffic updates — `http://developer.yahoo.com/traffic/rss/V1/index.html`

- News keyword searches — `http://news.search.yahoo.com`

# Hack 70: Quick Search Dependable Engines

Level....... **Medium**
Platform.... **All (Firefox)**
Cost ....... **Free**

Hack 25, "Search the Web in Three Keystrokes," describes how to execute a Google search without taking your hands off the keyboard using the Firefox search box on the upper-right corner of the browser. Another keyboard-driven method for searching the web is what Firefox calls Quick Searches — customizable, keyword-based searches from the Firefox address bar.

If you're a Firefox user who eschews the mouse where possible, give a Quick Search a try. In Firefox (`http://mozilla.org/firefox`), key up to the location bar (Windows: Alt+D; Mac: Cmd+L), type **dict eschew**, and press Enter. You'll be automatically transported to the definition of "eschew" (to avoid, shun). That's a Quick Search in action.

Firefox comes with the **dict** search preinstalled, along with the predictable **google** keyword search, but you can set up any number of Quick Searches. This hack includes 15 useful Firefox Quick Searches of dependable search engines, all ready to run from your keyboard.

> **NOTE** The Firefox search box can also contain any number of engines. However, the Quick Search interface is more like using a command line versus controlling a dropdown with your keys. As always, it's a matter of preference.

To set up a Quick Search, use Firefox to go to any search engine page with an input box (the Flickr photo search page at `http://flickr.com` is used in this example). To set up a Quick search for Flickr photos, right-click inside the tag search input box and choose Add a Keyword for this Search, as shown in Figure 9-3.

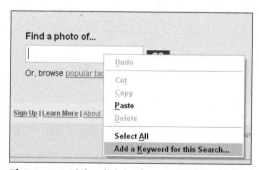

**Figure 9-3** Right-click in the search box and select Add a Keyword for this Search.

The Add Bookmark dialog box opens. Enter a title for the search and a keyword you'll use to execute it, as shown in Figure 9-4.

Press OK. In Firefox, press the Ctlr+L key combination to move your cursor to the address bar. Then type **flickr puppies** to search Flickr photos for — you guessed it — puppies.

Now you can go through and assign keywords to each search engine you use on a regular basis, or...

## Download Bookmark Set

My favorite Firefox Quick Searches are available for download. The file includes 15 keywords I use on a daily basis.

Here's how to get it installed:

1. Using Firefox, go to the Quick Search bookmarks file at `http://lifehackerbook.com/ch9/quicksearch.html`.

2. Select File → Save As, and save the file somewhere on your computer.

3. Select Bookmarks → Manage Bookmarks.

4. From the Bookmarks Manager File menu, choose Import → From File. Browse to and open the `quicksearch.html` file you just saved.

Now you have a `Lifehacker Quick Searches` folder in your Bookmarks, which includes all sorts of keyword searches, described in the following section.

**Figure 9-4** Assign a title and, most importantly, a keyword to your Quick Search.

# Lifehacker Quick Searches

Here's the full list of Quick Searches included in the Lifehacker file:

| QUICK SEARCH | TYPE THIS | DESCRIPTION |
| --- | --- | --- |
| Acronym Finder | `acronym <acronym>` | Finds an acronym for your word. |
| Amazon.com | `amazon <product name>` | Looks up an item on Amazon.com. |
| Dictionary.com | `dict <word>` | Finds definition of your word. |
| eBay | `ebay <item>` | Finds the item you want on eBay. |
| Flickr | `flickr <search term>` | Finds all the tags, titles, and descriptions of images at Flickr that match your search term. |
| Froogle | `froogle <product name>` | Looks up your product on the shopping search engine Froogle. |
| Google Maps | `map <address>` | Produces a Google map of a street address or location. |
| Google Image | `image <search term>` | Finds images that fit your search term. |
| Lifehacker | `lh <search term>` | Searches the Lifehacker site for information. |
| Technorati | `technorati <search term>` | Finds weblogs that are posting about your search term topic. |
| Thesaurus | `thes <word>` | Finds synonyms for your word. |
| Urban Dictionary | `slang <expression>` | Defines your slang expression. |
| Wikipedia | `wikiped <person|place|thing>` | Looks up your search item in the collaboratively edited encyclopedia Wikipedia. |
| Yahoo! Creative Commons | `cc <word>` | Finds Creative Commons-licensed items available for reuse. |
| Yahoo! Local | `local <business>` | Finds a local business listing.** |

** This bookmark must be edited to work in your area. Replace 92037 in the URL with your ZIP Code.

Customize your Quick Searches using the Bookmarks manager (Bookmarks → Manage Bookmarks). Browse to the `Lifehacker Quick Searches` subfolder and choose Properties of any bookmark. Here you can change a keyword shortcut or edit a URL. (Remember to edit the Yahoo! Local Search URL to include your ZIP Code.)

# Hack 71: Extend Your Web Browser

Level....... **Medium**
Platform.... **All (Firefox)**
Cost ....... **Free**

The best feature of popular open-source web browser Firefox is its openness: the browser was built so that anyone can write a feature-adding extension for it. As a result, developers all over the world have made thousands of these plug-ins available to enhance and streamline the way you use your browser.

Block banner ads, synchronize your bookmarks across several computers, track exactly how much time you spend on the Web, and back up files to your Gmail account with time-saving and feature-enhancing Firefox extensions. You've already seen some of these add-ins in action in earlier hacks.

## How to Install a Firefox Extension

In this example you install the excellent Greasemonkey extension, which enables you to associate custom scripts with certain web pages (as described in Hack 7, "Limit Access to Time-Wasting Web Sites"). Here's what to do:

1. Using Firefox, go to the Greasemonkey extension home page at `http://greasemonkey.mozdev.org`, and click the Install Greasemonkey link. Firefox displays a message across the top of the page that reads, "To protect your computer, Firefox prevented this site (greasemonkey.mozdev.org) from installing software on your computer," as shown in Figure 9-5.

2. Click the Edit Options button, and add `http://greasemonkey.mozdev.org` to your list of Allowed Sites, as shown in Figure 9-6, and click the Close button to return to the web page.

3. Click the Install Greasemonkey link again. Greasemonkey will install itself.

4. Quit Firefox and restart it to enable the new extension.

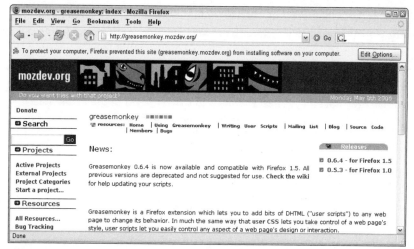

**Figure 9-5** Firefox warning when attempting to install the Greasemonkey extension.

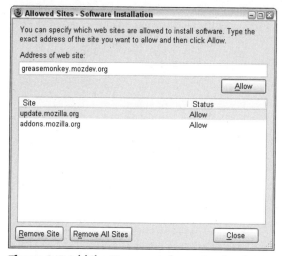

**Figure 9-6** Add the Greasemonkey extension home page to the Firefox list of sites allowed to install software.

When your new extension is installed, it may not be obvious what it does or how it works. If you don't see changes to Firefox's chrome or menus, select Tools → Extensions. From your list of installed extensions, you can right-click one and choose Visit Homepage to read the extension's instructions and often view screenshots of it in action. The Options menu item usually lets you configure the extension as well.

> **NOTE** Like all good software, Firefox is a work in progress, so new versions of it are constantly being released, which requires new versions of its extensions to update rapidly as well. At the time of writing, Firefox 2.0 is slated for release in the near future, which incorporates the functionality of many extensions by default. If you upgrade Firefox early, chances are some of your extensions will be disabled because they haven't yet had a chance to catch up. Go to the Extensions dialog box (select Tools → Extensions) to update your extension versions.

## Recommended Firefox Extensions

New versions of Firefox are released every few months, so the types and availability of extensions for the version you're running may vary. That said, the following table describes some examples of Firefox-enhancing extensions (for Firefox 1.5).

| EXTENSION | DESCRIPTION |
|---|---|
| Scrapbook<br>`http://amb.vis.ne.jp/`<br>`mozilla/scrapbook` | Clip, save, and annotate web pages to your own personal, local, searchable database of clippings. |
| BugMeNot<br>`http://roachfiend.com/`<br>`archives/` | Route around free web 2005/02/07/bugmenot site registration and sign-ins with this community database of auto-filled usernames and passwords. (See Hack 31, "Bypass Free Site Registration with BugMeNot.") |
| TinyUrl Creator<br>`https://addons.mozilla.org/`<br>`firefox/126` | Convert long web site addresses into short, more email-friendly URLs. (See Hack 43, "Craft Effective Messages.") |
| Gmail File Space<br>`http://rjonna.com/ext/`<br>`gspace.php` | Embeds an FTP-like interface inside Firefox to your Gmail email account, for easy backing up and saving files within Gmail. |
| Greasemonkey<br>`http://greasemonkey`<br>`.mozdev.org` | Customize web pages to your liking with JavaScript that can change the look and functionality of web sites. |

| EXTENSION | DESCRIPTION |
|---|---|
| SessionSaver<br>`https://addons.mozilla.org/`<br>`firefox/436` | Saves all the tabs and settings of your current browsing session if your browser crashes or you close it. (Great for users who often keep many tabs open at once.) |
| AutoCopy<br>`https://addons.mozilla.org/`<br>`firefox/383` | Bypass Ctl+C and automatically add selected text on a web page to the clipboard. (Great for researchers, bloggers, and writers who quote web pages often.) |
| Foxmarks<br>`https://addons.mozilla.org/`<br>`firefox/2410` | Synchronize your Firefox bookmarks across several computers. |
| Adblock<br>`https://addons.mozilla.org/`<br>`firefox/10` | Block banner advertisements from all or certain web sites with Adblock. |
| Googlepedia<br>`https://addons.mozilla.org/`<br>`firefox/2517` | Add search results from the Wikipedia automatically alongside your Google search results. |
| TimeTracker<br>`https://addons.mozilla.org/`<br>`firefox/1887` | Track how much time you spend browsing the Web with this Firefox-based timer that runs only while Firefox is in focus. |
| TabMix Plus<br>`https://addons.mozilla.org/`<br>`firefox/1122` | Enhance Firefox's tab behavior with an unread tab style and a close button on each individual tab. |
| DownloadThemAll<br>`http://downthemall.net` | Makes it easy to download all the files linked to a web page, pause and resume large file downloads, and increase speed and download performance. |

Be sure to visit the Firefox extension home base at `https://addons` `.mozilla.org` to find the most up-to-date extension recommendations and top downloads.

# Hack 72: Get 10 Must-Have Bookmarklets

Level....... **Easy**
Platform.... **All**
Cost ....... **Free**

A bookmarklet is a snippet of JavaScript that can be bookmarked (or saved as a favorite) on your web browser's bookmark toolbar. Bookmarklets can enhance web pages, add special functionality, and make your browsing experience a lot more efficient by offering one-click access to useful tools.

The following 10 bookmarklets will streamline work in your browser. Access them at http://lifehackerbook.com/links/bookmarklets.

- **Acronym lookup** — LOL, RTFM, YMMV AFAIK! If you stumble upon one of those nutty Internet-speak acronyms online, highlight it, click this bookmarklet, and automatically look it up using the Acronym Finder.

- **Translate text** — What do you do when you stumble across a web page that's definitely saying something you want to know, except it's in a language you don't speak? You translate it, of course. This bookmarklet runs a web page through Google's translation service, which automatically detects the language of the page and translates it to English.

- **Urban Dictionary lookup** — Similar to the acronym lookup, this bookmarklet looks up selected text on a web page in the Urban Dictionary, the collaboratively edited slang dictionary. Cool beans.

- **Wikipedia lookup** — Highlight text on any web page and perform a Wikipedia search.

- **Alexa site profile** — Find out everything you ever wanted to know about any web site you're currently viewing using Alexa's profile page. View traffic stats and charts, related sites, and inbound links to that site.

- **del.icio.us linkbacks** — See which del.icio.us users bookmarked a web page and what del.icio.us tags they assigned to it with one click.

- **View cookies** — Cookies are small text files that web sites plant on your hard drive to save the state of things, track where you have been on that site, or keep you logged in. Check out all the cookies a site has set for you with this bookmarklet.

- **Toss cookies** — When you see all the cookies a site has set for you, discard them using this bookmarklet. Warning: many sites may not work the way you expect without the cookies they set.

- **TinyURL** — Sometimes web page URLs are just too long to easily remember or type. Sometimes you want to email a web page address and it's so long it wraps around in the message, rendering it unclickable. That's where TinyURL comes in. Go to any web page with an extra long address, and hit up this bookmarklet to create a — well, tiny — URL for emailing, IMing, and sharing without the wrap.

- **View passwords** — You know when you're typing a password into a form, and it displays as *******, and it keeps telling you the password is wrong, and you're thinking, "No, what I typed is right!" and you just wish you could see exactly what characters were entered in the field? The View passwords bookmarklet reveals the contents of a password field. This bookmarklet is secure and client-side, so no worries about revealing your password to evildoers. It's just an easy way to verify that the pesky Caps Lock key didn't get hit accidentally.

**NOTE** Several of these bookmarklets are from Jesse's Bookmarklets Site (http://squarefree.com/bookmarklets), a fabulous index of all sorts of bookmarklet fun.

To install a bookmarklet, drag and drop the link that contains the JavaScript to your browser's Bookmarks toolbar, as shown in Figure 9-7.

If this toolbar is not visible in your web browser, simply enable it. In Firefox, select View → Toolbars and check off the Bookmarks. In Internet Explorer, choose View → Toolbars and check off Links.

To save toolbar real estate, create a bookmarklets — or the narrower bkmrklt — folder and drag and drop your bookmarklets there.

**TIP** Technology journalist and screencaster Jon Udell published a short film that demonstrates how bookmarklets work and how to install them. **It's available at** http://weblog.infoworld.com/udell/gems/bookmarklet.html.

**Figure 9-7** The Acronym lookup and Translate text bookmarklets on the Firefox Bookmarks toolbar.

## Hack 73: Get Your Data on a Map

Level....... **Easy**
Platform.... **Web**
Cost ....... **Free**

The launch of Google Maps (`http://maps.google.com`), the search engine's online geographical mapping application, ushered in a revolution in visualizing location-based data. Not only does Google Maps' built-in features help you find establishments, addresses, and driving directions (like its predecessor MapQuest), but Google opened up its maps interface to third-party developers for their own use. The result is a host of Google Maps mashups, which plot sets of data onto web-based maps.

These map mashups are an incredible way to see geographical information in a new way. This hack points you to several of the best mashups that can help you adjust your commute home from work for traffic, decide where to live, help you find a nearby used car for sale, and figure out how far your jog across the bridge this morning really was.

- **GeoWhitePages** (`http://geowhitepages.com`) — Look up an individual person's phone number and address in this maps-based white page, or see Census data for big cities, as shown in Figure 9-8.

- **Dude, Where's My Used Car?** (`http://dudewheresmyusedcar .com`) — In this eBay car auction maps mashup, browse used cars for sale on eBay near you.

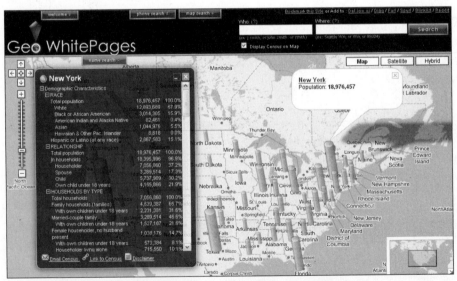

**Figure 9-8** The Geo White Pages maps more than Census data.

- **Garbage Scout** (`http://garbagescout.com`) — Dumpster divers in San Francisco, Philadelphia, and New York can find where someone just discarded an old couch on the curb with Garbage Scout's constantly updating map of useful trash.

- **Gchart** (`http://gchart.com`) — Look up the local time and area code of any location on the globe.

- **MapSexOffenders** (`http://mapsexoffenders.com`) — View the home addresses of people registered in the national database of known sex offenders, or search for known sex offenders who live near a specified address.

- **MapMyRun** (`http://mapmyrun.com`) — Plot running routes and calculate the distance and your speed based on time.

- **Home price records** (`http://homepricerecords.com`) — See how much homes sold for near a specified address or within a certain ZIP Code.

- **Fast food restaurants** (`http://fastfoodmaps.com`) — View all the locations of popular fast food chains by area.

- **WeatherMole** (`http://weathermole.com/WeatherMole/index.html`) — See the weather for a particular place on the map, as shown in Figure 9-9.

- **Universal Package Tracking** (`http://isnoop.net/tracking`) — View the progress of your DHL, UPS, USPS or FedEx package as it travels to your doorstep. This tracker also generates a feed you can subscribe to for updates.

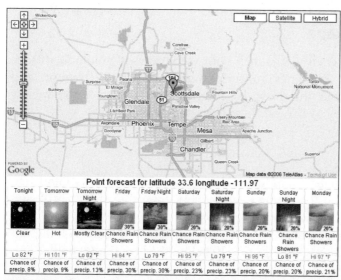

**Figure 9-9** The weather for Scottsdale, AZ, displayed on the WeatherMole maps mashup.

> **NOTE** New maps mashups appear every day. Two good sources to keep up on the latest and greatest maps development are the Google Maps Mania weblog (http://googlemapsmania.blogspot.com) **and Lifehacker.com's maps tag** (http://lifehacker.com/software/maps).

In addition to plotting various sets of data, Google Maps' open API allows a new breed of user-generated maps to flourish. Several of those applications enable users — or groups of users — to create annotated maps with photos and video. For example, a knitting group may publish a map of all the best yarn stores across the country. Or someone who just moved to Seattle may want to share a map with photos and videos of new favorite spots. These things are possible with this new breed of web application. See more on creating your own annotated online map in the Lifehacker.com feature, *Map Yourself*, http://lifehacker.com/software/google-maps/geek-to-live-map-yourself-165157.php.

## Hack 74: Set Multiple Sites as Your Homepage

Level. . . . . . . **Easy**
Platform. . . . **All (with Firefox or Internet Explorer 7)**
Cost . . . . . . . **Free**

The advent of tabbed browsing enables web surfers to work with sets of pages, instead of individual web sites. You can set several web pages as your homepage in tabbed browsers (like Firefox and Internet Explorer 7) and also bookmark and open sets of tabs.

### Multi-Tab Homepage

Say, for example, that when you launch your web browser, you look at three sites first thing: your Bloglines subscriptions, your Gmail account, and CNN.com. To make your three regular morning reads open automatically when you launch Firefox or IE7, set them as your homepage.

#### *Firefox*

To set multiple home pages in Firefox, select Tools → Options → General, and in the Location(s) field of the Home Page section, enter the addresses of sites separated by a pipe ( | ), as shown in Figure 9-10.

Alternatively, you can open all the addresses in tabs and then click the Use Current Pages button, shown in Figure 9-10 below the Location(s) field.

### Internet Explorer 7

Internet Explorer 7 also supports multiple, tabbed homepages. To set them, select Tools → Internet Options, and in the General Tab, enter the URL of each page on its own line (not separated by a | like Firefox). Alternatively, you can open the pages in tabs and click the Use Current button.

## Bookmark Sets of Tabs

You can also save and open sets of tabs as well. For example, say you're working on a research project for the next few months. The project involves a company intranet web page, an external client login page, and a weblog that you and your teammates use to keep each other updated. You can save this set of pages and easily launch all them with a click when it's time to work on the report.

To bookmark a set of tabs in Firefox, ensure that they're all open, and select Bookmarks → Bookmark All Tabs. Then enter the name of the folder in which the set should be stored. In Internet Explorer, select Favorites → Add Tab Group to Favorites, and then enter a folder name in which the set should be stored.

## Open a Set of Tabs

Once your set of tabs is saved, you can launch them all with one click in Firefox. From the Bookmarks menu, navigate to your set's submenu, and choose Open All In Tabs, as shown in Figure 9-11

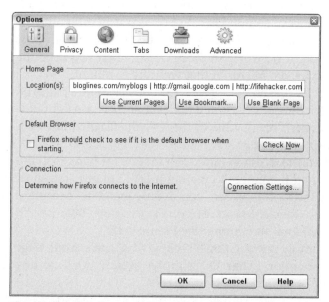

**Figure 9-10** Separate multiple URLs with a pipe (|).

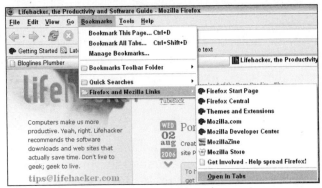

**Figure 9-11** Open a folder of bookmarks all at once with Firefox's Open in Tabs menu option.

As of this writing, Internet Explorer 7 does not offer the set-of-tabs feature.

## Hack 75: Access Unavailable Web Sites via Google

Level....... **Easy**
Platform.... **Web**
Cost ....... **Free**

Web sites go offline. They move, occasionally suffer from temporary unavailability or errors, or become slow to respond because of technical difficulties or a period of high user demand. Some web sites may not be reachable from your particular internet connection or network. In those cases, when you need the information right away, you need a mirror of that web site's content.

Unless a site explicitly denies it, Google creates a full copy of a site's pages on its servers. When you do a Google search, you'll notice that there are light blue links on the bottom right of each result. One of these — the Cached link — is the doorway to Google's copy of a site.

For example, if Lifehacker.com is down (although that never happens!) but you need the article published there about creating a DVD photo slideshow right away for Mom's birthday tomorrow, you'd only need to execute a Google search to find that article (`site:lifehacker.com DVD photo slideshow`). The results will look something like Figure 9-12.

Alternatively, you can simply view Google's copy of a site's front page by using the `cache:` operator. That is, simply search for `cache: lifehacker.com`.

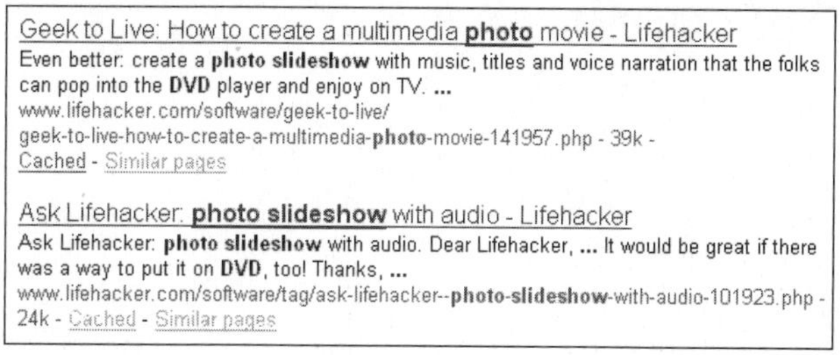

> Geek to Live: How to create a multimedia **photo** movie - Lifehacker
> Even better: create a **photo slideshow** with music, titles and voice narration that the folks
> can pop into the **DVD** player and enjoy on TV. ...
> www.lifehacker.com/software/geek-to-live/
> geek-to-live-how-to-create-a-multimedia-**photo**-movie-141957.php - 39k -
> Cached - Similar pages
>
> Ask Lifehacker: **photo slideshow** with audio - Lifehacker
> Ask Lifehacker: **photo slideshow** with audio. Dear Lifehacker, ... It would be great if there
> was a way to put it on **DVD**, too! Thanks, ...
> www.lifehacker.com/software/tag/ask-lifehacker--**photo-slideshow**-with-audio-101923.php -
> 24k - Cached - Similar pages

**Figure 9-12** Search results with Cached link to Google's copy of a web page.

## Hack 76: Take Your Browser Configuration with You

Level....... **Medium**
Platform.... **Windows (Firefox)**
Cost ....... **Free**

Now that you've tricked out your copy of Firefox with extensions, bookmarklets, sets of bookmarks, and Quick Searches, the last thing you want to do is have to set it all up again at another computer. If you get a new computer, or want to transport your settings at home to the office, a handy utility called MozBackup can help.

MozBackup packages all the Firefox settings, bookmarks, extensions, and other customizations that you've worked hard to perfect, and makes them available to a fresh, new copy of Firefox.

Here's how to take your Firefox browser configuration with you using MozBackup.

1. Download MozBackup from `http://mozbackup.jasnapaka .com/download.php`.

2. Install the application. Quit Firefox, and launch MozBackup.

3. Choose the Mozilla program you're backing up. (MozBackup can also package Thunderbird email settings, contacts, and other configuration information.) Choose the version of Firefox you're running from the list, as shown in Figure 9-13, and click Next.

4. Choose which Firefox profile you're backing up. Most likely, there will only be one choice: default. Select it and click Next.

5. Assign a password to your profile file to add extra security — a useful option for someone who carries files around on a thumb drive (see more on that in Hack 34).

6. Choose which of your Firefox settings you'd like to back up, as shown in Figure 9-14.

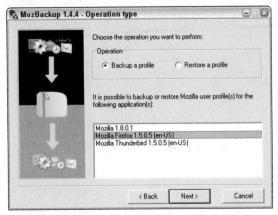

**Figure 9-13** Backing up a Firefox profile using MozBackup.

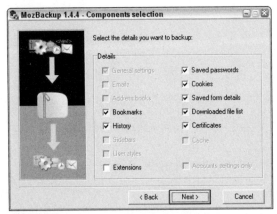

**Figure 9-14** You choose what to back up.

**WARNING** MozBackup's extensions backup does not support all extensions, so use this option at your own risk. To be sure you'll have the information you need to restore your extensions, export any extension data and if MozBackup is not compatible with an extension of yours, install the extension fresh and import the data.

The backup file will be named something like `Firefox 1.5.0.5 (en-US) - 2006-08-02.pcv`, including the software name, version, language, and date of the backup. That makes it easy to back up often — the file won't be overwritten provided you don't back up the settings more than once each day.

When you want to restore a backed-up profile at your other computer — or simply revert to an earlier configuration, launch MozBackup and select Restore a Profile from the Operation Type choices. Choose your `.pcv` backup file and restart Firefox.

That sets up Firefox exactly as you backed it up.

**TIP** Every time you consider installing a new extension — especially one in active development — back up your working copy of Firefox with MozBackup for extra insurance.

# Hack 77: Find out About a Web Site

Level........ **Medium**
Platform.... **Web**
Cost ....... **Free**

When you find information on the Web at a site you've never seen before, it's difficult to assess how trustworthy that source is. Although ultimately the decision is yours, there are several services that provide information about other web sites that can help you decide.

## View Site Traffic and Related Information with Alexa

Web site rankings service Alexa (`http://alexa.com`) provides quite a bit of meta-information about sites, including related sites, incoming links, traffic rank, screenshots, and ratings. To view information about a site — Wikipedia in this example — at Alexa, go to `http://alexa.com/data/details/main?q=&url=http://en.wikipedia.org`. To check out another site, just replace the `en.wikipedia.org` portion of that URL with the site you'd like to find out about.

Alexa also offers endlessly interesting web site traffic information, and enables you to compare sites' traffic against one another. This can be done through the Alexa.com site, but an easier-to-use interface is a site called Alexaholic (`http://alexaholic.com`), which enables you to enter up to five sites and compare their traffic to one another. For example, Figure 9-15 displays an Alexaholic traffic comparison between dell.com, apple.com, hp.com, ibm.com and sun.com.

**NOTE** Alexa's traffic graphs' accuracy is hotly debated because they're generated using data by web surfers who have the Alexa toolbar installed, a very small and most likely targeted segment of the Internet-surfing population at large. Take Alexa's traffic numbers with a grain of salt.

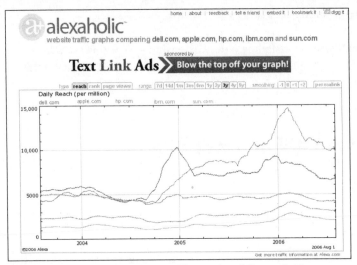

**Figure 9-15** Comparing Alexa traffic graphs of five web sites.

## See What Others Are Saying About a Site in Technorati

Technorati (`http://technorati.com`) is a blog search engine that indexes weblog posts across the Internet. You can use it to search for what bloggers are saying about a particular web page. For example, baseball fans can look for a list of blog posts that link to mlb.com on Technorati by using the URL `http://technorati.com/search/mlb.com`. Substitute the mlb.com bit of that URL with the web site you're researching. (Technorati specializes in weblogs, so it does not list every web site that links to a site.)

## View Past Versions of a Site in the Internet Archive

The Internet Archive is a non-profit project that's been saving snapshots of the Web since 1996. The Internet Archive's Wayback Machine search engine enables you to view a past incarnation of a site by entering its URL in the search box at `http://archive.org/web/web.php` and clicking the Take Me Back button. Then, choose from a dated list of site versions to view a snapshot from the past.

## See What Sites Link to a Site with Google and Yahoo!

Search engine giants Google and Yahoo! provide search operators that display which sites link into a particular site. On Google, use the `link:` operator. Here's a query that displays what sites link to `wsj.com`:

```
link:wsj.com
```

On Yahoo!, use the `linkdomain:` operator:

```
linkdomain:wsj.com.
```

Of course, not everyone is interested in links to *The Wall Street Journal*, but you can easily substitute another URL for `wsj.com`.

# Hack 78: Have a Say in What Google Says About You

Level . . . . . . . **Medium**
Platform . . . . **Web**
Cost . . . . . . . **Starting at $10 a month**

Someone out there's trying to find information about you right now, whether it's a potential employer, date, or a long lost friend. What happens when she Googles you?

More than half the time, she'll get information about someone else with the same name or a web site that you don't control. This hack provides the ins and outs of setting up a nameplate web site that makes you "Googleable" with a web page whose content *you* control.

## But I Already Have a Web Site

You may already have a personal blog with photos of your kids on it or a page dedicated to your monstrous Lego collection that comes up for your name. But is that the first point of contact you want a Google cold-caller to have? Consider your nameplate site your Internet business card, where you publish contact and professional info in a context insensitive way that'll help Googlers get a bird's eye view of who you are and what you do — beyond the Lego collection.

## Get Your Domain

Do what you can to register the yourname.com or .org domain. This will cost a small yearly fee, starting at around $10, depending on the top-level domain you choose (.com, .net, .org, .tv, and so on). There was a time you may have thought one domain to one individual person was egotistical and unnecessary, but that time is over. You will change jobs, move, go freelance, and switch email addresses more in your lifetime than any other past generation. Personal findability is more important than ever. Investing in a `yourname.com` domain is worth it. If you can't get `yourname.com` or `.org`, try `.net`, or even `.name`.

You don't absolutely have to get `yourname.com` to set up your nameplate site, but it's a better option than a page on a free host with a predetermined

---

**A NOTE ABOUT NAMES**

There are many people in the world who probably have the same exact name as you, and there will be more and more coming online each year. Do what you can to brand yourself uniquely online, either by including your middle name, initial, or using your full first name (James instead of Jim or Deborah instead of Deb). Of course you want to use the name people will most likely use to search for you, but if you decide to go with a more formal (read: unique) form of your name, be sure to also use it as your email name (James@JamesDoe.com) and on your resume and other paperwork.

You lucky people with unique names? Your domain name is waiting — its availability is payback for all the years of misspellings and mispronunciation.

---

URL, like at a university or Geocities because someday that service might change its address or go away. If you own `yourname.com`, you control it forever and you can point it anywhere you like — blog, static page, whatever — for as long as you pay for it.

**NOTE** Lifehacker.com readers recommend domain registrars at `http://lifehacker.com/software/ask-the-readers/ask-lifehacker-readers-good-domain-registrar-152014.php`.

## Author Your Nameplate

Now's the time to decide what to put on your "web business card." Your profession, location, and email address is a good start, maybe with links to your kids' pictures and your Lego collection site. Needless to say, do not give away your address, Social Security number, or phone number here — this is general info so others can identify you (as in, "Oh yes, John Smith the architect in Santa Cruz").

An HTML tutorial this hack is not, but do make sure your full name is prominent within a header tag `<h1>` at the top of the page, and within the title `<title>` of the document. Ensure that all the content of the page you want Google to know about is in text (not in images or Flash). Finally, be sure to mask your email address to keep it from spammers. (Google "email address obfuscator" for web sites that will help you mask your email address from spammers online.)

## Find a Web Host

The next thing to do is find a web host, which will entail a monthly fee. If your nameplate site is only one page (and it only has to be), this cost will be minimal. (See Lifehacker.com readers' recommendation for web hosting providers at `http://lifehacker.com/software/web-publishing/ask-lifehacker-readers-web-hosting-provider-139504.php`.) A nice side benefit of your own domain and host is a memorable email address, like joe@joesmith.com, which you can use as a future-proofed email address (see Hack 49 for more). Upload your new nameplate and associate it with your new domain name as per your hosting provider's instructions.

Dedicated do-it-yourselfers with always-on broadband can host their nameplate web site at home, but go this route only if your site is very low on bandwidth (no images), your computer is always on, and you're not concerned about site responsiveness, which will be slow for typical cable and DSL connections, especially if many visitors go to your site at once.

## Link up Your Name Site

Just because you build it, doesn't mean Google will come. Search engines will find your nameplate site and associate it with your name only if it is linked to your name on other, indexed pages. For example, if you're a member of an online community like MySpace, MetaFilter, or Slashdot and you want Google to find your nameplate site, just add it to your profile pages in those communities. You can also send a request to the webmaster of other sites that mention you to link your name to your new site.

## Hack 79: Capture Web Clippings with Google Notebook

Level . . . . . . . **Medium**
Platform . . . . **All (with Firefox or Internet Explorer)**
Cost . . . . . . . **Free**

Collecting bookmarks just isn't enough when you're doing serious web research. Web pages disappear, or the information you need is just one paragraph halfway down the page, or you want to annotate a page with your own notes for later reference.

Whether you're scouring the Web for information on your next vacation, a research paper, or an important client presentation, you can use Google Notebook (`http://google.com/notebook/`), to store and annotate your personal library of web clippings.

Here's how:

1. Register for a free Google account and log in to Google Notebook.

2. Google Notebook prompts you to install a notebook add-on for Internet Explorer or an extension for Firefox, depending on your browser. Click the Agree and Download button to do so.

3. Now you're ready to add a web page clip to your Google Notebook. Say you're collecting quotes on aviation. From the Amelia Earhart page on the Wikipedia (`http://en.wikipedia.org/wiki/Amelia_Earhart`), select an Earhart quote, right-click, and choose Note this (Google Notebook) from the context menu, as shown in Figure 9-16, to save the clipping.

In the bottom right of the current page, a Google Notebook dialog box appears. To add your own notes to the clipping, click the Edit button. Otherwise, simply click the X to close the dialog box. Your clipping (and the address of its source page) is neatly tucked away in your notebook for later reference.

At the Google Notebook site, you can manage your Notebook. There you can create multiple notebooks, edit and rename your current notebook, add section headings, notes, and move, edit, and delete current clippings. For example, you could rename the default "My Notebook" to "Quotes on Aviation," and then create a section called "Amelia Earhart." Simply click, drag, and drop the Earhart quote to that subsection to organize your clippings.

You can also make your Google Notebook(s) public for others to view. Search your own notebooks or all public notebooks by keyword using Google's world-class search technology as well.

**WARNING** Although it's convenient to make your Google Notebooks public to share information with others, do be careful when clipping text from private web pages, like email messages or your company's intranet. You don't want to inadvertently publicize private information.

The advantage to Google Notebook is that your clippings are available online from any computer, and you can use Google's excellent searching capabilities with them.

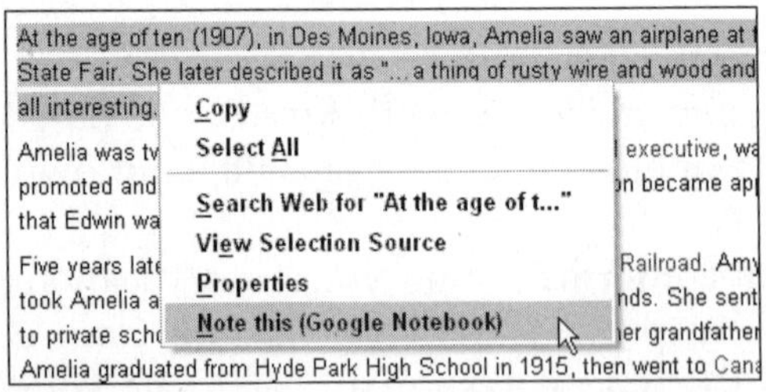

**Figure 9-16** Add a snippet of text on a web page to your Google Notebook.

However, you can also save a personal web clippings library on your own computer. The Scrapbook extension for Firefox is an excellent alternative to Google Notebook; it's free, and you can download it at `http://amb.vis.ne .jp/mozilla/scrapbook/`. Scrapbook has many features Google Notebook does not, such as the capability to capture whole web pages plus several levels of links; add yellow sticky notes onto a saved web page; insert inline comments on sections of text within a web page that appear when you mouse over them; and to save all the pages open in tabs. Watch a video demonstration of Scrapbook in action at `http://lifehackerbook.com/ links/scrapbook`.

## Hack 80: Clear Your Web Browsing Tracks

Level....... **Easy**
Platform.... **All (with Internet Explorer or Firefox)**
Cost ....... **Free**

Your web browser saves a lot of information about where you go and what you do online while you're surfing the web. The sites you visit, copies of the images and text you view, cookies, and information you type into form fields (like username and password or your mailing address and credit card number) are all saved to your computer's hard drive and web browser cache for the sake of convenience, so that those pages will load faster, or your browser can suggest auto-filling the address of a site you visited before.

However, if you're using a shared or public computer, you may not want the web browser to remember your web site logins, history, or even your usernames. Maybe you don't want your spouse to discover you ordered flowers for her at ftd.com when she types f into the address bar to visit froogle.com. Maybe you don't want your roommate to know that you searched for "apartments for rent" on Google last night.

This hack explains how to sweep away your browsing tracks after you're done surfing the web.

## Internet Explorer 6 (Windows XP)

In Internet Explorer 6, select Tools → Internet Options. On the General tab (see Figure 9-17), use the Delete Cookies, Delete Files, and Clear History buttons to wipe out your cookies, temporary files, and browsing history that IE6 saved while you surfed

To delete form field data — such as your shipping address at Amazon or Yahoo! username and password — that you may have entered while surfing, go to the Content tab in the Internet Options dialog and click the AutoComplete button. Here you can delete saved form information and passwords as well as web address suggestions based on sites you've already visited, as shown in Figure 9-18.

Simply check the items you want to delete, click the Clear Forms and Clear Passwords buttons, and then click Ok.

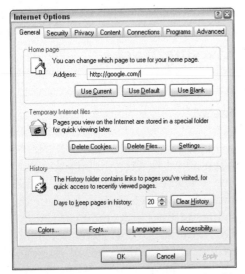

**Figure 9-17** Delete your saved browsing history and cookies in IE6.

**Figure 9-18** Clear saved AutoComplete information in IE6.

## Internet Explorer 7 (Windows Vista)

Internet Explorer 7 (which comes with Windows Vista) consolidated the interfaces for clearing your browsing tracks into one place. Select Tools → Internet Options, and under Browsing History on the General tab, click the Delete button. In the Delete Browsing History dialog (see Figure 9-19), you can remove all your browsing session information by clicking the Delete All button at the bottom.

You've erased your web tracks in one fell swoop.

## Mozilla Firefox

To delete your browsing tracks in Firefox, select Tools → Clear Private Data. Check the items you want to delete — Browsing History, Saved Form Information, Saved Passwords, Download History, Cookies, Cache, and Authenticated Sessions — and click the Clear Private Data Now button.

If you regularly use a shared computer with Firefox, configure the Clear Private Data tool to delete your tracks automatically at the end of every browsing session. Choose Tools → Options, and on the Privacy tab, click the Settings button next to the Clear Private Data tool information. Check the Clear Private Data When Closing Firefox box in the Settings area.

You can also use the Ctrl+Shift+Del keyboard shortcut (Cmd+Shift+Del for Mac users) to clear your private data in Firefox without navigating any menus or dialog boxes.

**Figure 9-19** Delete your browsing history in Internet Explorer 7.

# References

1. Search recipe courtesy of The Google Tutor & Advisor article, "Voyeur Heaven" (http://googletutor.com/2005/04/15/voyeur-heaven).

# CHAPTER 10

# Tune Your Computer

Like a soldier cleans and polishes her rifle to keep it in working order, you need to care for your computer. While operating system manufacturers have tried to create the self-cleaning, maintenance-free computer, power users have realized they must take PC upkeep into their own hands.

In an age of always-on PCs connected to the open Internet at high speed, rogue software tries to install itself on your computer at every turn. Viruses sent via email with inviting subject lines such as "Anna Kournikova pics ;)" and "I love you" threaten home computers as well as entire office networks. Pushy programs put themselves in your computer's startup and slow down overall performance. Toolbars voluntarily install themselves in your web browser and redirect you to advertising web sites. Your 9-year-old downloads and installs malicious software that looks a lot like Tetris onto your PC. Your toddler gets hold of the mouse and deletes a critical folder in one click.

Your computer is an essential tool in your work and life now more than ever before. As you become more dependent on it, the more wear and tear it suffers, and the more adept you should be at protecting, maintaining, and rescuing it from an unwanted end.

This chapter's hacks include simple methods for protecting your computer from malicious software; getting the most out of the disks that house your important data; reverting your broken PC to a past, working state; freeing up much-needed disk space; and restoring accidentally deleted files.

Several utilities are built right into modern operating systems to perform these tasks, but not all of them are the best ones available. These hacks contain information your operating system vendor won't tell you about, and they use some of the best (and usually free) software tools out there to keep your PC in tip-top shape.

# Hack 81: Save Your PC from Malware

Level....... **Medium**
Platform.... **Windows**
Cost ....... **Free**

The scourge of personal computing in recent years has been malware: malicious software that installs itself without your consent and undermines your computer's operation for various nefarious purposes, ranging from identity theft to aggressive advertising to common vandalism.

There are several different types of malware, but none of them is desirable. *Spyware* tracks what you do on your computer and sends information about that back to its originating service, which then uses that information to target ads to you, or worse, steal your credit card or identity. *Adware* pops up constant, unwanted advertising on your computer even when you're not browsing the web, interrupting your work. *Browser hijackers* take over your web browser's site requests and redirect them to unintended web sites, usually advertisements. *Viruses* (a different animal than spyware, but just as destructive) are usually spread via email (but not always) and can also wreak havoc on your PC's files and operation, and replicate by emailing themselves to all the addresses in your contacts list.

## Symptoms

Some unexpected behaviors you may see on a malware-infected system include:

- Constant advertising pop-ups.
- Unfamiliar or unknown programs running in the taskbar (that may or may not log your activity on the computer).
- Unknown web browser toolbars, or plug-ins that cause web pages to redirect to unintended web sites automatically.
- An overall system slowdown, or processes running in the background that were not started with your consent.

You can remove all these types of malware from your PC and protect it from future infection with a set of free software tools available for download.

## Malware Removal and Prevention Tools

Anti-spyware software either cleans existing spyware, prevents new malware installations, or both. Some of these tools include:

- **Lavasoft Ad-Aware** (must-have removal tool, free with paid upgrades available) — Ad-Aware SE Personal is the most popular malware-removal tool on the market. It scans and cleans infected computer systems. Pay-for versions of Ad-Aware include preventative protection and scheduled spyware scans. (`http://lavasoftusa.com/default.shtml.en`)

- **Spybot Search and Destroy** (removal, free) — Like Ad-Aware, Spybot Search and Destroy scans your system for existing spyware and removes it. (`http://spybot.info/en/spybotsd/index.html`)

- **Spyware Blaster** (preventative, free) — Spyware Blaster is preventative malware software that keeps browser hijackers and adware from installing themselves on your system. (`http://javacoolsoftware.com/spywareblaster.html`)

- **Windows Defender** (removal and prevention, free with Windows Vista) — Windows Defender is Microsoft's built-in spyware detection, removal, and preventative tool. Currently available as a beta download for Windows XP users (until December of 2006). Defender is built into Windows Vista. (`http://microsoft.com/athome/security/spyware/software/default.mspx`)

Each of these malware tools has two components: the scanning engine and the malicious software definitions. Because new types of malware are released every day, scanning software like Ad-Aware must have the latest list of known offending software to clean it up. Every single one of these tools has an Update feature that downloads the latest malware definitions for the engine to use.

## How to Clean an Infected System

A system that displays the symptoms listed previously is most likely infected with malware. To clean it, download Ad-Aware and Spybot Search and Destroy (to start). When the cleaners are installed, launch each and select Update to get the latest definitions.

**NOTE** If your web browser is hijacked, you may be unable to use the infected machine to download the software. Alternatively, download the software on a clean machine and burn it to CD or save to a USB drive. If no other machine is available, try downloading it using a non-Internet Explorer-based web browser, such as Mozilla Firefox (`http://mozilla.org/firefox`), which is less likely to be hijacked.

Before you scan your computer, you want to unload any spyware processes that are already up and running on your machine. To do so, disconnect your PC from the internet connection, then shut down. Start the computer again and press the F8 key while it is booting up (before you get to the blue-toned Windows welcome screens). Choose to start the computer in Safe Mode, which only runs the bare essential processes and drives to make a system work.

When the computer is up and running in Safe Mode, open Ad-Aware. Select Scan → Full System Scan, and click the Start button. The scanning process can take a while to run, but when it's finished, it displays a list of possibly malicious objects it found on your system, as shown in Figure 10-1.

Click the Next button to browse the list of detected adware and remove it from your system.

Next, open Spybot Search and Destroy. Choose Check for Problems. This scan might also take some time. Remove anything Spybot finds.

While you're still in Safe Mode, go to Add/Remove Programs in Control Panel, and comb through your installed software list. Uninstall anything you don't recognize or need. Any piece of software whose title contains the words *bargain*, *tracker*, *snoop*, or *monitor* should be removed immediately (and their authors roasted for long, painful hours over a hot fire).

Then, reestablish your Internet connection and reboot your computer normally (not in Safe Mode).

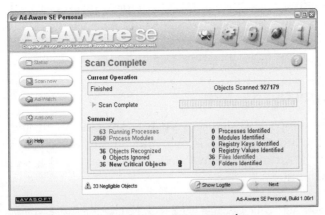

**Figure 10-1** Lavasoft Ad-Aware SE scan results.

When you're back in Windows, download Spyware Blaster, and then install and run it. Also, visit Windows Update (`http://windowsupdate .microsoft.com`) to make sure your copy of Windows has all the latest security patches and updates — at least all the critical updates, if not all recommended upgrades. This process can take a long time, depending on the speed and age of your computer, and it may require rebooting your PC (sometimes, more than once). When given the option, turn Automatic Updates on, as shown in Figure 10-2.

If it isn't already on your computer, install and run Microsoft Windows Defender. Fix any problems it finds.

Finally, weed out any unnecessary programs that are starting up with your computer. (The next hack provides more on how to do that.)

## Virus Protection

Most PCs ship with a preinstalled antivirus tool, one that usually starts nagging you to pay for a subscription after the three-month trial is over. Pay-for antivirus solutions do a fine job, but less costly, open-source options also get the job done. My favorite, ClamWin, is available as a free download at `http://clamwin.com`. ClamWin integrates into Windows Explorer and Microsoft Outlook and can perform scheduled virus scans. Download and launch ClamWin to scan your computer for viruses. Select the disks you want to scan (your hard drives, and/or removable disk drives) and press the Scan button, as shown in Figure 10-3.

**Figure 10-2** Microsoft Windows Automatic Updates keep your PC's system patched and secure.

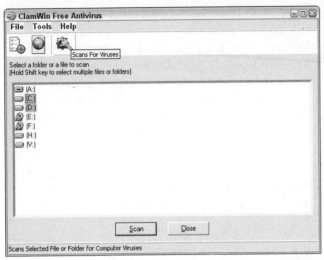

**Figure 10-3** The ClamWin Free AntiVirus console.

Unlike many popular commercial products, ClamWin does not provide an on-access real-time file scanner. You must manually scan your files for viruses with it (or schedule a scan to run on a regular basis).

## Web Browser Hijacking

The best indicator that your PC is host to malicious software is unexpected Web browser behavior. If an unfamiliar toolbar has suddenly appeared, if your home page has mysteriously changed, if the built-in search functionality uses "Joe's Super-Duper Marketing-Enhanced SearchIt!" instead of your usual search engine, chances are your web browser has been hijacked.

If scanning with Ad-Aware and Spybot Search and Destroy didn't resolve your Web browser's erratic behavior, a free diagnosis tool called HijackThis is available at http://spychecker.com/program/hijackthis.html.

The HijackThis freeware does not identify browser-hijacking programs, it only lists all the add-ons, buttons, and startup items associated with your browser. Using it, you can disable whichever items you choose — the trick is identifying unwanted items. The list includes every browser startup object, including the benign ones, so using HijackThis requires research or expert review of your log before you decide what to remove. A free tool that will analyze your HijackThis log and point out known malicious browser add-ons listed there is available at http://hijackthis.de/#anl.

Typically, the Microsoft Internet Explorer browser is targeted by malicious browser-hijacking programs. One way to avoid future infection is to switch your system's default web browser to Firefox. (Firefox can easily import your current Internet Explorer bookmarks.)

# Hack 82: Clean up Your Startup

Level. . . . . . . **Easy to Advanced**
Platform. . . . **Windows**
Cost . . . . . . . **Free**

Does your computer seem a lot slower starting up now than it did the day you took it out of the box? When it comes to computer slowdowns that get worse over time, one of the biggest culprits is software installations that plant themselves in your PC's login sequence and start up automatically with your computer. This means these programs — that you may or may not use during your session — are taking up memory and CPU cycles they don't have to.

Say you install a media player like Apple's popular QuickTime player. QuickTime wants to be your media player of choice, and it wants to start up fast whenever you need it. To that end, QuickTime places a link to start itself up in the background *whenever you start your computer*, whether or not you need to run QuickTime, so it can detect when you come across a QuickTime playable file and run. When several different pieces of software do this, the result is a much longer lag between the time you log into your PC and the time it's ready to get to work for you.

There are a few simple methods and utilities available to prune those unneeded programs from your computer's Startup directory and speed it up again.

## Start Menu (Easy)

A special folder in your PC's Start → Programs menu contains shortcuts to programs that start automatically when you log in. This folder is called, appropriately, Startup (see Figure 10-4).

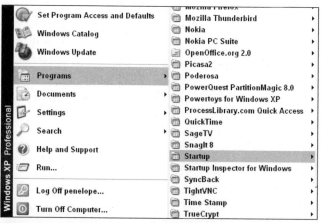

**Figure 10-4** The Startup group in the Programs menu contains shortcuts to programs that automatically start with your computer.

To edit these auto-starting programs, right-click the Start button, and choose Explore. Browse to your user's Programs folder, then the Startup subfolder. You can delete any shortcuts that appear there. Then, go to the Startup folder for All Users, which is located at `C:\Documents and Settings\All Users\Start Menu\Programs\Startup` by default. Audit the programs listed there, deleting anything you don't use on a regular basis.

## System Configuration Utility (Medium)

Not every auto-starting program is listed in the Startup folder. View additional startup items using the built-in Windows System Configuration. To get to it, select Start → Run, type `MSCONFIG`, and press Enter.

In the Startup tab of the System Configuration Utility (see Figure 10-5), uncheck anything you don't need to load automatically on boot.

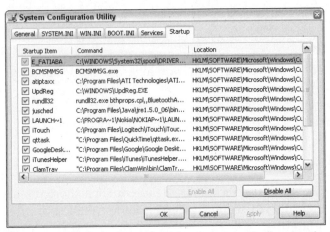

**Figure 10-5** View the items that start up automatically using the System Configuration Utility.

You'll notice most of these programs have opaque names that give little hint to what they do or whether you really need them. One strategy for deciding is expanding the width of the Command column and viewing the entire path. If `qttask` is in the `Program Files/QuickTime` folder, chances are it starts up QuickTime. If you don't want QuickTime to start automatically (there's little reason why you would; it works without getting started up first), uncheck that task.

Using the System Configuration Utility is a bit of a hit-or-miss proposition. Many of the programs listed there are unidentifiable on sight. If the file path doesn't help, Google the process name for more information. When in doubt, keep it checked.

**TIP** It's a great idea to create a System Restore Point first — before you make any system changes — just in case you have to roll back to the original state. Hack 83, coming up next, provides more information on that.

## AutoRuns (Advanced)

A third-party freeware utility called AutoRuns can also help you weed out any unneeded tasks from starting automatically. Download the free AutoRuns from `http://sysinternals.com/Utilities/Autoruns.html`. When AutoRuns is installed and running, view items that automatically start up with your computer in several different categories, including services, drivers, Internet Explorer add-ons, Start menu items, scheduled tasks, and more, as shown in Figure 10-6.

One of the more convenient features of AutoRuns is a built-in Google lookup for an entry. To use it, select an entry for which you'd like more information and select Entry → Google to go directly to Google search results for it.

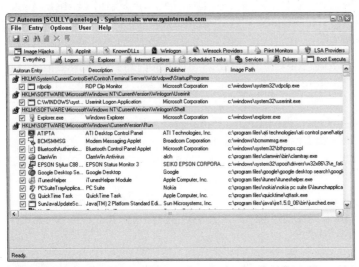

**Figure 10-6** AutoRuns provides a thorough, detailed list of items set to automatically start with your computer.

# Hack 83: Undo System Configuration Changes

Level. . . . . . . **Medium**
Platform. . . . **Windows**
Cost . . . . . . . **Free**

You installed buggy software or changed a setting on your PC, and things got ugly — now nothing works. But all is not lost. Luckily, you can save your PC from that bad decision with a powerful tool that's built into Windows XP and Vista. It's called System Restore.

You know how it goes: you're editing your registry, you're installing beta — OK, alpha — software, you're throwing caution to the wind and testing unstable applications and drivers all willy-nilly. But one false move can render your machine unusable — or make it start popping up 30 `missing .dll` alerts every time you log in.

System Restore takes snapshots of your computer's configuration over time. In the event of a disastrous installation or configuration change that didn't go your way, System Restore can roll back a current Windows state to a working version, without affecting any of your data.

By default, System Restore in Windows is turned on for all your computer's hard drives, if you had more than 200 MB (300 MB for Vista) of disk space available after Windows was installed (and most likely, you did). To see if System Restore is enabled:

- Windows XP — Open the Control Panel and select Performance and Maintenance → System. On the System Restore tab, clear the Turn Off System Restore On All Drives check box.

   Windows Vista — Open the Control Panel and select System Maintenance → Backup and Restore Center. Under Restore Files Or Your Entire Computer, click Use System Restore to Fix Problems And Undo Changes To Windows.

Make sure that your computer's drive — at least the one that contains your system and program files (usually the `C:` drive) — status is listed as Monitoring, as shown in Figure 10-7.

**NOTE** If your hard drive doesn't have enough space to enable System Restore, see Hack 85, "Free up Disk Space."

System Restore tracks changes in the Windows registry, user profiles, `.dlls`, and other internal Windows files over time. If you have multiple drives or partitions on your computer, but only one runs Windows, it makes sense to just set System Restore to monitor the drive where your operating system and applications reside.

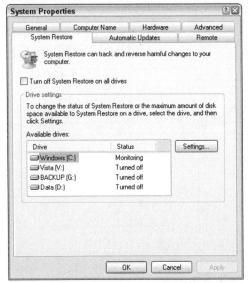

**Figure 10-7** Enable System Restore in the System Properties dialog box.

## Create or Restore a Saved Point with System Restore

To run System Restore, select Start → Programs → Accessories → System Tools → System Restore. From there choose whether you want to restore a previous state or create a new saved state, which you can name — for example, "Pre-startup cleanup."

If you restore your computer to a previous state, note that current documents, files, and email are *not* affected. Choose your previous state from a calendar, as shown in Figure 10-8.

Also, a restoration can be undone. To reverse your restoration, start up System Restore, choose Undo My Last Restoration, and click Next.

**WARNING** System Restore is not a replacement for file backup; it takes snapshots of your computer's configuration and program files, *not* your personal data and information. (See Hack 18, "Automatically Back up Your Files," for more on backing up your personal data.)

## When System Restore Takes Snapshots

System Restore takes system snapshots every day the computer's on during idle time, as well as *before* system changes such as Windows Automatic updates, driver installations, software installations, and system restorations. The Microsoft web site lists specific times and instances in which System Restore snapshots are taken at `http://lifehackerbook.com/links/systemrestore`.

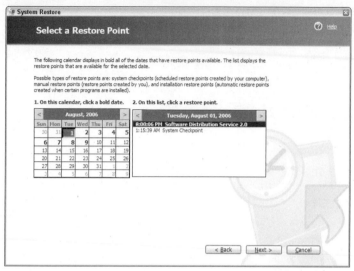

**Figure 10-8** Return your system to a past working state with System Restore.

## Limit System Restore's Disk Usage

One of the gripes about System Restore is that its snapshots can take up a significant bit of hard drive space. By default, System Restore is given 12 percent of disk space in Windows XP (15 percent in Vista.) To reduce that amount, right-click on My Computer and choose Properties. From the System Restore Tab, adjust the disk space slider in the Settings area, as shown in Figure 10-9.

**Figure 10-9** Adjust the amount of disk space allocated to System Restore points.

New snapshots age and overwrite old ones, so if you can spare the maximum 12 percent (or 15 percent), do so. The more space you allocate to System Restore, the more restore points you'll have available in the event of a system misconfiguration.

# Hack 84: Truly Delete Data from Your Hard Drive

Level....... **Medium**
Platform.... **Windows, Mac OS X**
Cost ....... **Free**

You're about to sell, donate, pass on, or give away your old computer. Did you know that file undelete software can easily resurrect those files you just emptied out of the Recycle Bin? Even though it *looks* like you've erased the files, in reality your computer has only marked the space they took up on disk as available — the 1s and 0s that make up those deleted files still exist.

The only sure way to securely and permanently delete sensitive files — like a customer database, secret company documents, or personal photos you don't want the guy who buys your hard drive on eBay to see — is to overwrite them several times with new data. Utilities to do this are available for both Mac and Windows systems.

## Windows

Free, open-source Windows software Eraser (`http://heidi.ie/eraser/download.php`) permanently deletes files from disk using your choice of methods, including a Defense Department standard (DoD 5220.22-M). Eraser can do both on-demand and scheduled scrub-downs of unused disk space on your entire hard drive; either way, it permanently deletes files.

If you're passing a computer on to a co-worker or family member or selling it, delete your data as usual, and then use Eraser to permanently remove any trace of that data from the free space on your disks. To do so, open Eraser, and in the On-Demand section, select File → New Task. From the drop-down menu, choose the drive, folder, or file you want to permanently delete and click OK. The location is added to Eraser's task list, as shown in Figure 10-10.

To go ahead with the delete action, select Task → Run All.

Eraser is also integrated with Windows Explorer. With Eraser installed, right-click any file, choose Erase from the context menu, and confirm deletion.

> **WARNING** When you erase a file with Eraser, it does not go into the Recycling Bin; nor can it be recovered using undelete software. It is permanently deleted, so use it sparingly and with caution.

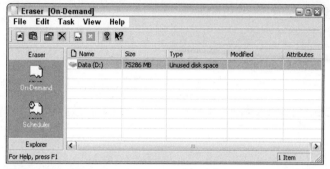

**Figure 10-10** Eraser can permanently delete any trace of files on the unused portions of a disk, or delete specific existing files.

## Mac OS X

To permanently delete sensitive data in the Trash on a Mac (OS X 10.4 and higher), choose Finder → Secure Empty Trash. (That menu option is enabled only if there are files in the Trash bin.)

To white out all the current free space on your Mac, launch Disk Utility and choose your Mac's hard drive. Then, on the Erase tab, click the Erase Free Space button to choose your erasing method, as shown in Figure 10-11.

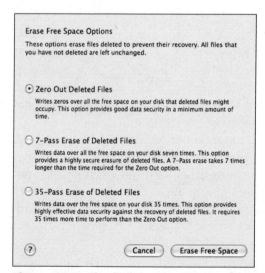

**Figure 10-11** The built-in Mac OS X erase feature scrubs deleted file fragments from unused disk space.

# Hack 85: Firewall Your Computer

Level....... **Medium**
Platform.... **Windows**
Cost ....... **Free**

A home PC connected directly to the Internet — especially with an always-on broadband connection like cable or DSL — is a prime target for malicious software attacks. Malware such as viruses, worms, key loggers, and Trojan horses constantly scan public networks (like your ISP's network) looking for insecure computers to attack, take over, and use for their own purposes. A criminal hacker can use an unsecured home PC to send out spam email, steal credit card or other identity information, or simply delete data or crash a machine for the fun of it.

A firewall can protect your computer against these types of attacks. Without a firewall, a computer connected directly to a cable modem is exposed to the wilds of the Internet — which runs rampant with infected PCs just waiting to spread their viruses and key log your credit card numbers.

## Does Your Computer Need a Firewall?

If you're on a secure network — like at the office — or if your home computer is connected to a wireless router with a built-in firewall, it may already be protected. If not, running a software firewall can greatly reduce the chances of an outsider gaining access to your PC without your knowledge or consent.

Open ports on your computer represent possible entry points and vulnerabilities on your machine. Test out how secure your PC is by using a free online port scan application at `http://dslreports.com/scan`.

If your machine has open ports, run a firewall to explicitly allow and disallow traffic from the Internet in and out of your computer.

> **NOTE** If you're running a home server as described in Hacks 35 and 36, you will have purposefully opened ports on your machine. Make sure those servers are secured with difficult-to-guess passwords. When you're not using the servers, shut them down to close their open ports.

If you can, get a hardware firewall to protect your home desktop computers. (Most modern wireless network routers come with a firewall built-in.) A hardware firewall is preferable because it frees up CPU cycles (because your computer doesn't have to run the firewall itself) and is often more effective than a software firewall. However, software firewalls are sometimes necessary, especially for roaming laptops that connect to open wireless networks like at the local coffee shop or airport.

## ZoneAlarm Software Firewall

Several commercial firewall applications are available for home use. Zone Labs offers a free version of its feature-full ZoneAlarm firewall for download at `http://zonelabs.com/store/content/catalog/products/sku_list_za.jsp`.

When ZoneAlarm is installed, it monitors and asks you to confirm or deny incoming and outgoing internet traffic from your computer. Also, for troubleshooting purposes (and a great sense of satisfaction), ZoneAlarm reports the details and total of how many possible intrusions it blocked — attempts from other computers to connect to yours, as shown in Figure 10-12.

## Control What Programs Can Connect to the Internet

After ZoneAlarm is installed and you've begun using your computer as usual, you'll notice that it will interrupt you every time a program tries to connect to the Internet. (These days, most software applications do — mostly for legitimate purposes, like checking to see if they're the most updated version.) Allow or deny Internet access to those programs using ZoneAlarm's (somewhat annoying) pop-ups, like the one shown in Figure 10-13, which appears when you click a link in a Microsoft Word document.

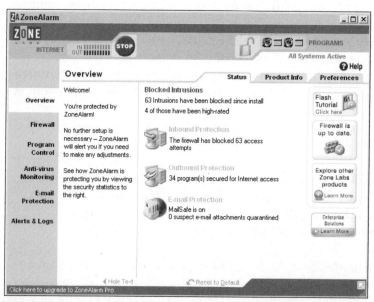

**Figure 10-12** The ZoneAlarm firewall's main console displays how many possible intrusions it has blocked and how many programs are secured for Internet access.

To avoid constant ZoneAlarm interruptions, edit the program whitelist and blacklist all at once. In ZoneAlarm's Program Control section, choose the Programs tab. There, click each program and choose Allow, Deny, or Ask as shown in Figure 10-14.

With ZoneAlarm running, you can rest easy knowing no one can connect to your computer without your explicit permission.

**NOTE** Starting in Windows XP Service Pack 2, a built-in firewall is available in the Control Panel Security Center. The Windows Firewall offers similar protection as ZoneAlarm, but it's not as informative or configurable. Get more information about the Windows Firewall and the benefits of firewalls in general at `http://microsoft.com/athome/security/protect/firewall.mspx`.

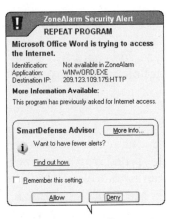

**Figure 10-13** ZoneAlarm asks you to authorize or deny individual programs' access to the Internet.

| Programs | Access | | Server | |
| --- | --- | --- | --- | --- |
| | Trusted | Internet | Trusted | Internet |
| ClamWin Antivirus | √ | √ | ? | ? |
| Client.exe | ? | ? | ? | ? |
| EditPlus | ? | ? | ? | ? |
| Firefox | √ | √ | ? | ? |
| Generic Host Process for Win32 Se... | √ | √ | √ | X |
| Google Desktop | ? | √ Allow | | |
| Google Desktop | ? | X Block | | |
| Google Desktop | ? | ? Ask | | |
| ImageReady | ? | ? | ? | ? |
| iTunes | ? | X | ? | X |

**Figure 10-14** Update the Access control setting for each program on your computer within ZoneAlarm.

# Hack 86: Free up Hard Drive Space

Level. . . . . . . **Easy**
Platform. . . . **Windows, Mac OS X**
Cost . . . . . . . **Free**

When you bought your computer two years ago, you thought it had a much bigger hard drive than you'd ever need. However, as your computer aged, all that space got eaten up by who-knows-what. Hard drive space is cheap and plentiful, but you don't have to run out to buy a whole new drive the minute you start pushing your current disk's space limits. There are easy ways to inventory what's hogging up your hard drive and then offload some of it to external disks or simply delete it.

## Visualize Disk Hogs

Two utilities — WinDirStat and JDiskReport — analyze your hard drive and map out its usage statistics. They're discussed in the following sections.

### WinDirStat (Windows)

The free, open-source utility WinDirStat (http://windirstat.sourceforge .net, Windows only) displays your disk usage in a color-coded map that shows what file types and folders take up the most space on your hard drive.

Using WinDirStat, it's easy to identify the biggest space hogs on your disk. The utility provides a three-paned view: tree view, list view, and treemap view, as shown in Figure 10-15.

The treemap represents each file as a colored rectangle, the area of which is proportional to the file's size. The rectangles are arranged so that directories make up rectangles that contain all their files and subdirectories. Select files by folder name, file type, or colored rectangle, and delete or move them from within WinDirStat.

### JDiskReport (Windows or Mac)

Freeware JDiskReport (http://jgoodies.com/freeware/jdiskreport, Mac/Windows/Linux), like WinDirStat, provides graphical disk usage statistics using more common pie/line/bar charts, as shown in Figure 10-16.

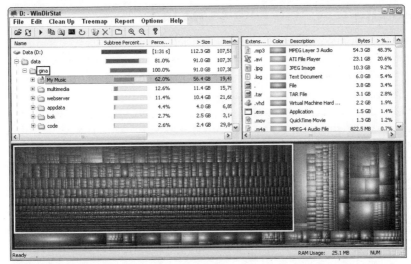

**Figure 10-15** WinDirStat graphs disk usage based on a color-coded map.

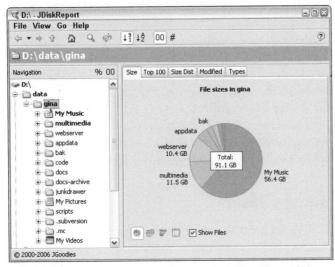

**Figure 10-16** JDiskReport, for Mac or Windows, charts disk usage to easily identify hard drive space hogs.

JDiskReport is cross-platform but does require Java (http://java.com/en) to run.

## Clean Your Entire System with CCleaner

Another free utility for Windows, CCleaner (which stands for Crap Cleaner), identifies system files — such as Internet browsing history, temporary setup files, and logs — which can be deleted to free up space on your hard drive. CCleaner includes an interface for uninstalling programs (also available in the Control Panel Add/Remove Programs area), fixing broken shortcuts, and removing unused registry items and outdated software. Download it from `http://ccleaner.com`.

# Hack 87: Resurrect Deleted Files

Level....... **Medium**
Platform.... **Windows**
Cost ....... **Free**

When you delete files from your computer's hard drive, the data is not actually erased. In reality, the space it occupies is marked as available for your operating system to overwrite with new data.

As a result, special file recovery undelete programs can often resurrect deleted files from the space on your disk marked as free (which still holds fragments of the old file). Although there are times when you don't want your deleted files to see the light of day again, in the case of accidental deletion, an undelete process can retrieve what you thought was permanently lost data.

Free software Restoration can restore deleted files on your Windows PC's hard drive, or on external disks such as a digital camera memory card and USB stick.

## How to Restore Deleted Files

The moment you realize you've accidentally deleted files you want back, stop. Those files may still be on disk, but any computer activity that writes to disk may overwrite whatever's left of them and render them unrecoverable. Don't restart your computer (boot up writes temp files to disk) and don't do any other work on the machine — get straight to the recovery process.

Download free undelete utility Restoration from `http://snapfiles` `.com/get/restoration.html` and unzip it, preferably using a computer other than the one where your deleted files live. If that's not possible, save and unzip the file to an external drive (such as a USB drive).

**TIP** Restoration is an excellent addition to a PC helper's USB drive, along with spyware and virus cleaning utilities. (See Hack 81, earlier in this chapter, and Hack 34, "Carry Your Life on a Flash Drive.")

Launch Restoration, and choose the disk and filename of the document you want to recover. Say you deleted a Word document called `chapter10.doc` from the Desktop and emptied the Recycle Bin. In Restoration, enter some part of the filename — even if it's just the extension, like `.doc` — and its location, as shown in Figure 10-17.

Restoration lists all the deleted files that match your search term. (Alternatively, view all the available deleted files by not entering any search term.) To get a deleted file back, select it, click the Restore by Copying button, and choose a location for the restored copy.

**TIP** If you've accidentally deleted photos from your digital camera, connect it to your PC. Many modern digital camera memory cards will appear as an external hard drive in My Computer. Use Restoration to scan your camera as if it were an external disk and recover deleted pictures.

Keep in mind that restoring deleted files is a hit-or-miss operation that can miss often, especially in the case of large files such as video or music that Windows might overwrite quickly.

This type of file restoration is no excuse or replacement for a solid backup system.

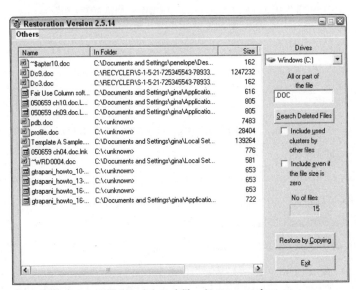

**Figure 10-17** Searching deleted files in Restoration.

# Hack 88: Recover Files from an Unbootable PC

Level....... **Advanced**
Platform.... **Windows**
Cost ....... **Free**

Few moments in computing are as heartbreaking as when you turn on your trusty PC only to receive that bone-chilling message: Boot sector corrupt. Config.sys missing. Disk cannot be read.

In other words, you're dead in the water.

Or are you? Just because your computer can't boot up Windows from your hard drive doesn't mean you can't boot it up with another operating system on another disk just long enough to rescue your important files. This hack uses the completely free Knoppix Linux Live boot disk (http://knopper.net/knoppix/index-en.html) to safely move your files from a failing hard drive to a healthy USB drive — no Windows required.

> **NOTE** There are lots of flavors of bootable CDs and DVDs that you can use to get your computer running long enough to grab your files. Some of them require your original Windows installation disk to build, though. Knoppix is for users who have lost or no longer have access to their original Windows disks, don't want to build a boot disk, and who aren't afraid of a different-looking operating system.

## What You Need

For the latest version (as of writing, 5.01) of Knoppix to run, you need:

- Intel-compatible CPU (i486 or better)
- At least 82 MB for graphic mode (which is what you want)
- A bootable CD-ROM/DVD drive (IDE/ATAPI, FireWire, USB, or SCSI)
- A standard SVGA-compatible graphics card
- A standard serial or PS/2 mouse, or IMPS/2-compatible USB Mouse

If you use a USB mouse and keyboard, they may work with Knoppix, but it's smart to have a PS/2 option available just in case. Be sure to check the Knoppix site (http://knopper.net/knoppix-info/index-en.html) for updated system requirements for new versions.

Ready to turn your machine into a Linux-CD booted powerhouse?

## Prepare Your Knoppix Disk

There are two options for getting the Knoppix bootable disk: download and burn one yourself, or order one by mail.

Do-it-yourselfers in a hurry can use another computer to download an `.iso` file (`http://knopper.net/knoppix-mirrors/index-en.html`) and burn it to their own CD or DVD. (This, naturally, requires a CD or DVD burner and burning software.) If you opt to go this route, make sure you choose the most recent `.iso` file available (currently `KNOPPIX_V5.0.1CD-2006-06-01-EN.iso`). The DVD files are available from the `knoppixdvd` folder on the download server.

Alternatively, if you have time (or no friend with an available burner), order a Knoppix CD via mail for anywhere from $1.50 to $5.00 from a vendor listed at `http://knopper.net/knoppix-vendors/index-en.php`.

## Set Your Computer to Boot from the CD or DVD Drive

Here things get as tricky as they're going to get. When your computer starts up, it boots itself on disks in a particular order (usually the floppy `A:` drive, then the `C:` drive) as set in the computer's base configuration (called the BIOS). To boot from CD or DVD, you have to edit the disk order to make your computer go to the CD or DVD *first*. How you do so will differ from machine to machine. For example, when my Dell first starts up, there's a message to `Press F2 to enter setup`. That's what you want.

So here's what to do:

1. Insert the Knoppix CD into your CD/DVD drive.
2. Shut down your computer.
3. Disconnect any peripherals you don't need to grab your files (printer, Wi-Fi adapter, remote control IR device — anything unnecessary).
4. Connect the drive to which you want to move your files — like a USB drive or external hard drive.
5. Start up your computer and watch carefully for the message on how to enter your BIOS settings (like the F2 message), and then press the correct key.
6. When you're in the BIOS settings, find the Boot Sequence option. Go into it, and select the CD drive as the first bootable option.

**WARNING** One false move inside your BIOS can seriously affect your computer's operation. Be careful, and edit only the boot sequence settings.

7. When your PC is set to boot from CD first, save and quit the BIOS.

## Start Knoppix

The CD is in the drive and your computer is set to boot from it; you're golden. When you restart, you'll hear the Knoppix CD or DVD spinning right away. Your computer will bypass your crippled hard drive and begin booting up Linux. First thing you'll see is the Linux Penguin, and progress messages as Knoppix gets itself started. It will take some time to detect your devices, but eventually you'll get a message to press Enter to continue with the Linux boot.

Press Enter and eventually you'll get to the full-on Knoppix desktop, as shown in Figure 10-18.

> **NOTE** My first time out with Knoppix, I had to reboot three times before it ran successfully. The first time the boot sequence got stuck in the Auto-Detecting Devices process. After 20 minutes, I restarted and tried again. The second time I got to the desktop but was told the computer didn't have enough memory for graphical mode (which it most certainly does.) The third try was a charm — startup happened in a minute and a half with all my disk drives mounted and the full Knoppix desktop. Moral of the story: if bootup ain't going well, try, try again.

**Figure 10-18** The Knoppix desktop booted from CD or DVD.

## Rescue Your Data

If you have no Linux experience, Knoppix may look odd and scary, but it isn't. See the hard drive icons on the desktop? Click on one to browse its contents — your Windows files. To copy your important documents, just open your USB drive (click its icon) and simply drag and drop files onto it.

When you attempt the copy, you may receive a message saying, "You cannot drop any items in a directory in which you do not have write permission." If you do, change the permissions by right-clicking on the USB drive, and choosing Change Read/Write Mode, as shown in Figure 10-19.

Then, you can simply drag and drop files from your hard drive to your USB drive. When you're finished, you can shut down, reset your boot order to where it should be, and rebuild or repair your PC knowing that your data is safe and sound.

**Figure 10-19** Change the permissions to write to your external drive in Knoppix.

A Linux boot CD or DVD like Knoppix is also a low-overhead way for the curious to try out Linux without having to install it. Just pop in the CD, reset your boot order, and go.

**TIP** Another popular bootable Linux distribution, Damn Small Linux (`http://damnsmalllinux.org`), can run within Windows from a USB drive or can boot from CD or DVD.

# Index